DATE DUE

DEC 0 4 '98			

HIGHSMITH 45-220

International Financial Markets

International Financial Markets

Harmonization versus Competition

Edited by Claude E. Barfield

WITHDRAWN

The AEI Press

Publisher for the American Enterprise Institute
WASHINGTON, D.C.

1996

The American Enterprise Institute would like to thank the American Express Foundation and the Sasakawa Peace Foundation for support for this project. The authors of the individual chapters also benefited greatly from the views and comments expressed at a joint conference with the Federal Reserve Bank of Chicago in July 1995.

Available in the United States from the AEI Press, c/o Publisher Resources Inc., 1224 Heil Quaker Blvd., P.O. Box 7001, La Vergne, TN 37086-7001. Distributed outside the United States by arrangement with Eurospan, 3 Henrietta Street, London WC2E 8LU England.

Library of Congress Cataloging-in-Publication Data

International financial markets : harmonization versus competition / edited by Claude E. Barfield.
    p. cm.
   Includes bibliographical references and index.
   ISBN 0-8447-3926-X (cloth : alk. paper)
   1. Financial services industry.   2. Financial services industry—Law and legislation.   3. International finance.   4. Competition, International.   I. Barfield, Claude E.
   HG173.I57 1996
   332.1—dc20   96-15326
                                    CIP

Printed in the United States of America

Contents

CONTRIBUTORS   xi

1   INTRODUCTION   *Claude E. Barfield*   1

2   COMPETITION VERSUS HARMONIZATION—AN OVERVIEW OF
INTERNATIONAL REGULATION OF FINANCIAL
SERVICES   *Lawrence J. White*   5
   Types of Regulation   8
   Market Failure and Government Failure   12
   Competition versus Harmonization   24
   Conclusion   41
   References   42

3   INTERNATIONAL TRADE IN BANKING   *Jean Dermine*   49
   The Banking Industry   52
   The Economics of Banking Regulations   63
   Reciprocity and Nondiscriminatory Barriers   71
   The European Union Approach to International
     Integration   74
   Conclusion   79
   References   81

4   GLOBAL COMPETITION AND MARKET ACCESS IN THE
SECURITIES INDUSTRY   *Ingo Walter*   84
   Stylized Process of Financial Intermediation   87

Character of the International Securities
Industry   97
Regulatory Determinants of Financial
Structures   107
Trade Policy Aspects of Investment Banking
Regulation   114
Conclusion   143
References   147

5   INTERNATIONAL TRADE IN INSURANCE   *Harold D. Skipper, Jr.*   151
The Nature of Insurance   152
The Structure of Insurance Markets   157
Government Intervention into Insurance
Markets   184
Is Regulatory Harmonization Necessary for
Insurance Liberalization?   197
Conclusion   212
References   218

6   FOREIGN BANKS, FINANCIAL DEVELOPMENT, AND ECONOMIC
GROWTH   *Ross Levine*   224
Does Finance Matter?   227
What Role for Foreign Banks?   235
Conclusion   248
Appendix 6–A: McFadden's Study of Foreign
Banks in Australia   249
References   251

INDEX   255

LIST OF TABLES
3–1   Percentage of Labor Force in Banking,
Insurance, or Real Estate in Selected
OECD Countries, 1980 and 1989   54
3–2   Percentage of Bank Ownership Allowed to
Foreign Investors in Selected Countries,
1992   55
3–3   Trade in Financial Services in Selected
OECD Countries, 1988 and 1991   56
3–4   The Interbank Market within the BIS
Reporting Area, 1983 and 1994   57
3–5   International Bank Assets by Nationality of
Banks in Selected OECD Countries, 1983,
1991, and 1993   57

3–6 Assets and Market Value of Equity of Selected International Banks, 1994 58

3–7 Nationality Distribution of Open Positions in the Eurodollar Futures and Options Contracts Traded on the Chicago CME-IMM Exchange, 1991 59

3–8 Open Positions in Futures and Options Contracts Traded on the MATIF, 1991 60

3–9 Market Share of Foreign Institutions in Selected OECD Countries, 1986 and 1989 60

3–10 Deposit Insurance Systems in Selected Countries 67

3–11 Permissible Activities in Insurance in Selected OECD Countries, 1993 72

3–12 Permissible Activities of Banks in Securities in Japan, 1993 73

3–13 Liabilities of National Banks vis-à-vis the Nonbank Sector, 1989 and 1994 79

4–1 Functions and Products of the Financial Services Industry, circa 1950 92

4–2 Functions and Products of the Financial Services Industry, circa 1995 93

4–3 Percentage Shares of Assets of Financial Institutions in the United States, 1860–1993 94

4–4 Products and Services of Securities Firms 99

4–5 U.S. and International Capital Market Activity, 1990–1994 105

4–6 U.S. and International Volume of Transactions in Global Merger and Acquisitions Developments, 1985–1994 106

4–7 Range of Permissible Securities Activities for U.S. and Foreign-based Commercial Banks, 1968–1987 117

4–8 Global Wholesale Banking and Investment Banking, Full Credit to Book Running Manager Only, 1995 122

4–9 Weighted Composite Score of Underwriting, Trading, Research, and Advisory

Activities of Investment Banks, 1993 and 1994   124

4–10   Access of Foreign-based Securities Firms to National Markets, 1994   144

5–1   Number and Types of Insurance Companies in OECD Member Countries, 1993   166

5–2   Twenty-five Largest Insurance Companies Worldwide, Ranked in Asset Order, 1994   167

5–3   Estimated Number of Captive Insurers in Major Captive Domiciles, 1994   168

5–4   U.S. Cross-Border Trade in Insurance, 1990–1992   170

5–5   U.S. Reinsurance Market, 1987–1991   170

5–6   Twenty Largest Insurance Brokerage Firms Worldwide, Ranked in Order, 1993   182

5–7   Banks' Percentage of Total Insurance Premiums for Selected Countries, 1992   183

5–8   Potential Scheme for Permitting Greater Liberalization   217

6–1   Bank Operating Ratios, Industrial Countries, 1977   239

6–2   Selected Deposit Rates of Foreign and Domestic Banks in Indonesia, 1978–1985   241

LIST OF FIGURES

4–1   Intermediation Dynamics for Financial Contracting   88

4–2   Diagram of a Full-Service Securities Firm   98

4–3   Policy Trade-offs and Techniques of the Regulatory Overlay   108

4–4   Percentage of Market Share of International Equity Issues, by Institution Type, 1984–1993   120

4–5   Percentage of Market Share of European and International Bond Issues, by Institution Type, 1984–1993   121

5–1   Percentage of Household Savings through Life Insurance among the G-7 Countries, 1980 and 1990   154

5–2   Insurance Market Shares Worldwide, Total
       Business, 1985 and 1993   157

5–3   Percentage Change in Nonlife and Life
       Insurance Market Shares Worldwide,
       1985 and 1993   158

5–4   Insurance Market Shares Worldwide, by
       Selected Country Groupings, 1993   160

5–5   Insurance Density and Penetration, by
       Country, 1993   162

5–6   Market Share of Foreign-controlled
       Undertakings among Selected OECD
       Countries, as Percentage of Life and
       Nonlife Business, 1992   172

5–7   European Cross-Border Acquisitions of
       Financial Institutions, 1984–1990   173

5–8   American Cross-Border Acquisitions of
       Financial Institutions, 1985–1993   174

5–9   Cross-Border Insurance Merger and
       Acquisition Transactions into and out of
       the United States, 1987–1993   175

5–10   Revenues of Foreign-owned Insurance
       Companies, from U.S. Perspective,
       1993   176

5–11   Market Concentration Indicators for Life and
       Nonlife Insurers, for Selected OECD
       Countries, 1989   186

5–12   Relative Levels of Insurance Market
       Liberalization   199

5–13   The Case for Strengthened Competition
       Regulation   201

5–14   The EU Chain Approach to
       Liberalization   208

6–1   Real per Capita Income and Financial
       Development for Selected Developing
       Countries, 1970   234

6–2   Growth and Financial Development for
       Selected Developing Countries,
       1960–1989   235

6–3   Initial Depth of Financial Development,
       1960, versus Future Growth, 1960–1989,
       for Selected Countries   236

Contributors

Claude E. Barfield is a resident scholar at the American Enterprise Institute and the coordinator of its trade policy studies program. He is also the director of science and technology policy studies at AEI. He is the editor of many books on trade policy, including most recently *Expanding U.S.-Asian Trade: New Challenges and Policy Options* (AEI Press, 1996), and, with Bruce L. R. Smith, *Technology, R&D, and the Economy* (AEI-Brookings, 1996). His articles on international trade, science and technology policy, and U.S. competitiveness frequently appear in the *Wall Street Journal*, the *New York Times*, and the *Washington Post*.

Jean Dermine is Professor of Banking and Finance at the European Institute of Business Administration (INSEAD), in Fontainebleau, France. He has taught at the Wharton School of the University of Pennsylvania and at the Salomon Center at New York University. Mr. Dermine is the author of numerous books and articles on asset liability management, deregulation in the European financial industry, and the theory of banking, and he serves as associate editor of the *Journal of Banking and Finance* and of *The Financier*.

Ross Levine is a senior economist at the World Bank. He has taught at Johns Hopkins University and at the University of California, Los Angeles, and has published numerous articles and book chapters on international finance.

Harold D. Skipper, Jr., is the C. V. Starr Distinguished Professor of International Insurance in the Department of Risk Management and

Insurance at Georgia State University. He serves on the boards of the Boettner Institute of Financial Gerontology at the University of Pennsylvania, of the U.S. chapter of the International Insurance Law Association, and of the American College.

INGO WALTER is the Charles Simon Professor of Applied Financial Economics at the Stern School of Business, New York University. He also serves as director of the Salomon Center, an independent academic research institute. He holds a joint appointment as Swiss Bank Corporation Professor of International Management, INSEAD.

LAWRENCE J. WHITE is the Arthur E. Imperatore Professor of Economics at New York University's Stern School of Business. He is widely published in the fields of banking and regulation; his most recent books include *The Antitrust Revolution* (2d ed., 1994), *Bank Management and Regulation* (1992), and *Structural Change in Banking* (1993).

1

Introduction

Claude E. Barfield

Just after the Uruguay Round of trade negotiations concluded, the Organization for Economic Cooperation and Development (OECD) issued a ministerial communique looking to future trade issues for the 1990s. It stated:

> Looking beyond the Uruguay Round to the trade issues of the 1990s, Ministers emphasize the need to address the new dimensions of trade policy. . . . The increasingly international scope of economic activity has seen the emergence of areas in which the needs of private agents and governments have run ahead of the existing "rules of the game." There is a perceived need for better understanding of these issues and, where appropriate, convergence of policy approaches and consideration of fresh rules.

Among the goals specified by the communique was completion of financial services and telecommunications agreements from the Uruguay Round. It also addressed a group of new issues, including the trade-related aspects of investment policy, competition policy, technology policy, and the environment, as the top priorities for future multilateral trade negotiations.

Policy questions related to trade in financial services form a bridge between the policy issues discussed in the Uruguay Round and the new issues that present the challenges to trade negotiators for the balance of the 1990s. Trade in financial services directly intersects both trade-related investment issues and questions related to

1

competition policy. For instance, financial services—banking, securities markets, and insurance—provide the indispensable infrastructure for foreign investment. Negotiations leading to a more liberal international-investment environment will necessarily address the multilateral rules governing this financial-service infrastructure. For policy on competition, the corporate relations between financial services providers and other service and manufacturing concerns (such as the role of banks in corporate control and governance of German industrial firms) will pose large and complicated issues for negotiators attempting to construct a new multilateral regime in this area.

As noted above, the Uruguay Round began the process of creating new multilateral rules for financial services trade and investment. These deliberations, however, represented only the beginning of an effort to work through the issues raised by the potentially huge markets for international banking, securities, and insurance activities. The Uruguay Round negotiators failed to achieve a consensus about new rules for financial services, and negotiations were extended for several years. In the summer of 1995, the multilateral negotiations suffered an important setback when the United States withdrew its offer for liberalization, arguing that other countries—particularly East Asian nations—had failed to come up with significant market-opening plans.

The goal of this volume is to set forth criteria for a financial services multilateral regime and to make sector-specific recommendations to provide future international trade and investment rules for banking, securities, and insurance. The central question addressed by each chapter is the degree to which a future financial services regime must be harmonized, with common rules governing all participants. The OECD ministerial communique looks to a "convergence of policy approaches . . . where appropriate"; but it gives no guidance as to criteria for appropriateness.

Underlying the questions of harmonization are fundamental policy choices and competing visions of the substance and mechanics of a new multilateral system that extends to hitherto domestic regulatory systems, such as those governing financial services. On the one hand, some economists and many trade negotiators lean heavily toward substantial harmonization, citing the problem of nonlevel playing fields and the danger that increased system friction will result in substantial disruption and weakening of the new World Trade Organization (WTO). On the other hand, many economists and some trade negotiators are skeptical of the benefits of forced harmonization. They argue that competition among national regulatory systems will ultimately produce a more efficient, as well as more equitable, system.

The authors in this volume generally agree with the skeptics. The common theme is best expressed by Lawrence White in chapter 2:

> In this author's judgment, competition—whether among firms, among markets and exchanges, or among national regulatory regimes—ought to be the "default option"; that is, in the absence of a strong showing that there is a substantial market failure and that the problems of government failure can be overcome to create a reasonable likelihood that government intervention will improve outcomes, the competition outcome should prevail. For the international competition-versus-harmonization controversy, this position would imply that those who favor the international harmonization of specific national regulatory provisions should bear a substantial burden of making a convincing case. As is discussed below, there do seem to be specific instances where international harmonization may well be desirable; but the presumption should be in favor of competition, and a strong affirmative case for harmonization must be made in these specific instances.

The volume is organized as follows: Lawrence White presents an overview chapter, defining an approach to analyzing the issues of harmonization versus competition in international trade in financial services. He delineates the potential conditions of market failure that would call for public intervention, but he also carefully balances these conditions with possibilities of "government failure" and warns of the "danger that harmonization efforts could be subverted and become a vehicle for reinforcing the protectionist tendencies of many national regulatory regimes."

Using White's criteria as general guidelines, the next three chapters present detailed analyses of the current competitive structure and activities of the three main financial-service sectors: banking, by Jean Dermine of INSEAD; securities, by Ingo Walter of New York University; and insurance, by Harold Skipper of Georgia State University. For each sector, the authors present more detailed recommendations for trade liberalization.

Finally, Ross Levine of the World Bank contributes a chapter describing the particular problems faced by developing countries in overcoming barriers of financial-service liberalization. Levine also presents a more general case for the role that both domestic and foreign financial-service institutions can play in economic development. Indeed, his conclusions regarding the seminal role of financial

3

services in promoting faster economic growth hold true not only for developing countries but for developed countries as well. He describes five functions that provide the means for more efficient capital accumulation and utilization. Financial services (1) facilitate trade and allow specialization in production functions, (2) facilitate risk management, through pricing risk and allowing mechanisms for pooling and ameliorating risk, (3) mobilize resources, through channeling disparate savers into growth-enhancing investment projects, (4) obtain information, evaluate firms, and allocate capital more efficiently than individual savers can, and (5) provide a check and outside regulator of corporate governance.

Thus, as Levine points out, "financial services are not simple balance sheets, and financial markets are not simple veils for the functioning of the real sector. The financial system provides 'real' services that are crucial for economic activity and long-run growth." For these reasons, as the authors of these chapters make clear, it is imperative that future trade negotiations aimed at liberalizing financial services strike the right balance between essential central rules and free competitive play, to allow the most efficient firms and national regulatory systems to flourish.

2

Competition versus Harmonization—An Overview of International Regulation of Financial Services

Lawrence J. White

Rapid improvements in the technologies—data processing and tele-communications—that underlie financial services are dramatically broadening the markets for these services. Firms are able to offer a wider array of financial services to more customers over larger geographic areas. For many financial services the effective market boundaries now extend beyond national borders.[1] Borrowers and securities issuers are increasingly seeking funds across national boundaries; savers and investors are increasingly prepared to channel their capital flows across those same national boundaries; and the financial services firms that intermediate or facilitate the flows of funds between

Thanks are due to Jonathan Aronson, Claude Barfield, Jean Dermine, Franklin Edwards, Geza Feketakuty, William Haraf, Roberta Karmel, Ross Levine, Harold Skipper, Ingo Walter, and Dana Jaffe for valuable comments on an earlier draft of this chapter.

1. For general discussions, see Stoll (1990), Kosters and Meltzer (1990), Siegel (1990), Fingleton (1992), Edwards and Patrick (1992), Stansell (1993), and White (1995b).

the users and the providers of capital are increasingly operating and offering their services in multiple countries.

In this new world of internationalized financial flows, the *national* regulatory regimes that have hitherto governed financial services are increasingly under strain. Whether their concerns are orderly markets, the safety and soundness of financial institutions, or the protection of depositors and investors, regulators fear that the pressures of these international capital flows may undo or overwhelm their efforts.[2] Their usual plea is for international harmonization of national regulatory regimes, so as to coordinate their efforts, create a "level playing field," and prevent a competitive "race to the bottom" among national regulators that would ultimately harm the participants in these markets.[3]

Some critics, however, are skeptical of such arguments.[4] They view much of national financial regulation as interfering with the efficient operation of financial markets, and they fear that international harmonization would solidify these inefficiencies and prevent international competition from circumventing them. In essence, these critics view international competition—among regulators, as well as among firms—as a "race to the top" that will enhance the efficient allocation of capital and financial services, rather than as a race to the bottom.

This chapter will provide an overview of these issues and an analytical framework for evaluating the conflicting claims as to the relative merits of harmonization or competition among national regulatory regimes.[5] The chapter also serves to integrate the chapters on specific topics that follow in this volume—banking, securities, insurance, and the telecommunications networks that link financial services participants. Here we will focus on these same three financial sectors—banking, securities, and insurance—but the principles and conclusions of this discussion are valid for other financial services as well.[6]

---

2. See, for example, Walker (1992), Breeden (1992), Guy (1992), and Quinn (1992).

3. See the references cited in footnote 2. See also Grundfest (1990), Steil (1992, 1993), Worth (1992), and Karmel (1993).

4. See, for example, Kane (1991, 1992), Benston (1992a), and Steil (1992, 1993).

5. This chapter expands and extends the discussion found in White (1995).

6. Unless otherwise indicated, by banking I mean all financial intermediaries that offer deposit liabilities. In the United States, this would encompass commercial banks, savings and loan institutions, savings banks, and credit

Competition among regulatory regimes can be analyzed in ways that are similar to the standard microeconomics analysis of competition among firms. Accordingly, we employ the concepts of *market failure*—the conditions under which a market fails to achieve the efficiencies promised by the textbook model of a competitive market—and *government failure*—the reasons why government agencies fail to provide the improvements to and may even exacerbate the market imperfections that a textbook model of a benevolent and omniscient government would eradicate—to evaluate arguments for multilateral governmental efforts to regulate the competition that would otherwise occur among these same governments' national regulatory regimes.[7]

Using this framework we find that competition—among firms, exchanges, markets, *and* regulators—is generally beneficial and should be encouraged. In certain circumstances, however, the international harmonization of specific national regulations may be capable of improving the efficiency of financial services markets. Specifically, harmonization may be beneficial if it is the guise for a general lowering of protectionist barriers; if it serves as a means of limiting subsidies to domestic firms; or if it sufficiently reduces the transaction costs that financial services firms or users would otherwise incur in dealing with separate national regulatory regimes. An irony should be noted: the first two instances involve international harmonization's having value because it overrides the domestic government failures of national regulatory regimes.

In many other circumstances, however, international harmonization is unnecessary. Further, there is always the danger that harmonization efforts could be subverted to become a vehicle for reinforcing the protectionist tendencies of many national regulatory regimes. And even the apparent gains that harmonization might achieve by reducing transaction costs might be illusory if the regulatory uniformity thereby achieved translates into inefficient limits on local diver-

---

unions. By securities markets I mean the markets (which need not be organized around an exchange) for financial instruments of all kinds, including foreign exchange; in essence, I am excluding primarily the financial intermediation that occurs directly through banks, insurance companies, and pension funds (although these institutions are often involved in transactions that encompass the instruments that are the focus of this chapter). The discussion of insurance will similarly be broad, encompassing both the property-casualty and life insurance categories.

7. This discussion will follow the arguments developed in Wolf (1989) and White (1994).

sity or simply yields a globally inappropriate and inefficient regulatory standard.

The next section of this chapter provides a description and taxonomy of the major types of governmental regulation and illustrative examples from nonfinancial areas. The subsequent section discusses the main categories of market failure and relates these categories to the types of regulation that might be used to remedy them; it also outlines the major sources of government failure. The next section combines these elements and analyzes the arguments for harmonization and for competition. The final section offers a brief conclusion.

Types of Regulation

For the purposes of this chapter we define regulation to mean any nonfiscal governmental intervention (thus excluding specific taxes or subsidies) in the operation of private-sector markets. Regulation can be in the form of laws passed by legislatures, formal edicts issued by regulatory bodies, or informal guidance or interpretations offered by a government agency.

This definition of regulation clearly encompasses a broad range of governmental intervention in markets. But regulation is not simply an undifferentiated mass of governmental intervention. It is possible to find commonalities among major types of regulation, and these will prove useful for the discussion in the later sections in this chapter. We offer three major categories:

Economic Regulation. This form of regulation usually involves limitations on prices, profits, or entry into or exit from an activity, including "must-serve" requirements.[8] Familiar examples outside the financial services arena would include the pre-1980s regulation of airline prices and routes by the U.S. Civil Aeronautics Board (CAB); the regulation of local electricity, natural gas, and telephone company prices and profits by individual state regulatory commissions; and limitations on local taxicab entry and fees by many cities.

The application of economic regulation to banking in the United States has been and continues to be pervasive, even after the era of deregulation of the late 1970s and early 1980s. Examples, past and present, include:

- the federal limitations (before the mid-1980s) on the interest rates that banks could pay on most types of deposits[9]

---

8. For an overview, see Braeutigam (1989) and Joskow and Rose (1989).

9. This was frequently described as the "Regulation Q" interest rate ceilings.

- the continuing federal prohibition of the payment of interest on commercial checking accounts
- usury ceilings by some states on some categories of loans
- limits by some states on various categories of credit card fees
- restrictions by some states on intrastate branching
- restrictions by most states and by the federal government on interstate branching[10]
- the federal Glass-Steagall Act's limitations on the ability of banks to enter the securities business[11]
- the federal Bank Holding Company Acts' severe limitations on banks' (and their holding companies') activities outside of banking
- the federal Community Reinvestment Act's requirement that banks "serve the needs" of their communities

Outside the United States, limitations on banks' interest rates charged on loans and paid on deposits are common, as are limitations on banks' activities. Also, many governments restrict entry into banking generally and are especially restrictive with respect to banks that are headquartered outside the country.[12]

Economic regulation of the securities industry is much less widespread, but examples can be found. In the United States the pre-1970s support by the U.S. Securities and Exchange Commission (SEC) for the New York Stock Exchange's (NYSE) system of minimum fixed commissions was one such instance. The Glass-Steagall Act's reciprocal limitations on the ability of securities firms to operate commercial banks are a second. As is true of banking, outside the United States many governments restrict entry by firms into securities activities, especially by nonnational firms.[13]

The insurance industry in the United States is regulated exclusively at the level of the individual states. One form of economic regulation is the price ceilings that some states impose on some lines of property-casualty insurance (for example, automobile liability insurance) and on health insurance. Another form is the must-serve

---

10. The Riegle-Neal Interstate Banking and Branching Act of 1994 will eliminate many, but not all, of the restrictions on interstate branching.

11. Loopholes, discovered by sharp-eyed lawyers in the 1980s, have allowed a few commercial banks to engage in securities underwriting and have allowed some securities firms to operate "nonbank banks."

12. These limitations are those that extend beyond considerations of safety and soundness.

13. Again, these restrictions extend beyond considerations of safety and soundness.

requirements imposed by some states. And the Bank Holding Company Acts' severe limitations on the ability of banks to offer insurance have a reciprocal effect in prohibiting insurance companies from offering banking services. And outside the United States similar limitations, as well as price floors and limitations on entry, are frequently found.

Health-Safety-Environment (H-S-E) Regulation. This type of regulation typically involves mandated changes in production processes or product qualities or types.[14] Nonfinance examples include the U.S. Federal Aviation Administration's safety requirements for airlines, including minimum requirements for their aircraft, pilots, and procedures; the U.S. Food and Drug Administration's safety requirements with respect to pharmaceuticals and food additives; the U.S. Environmental Protection Agency's maximum limits on the emissions of air pollutants from electric utilities (and other stationary sources) and from motor vehicles; and the U.S. Occupational Safety and Health Administration's requirements for workplace safety.

Again, in U.S. banking this type of regulation is pervasive. It is typically described as "safety-and-soundness" or "prudential" regulation. Some of the features of federal and state safety-and-soundness regulation include:

- minimum capital (net worth) requirements
- limitations on the types of assets, and their percentages, that a bank can hold
- limitations on the types of liabilities that a bank can issue
- limitations on non-asset-based activities in which a bank can engage
- requirements that banks' deposits (up to a maximum of $100,000) be federally insured
- limitations with respect to the "character," financial capability, and business competence of those who own and control banks

Similar forms of prudential regulation are applied by virtually all governments to their banking systems.

As was true of economic regulation, the securities area has a relatively lighter load of H-S-E regulation than has banking. Examples in the United States include the SEC's minimum capital requirements for broker dealers; its requirement that securities firms' "registered

---

14. Together with information regulation, this form of regulation is sometimes described as "social regulation." For an overview, see Gruenspecht and Lave (1989).

representatives" should be licensed, should "know their customers," and should recommend only investments that are suitable for the specific circumstances of their customers; its requirement that only accredited investors (institutions) be allowed to purchase private placement securities; and its requirement that money market mutual funds limit their holdings of low-quality commercial paper.

With respect to insurance—both property-casualty and life-health—safety-and-soundness regulation by the individual states takes forms quite similar to those imposed on banks: for example, minimum net worth (capital or surplus) requirements, limitations on the suitability of assets, and limitations on activities.[15]

Information Regulation. This type of regulation typically involves the requirement that sellers attach specified types of information to the goods and services they sell. Nonfinance examples include the U.S. Department of Transportation's requirement that an airline's ads for special fares should include (in fine print) the major details of the special fares' limitations; a state utility commission's requirements that electric or telephone utility bills include specified types of information; the FDA's requirements for labeling to accompany pharmaceuticals and processed foods; and a local taxicab commission's requirement that a cab driver's name and license number be prominently displayed.

In the finance area banks bear a relatively lighter load of information regulation. In the United States, banks are expected to inform their depositors and their borrowers as to the relevant interest rates and fees, using a standardized format. Banks must also make available to any requesting party a statement of condition, providing a summary of its recent profit-and-loss and balance sheet results.

By contrast, the domain of securities issuance and trading bears a heavy load of information regulation. Examples for the United States include the SEC's requirements that issuers of publicly traded securities should disclose extensive information at the time of issuance and then disclose extensive information at periodic intervals and on a uniform basis—that is, according to generally accepted accounting principles (GAAP). Further examples include the SEC's requirement that mutual funds should report yield information on a specific and standardized basis, and its requirements that a publicly traded company's insiders disclose their holdings and trading activities.

Insurance companies are similarly required to provide extensive information concerning terms and conditions to their policy holders.

---

15. See, for example, Kopke and Randall (1991).

And many governments have similar information-disclosure requirements that apply to their banking, securities, and insurance sectors.

The three aforementioned regulatory categories are not mutually exclusive and may blur at the edges. Some forms of economic regulation may have some real or alleged H-S-E justifications or effects—for example, the CAB's airline regulation or the Glass-Steagall restrictions. Also, the CAB's entry restrictions on airlines clearly impeded the development of an important production technology ("hub and spokes" scheduling), which emerged only after deregulation. And profit limitations in the form of rate-of-return restrictions are likely to influence input choices in production.[16] Further, virtually all forms of H-S-E and information regulation have some cost consequences, with implications for prices, profits, and possibly even entry. Nevertheless, the intent, form, and direct consequences of these three types of regulation are generally distinct enough that this typology is useful for furthering our understanding of regulatory goals, processes, and effects.

Market Failure and Government Failure

What might justify the forms of regulation just described? In principle, perfectly competitive markets ought to achieve efficient outcomes without the need for any governmental intervention. But real-world markets may exhibit one or more types of "market failure" that would preclude their achieving those efficient outcomes.

Market Failure. These market failures can be categorized in the following eight ways.

Market power. If one or a few sellers are present in a market and entry is not easy, the quantity sold is likely to be smaller and the equilibrium price is likely to be higher than would be true for an otherwise similar competitive industry. This is frequently described as the problem of monopoly or oligopoly.

Market power can arise (when entry is not easy) through explicit or implicit collusion among sellers (price-fixing conspiracies); through mergers that significantly reduce the numbers of firms and increase their market shares, thereby making explicit or implicit collusion easier; through technological conditions (economies of scale) that limit the number of efficient-size firms that can serve a market (for example, the monopolies of local exchange telephone service or of local

---

16. This is frequently described as the "Averch-Johnson effect"; for a summary, see Baumol and Klevorick (1980).

electricity distribution); or through government restrictions that prevent entry and thereby protect market incumbents (for example, the CAB's restrictions on entry into the airline industry).

Examples of market power can be found in financial services, though they were more frequent in the past than in the present. Before the 1980s, banks were protected both by economic regulation (for example, limitations on branching, on entry, and on the interest that could be paid on most deposits) and by technology (limiting the ability of banks to offer services and therefore to compete over wide geographic areas and limiting the ability of nonbanks to offer loan or deposit services that could compete with those of banks). Consequently, banks in local geographic areas where rivals were few were often able to exercise market power: to pay lower interest rates on deposits or charge higher interest rates on loans.[17] As was noted in the introductory section of this chapter, the rapid improvements in financial services technologies have been widening markets and increasing competition;[18] often this has been reinforced by a loosening of key regulatory restrictions. Even in this new environment, however, the markets for some bank products and services (such as loans to small and medium-size businesses, checking account deposits, safe deposit boxes) may still be local, and banks may still be able to exercise market power when their numbers are small and entry is difficult.[19]

Similarly, in the securities area, the pre-1970s agreement among NYSE member firms as to minimum brokerage commissions collectively gave those firms market power. The protected position of specialist market makers in most stocks listed on the NYSE similarly gave them market power. Specialists today in stocks where trading volumes are insufficient to permit competitive market makers may still enjoy some residual market power.

In insurance, with thousands of firms offering lines of products in the United States and with relatively easy entry, the major source of market power has been economic regulation in some states that has placed limitations on price competition in some lines of property-casualty insurance and title insurance.[20]

Economies of scale. The presence of economies of scale may serve as a source of pricing inefficiency even if the seller is not exploiting

---

17. For a survey of the evidence as of the early 1980s, see Gilbert (1984).

18. See also Aronson (1995).

19. For recent evidence, see Weiss (1989), Berger and Hannan (1989, 1992), and Hannan (1991).

20. See Pugel and Saunders (1992); see White (1984).

market power. If the technology of production in a relevant market is such that larger volumes (per unit of time) always imply lower unit costs,[21] then the efficient outcomes of setting price equal to marginal costs may not be feasible, since they would not allow the firm to recover its full costs. Systems of local telephone service or electricity distribution may be of this nature.

In financial services, the broadening of markets has reduced the practical importance of economies of scale as a source of market failure. Even comparatively small banks, securities firms, and insurance companies appear to be able to achieve sufficiently low-cost levels to allow them to compete effectively with larger firms;[22] size does not appear to be an important efficiency factor. Consequently, in all but the smallest of local geographic areas, economies of scale are unlikely to be a significant influence on pricing. Securities markets themselves, however, appear to exhibit economies of scale, since greater volumes of transactions (greater liquidity) are usually accompanied by smaller transaction costs (narrower spreads). For small (thin) securities markets, greater volumes may still bring significant scale effects.

Similarly, larger insurance markets may yield more actuarial data with respect to risks, allowing insurance companies, if they pool their data, to price their services more accurately.

Externality (spillover) effects. If, as a consequence of a firm's production or an individual's consumption, there are direct and uncompensated effects on others—negative or positive—outside a market framework, then the market outcome (even with a competitive structure) will not be efficient. With negative externalities (such as air or water pollution or traffic congestion), too much of the good or service will be produced or consumed, the price will be too low, and too little effort and too few resources will be devoted to correcting or reducing the externality. With positive externalities (for example, when one firm learns about improved production processes because of the efforts of other firms), too little of the good or service will be produced, and its price will be too high; also, too little effort will be devoted to enhancing the externality.

The usual source of externalities is the absence or poor specification of property rights or difficulties in enforcing them. For example,

---

21. This is a separate phenomenon from that of a learning curve, which involves reductions in unit costs as a consequence of the accumulated production volume over any extended period of time. This latter phenomenon more closely resembles a process of gradual technological change.

22. For a recent summary and survey of the relevant evidence, see Berger, Hunter, and Timme (1993).

problems of air or water pollution can arise from the absence of clearly defined property rights in clean air or water or the free-rider problems that would accompany any single party's efforts to enforce its property rights.

Negative externalities can be found in financial services in a number of areas. For banks, the phenomenon of a depositor run has at its heart a negative externality. Depositors either fear (correctly or incorrectly) that the insolvency of their bank will cause a loss in the value of their deposits or fear that other (fearful) depositors will rush to the bank and impair the first depositors' options to claim liquidity on demand; either reason causes depositors to run to the bank to withdraw their deposits.[23] In essence, each depositor's withdrawal has a negative effect on the others, reducing the likelihood that the others will be able to withdraw their deposits. Similarly, the failure of one bank may cause poorly informed depositors to run on a neighboring bank. Or the fraudulent actions of one securities firm may cause the public to believe that other firms could or would act fraudulently. Similarly, the failure or fraudulent actions of one insurance company may have detrimental effects on policy holders' perceptions of other insurance companies. An example of positive externalities would be one firm's learning about another firm's development of a new banking, securities, or insurance product and thereby being able to develop and offer a similar product.

Public goods. A "public good" is one in which the marginal costs of an extra party's enjoying the benefits of the good are relatively low or zero and exclusion from those benefits is difficult or impossible. In essence, a public good is one in which the positive externalities are substantial and pervasive.[24] Again, competitive markets will produce too little (or none) of the good or service, and its price will be too high. The provision of national defense, a police force's accomplishments in reducing the level of criminal activity in a community, a community's efforts to control or eradicate mosquitoes, and an individual's creation of an idea (information) that is useful to others would all be examples of public goods.

In the financial services area, the previous example of one firm's developing a product that other firms can copy would qualify as an example of a public good; similarly, the price established in one mar-

---

23. See Diamond and Dybvig (1983) and Postlewaite and Vives (1987). A similar phenomenon could develop among life insurance policy holders; see Skipper (1995).

24. Many of the phenomena that are identified as negative externalities, such as air and water pollution, are thus really "negative public goods."

ket for a security may be useful to participants in other markets and would constitute a public good, as would the information that financial services firms regularly generate: for example, a securities analyst's recommendations for his clients, an insurance company's actuarial information, or the credit histories of specific bank customers.

Uncertainty and the absence of complete knowledge. If individuals do not have complete knowledge about the present and future choices that are before them, they face uncertainty and risk as to the consequences of their choices and actions. Since most individuals are likely to be risk-averse, they are likely to take ameliorating or offsetting actions—such as acquiring information, forming portfolios, hedging, or purchasing insurance—to reduce their risk exposure. These offsetting actions often mean that additional resources must be expended. Also, with the presence of any uncertainty, individuals' ex ante choices may yield ex post mistakes.

The financial services area—especially securities—is one in which uncertainty and incomplete information are pervasive; but it is also one in which a major fraction of the services offered are designed to ameliorate or offset the effects of uncertainty. Such services include the insured deposits offered by banks; the services of research firms and of rating firms; the diversified portolios offered by mutual funds; the options, futures, and swaps instruments that are now an active part of the banking and securities world; and the wide range of insurance products offered by insurance companies.

Asymmetric information. Problems of "asymmetric information" arise when a party on one side of a transaction has relevant information that the other side does not have.[25] For example, a seller of a good or service is likely to know more about its qualities and properties than does the buyer; an agent (such as a lawyer) is likely to know more about its actions than is the principal (a litigant) on behalf of whom the agent is expected to perform services; a borrower is likely to know more about its own prospects of repaying a loan than is a lender; a buyer of insurance is more likely to know about its own risk characteristics and the risk consequences of its prospective behavior than is a seller of insurance.[26]

---

25. For an overview, see Stiglitz (1989).

26. These asymmetric information phenomena can usefully be grouped as "hidden information" problems (the "lemons" problem of the buyer's knowing less about the qualities of the seller's product than does the seller, or the "adverse selection" problem of the insurance company's knowing less about

In the absence of any amelioration of these conditions, market participants may initially be adversely affected by the outcomes of these transactions but then learn to adjust their behavior—perhaps by participating less often in these transactions. Output of the relevant good or service is likely to be lower than if the asymmetric information phenomenon did not exist. Over time markets may develop institutions and practices—such as information-generating entities, certifying agencies, reliance on reputation, reliance on "signals"—that can ameliorate the problems of asymmetric information. But these institutions and practices, in turn, involve costs and imperfections that would not be present if the asymmetric information problem were somehow absent.

Financial services markets are an area where the problems of potential or actual asymmetric information are pervasive. Borrowers know more about their prospects for repayment than do lenders. Insured parties know more about their riskiness than do insurance companies. Bank managers know more about the values of their portfolios and their solvency than do depositors; the same is true for insurance company managers vis-à-vis their policy holders. Securities issuers know more about themselves than do prospective purchasers of the securities. Corporate managers know more about the quality of their services and recommendations than do their customers. Various information-based institutions have developed and flourished in efforts to ameliorate these problems of asymmetric information—banks and insurance companies as information and monitoring specialists with respect to their loan portfolios; deposit insurance; accounting firms; securities analysts; research firms; rating agencies; investment advisors. These institutions in turn, however, are likely to embody their own potential problems of asymmetric information.

Individuals who are unable to know their own best interests. If individuals do not know their own best interests, then even complete information will not prevent mistaken choices. This form of market failure is generally different from the problem of asymmetric information. If individuals are overwhelmed by the complexity of choices—for example, judging the safety of an airline or the quality of a hospital's services—they may rely on agents to help them (but with concomitant agent-principal problems). But if individuals do not know their own

---

the risk attributes of its insureds than do the latter) or as "hidden action" problems (the "agent-principal" problem of the buyer of services' knowing less about the agent's actions than does the latter, or the "moral hazard" problem of the buyer of insurance engaging in more risky behavior because it is covered by insurance than if it did not have coverage). See Arrow (1985).

best interests, they may not even realize that they should be relying on agents, and they are unlikely to learn from their mistakes.

This "widows and orphans" approach to individuals' behavior is clearly a popular one for legislators, as is evidenced by numerous regulatory laws that require that "unsafe" products and services—including financial products and services—be banned from markets, rather than allowing individuals, or their agents, to make their own choices and trade-offs. Even if it is an accurate characterization of a portion of a society (beyond the categories of children and the mentally incompetent to which it clearly would apply), the presence of others who are capable of making sensible choices then poses a difficult problem of how best to deal with safety issues in a society with diverse decision-making capabilities.

Problems of "second best." If an uncorrected market imperfection or failure exists in one market, then it will generally be true that unhindered competition in that market or in a related market—one in which there are demand or supply consequences from the initial imperfection—will not yield socially optimal results.[27]

A Caveat and a Linkage. This listing of the major forms of market failure may initially encourage the impression that virtually all markets are ripe for governmental intervention. After all, few if any real-world markets would fit the textbook ideal of a perfectly competitive market. As will be argued below, however, governments are also far from perfect. The notion of the omniscient and benevolent governmental agency that can perfectly correct the failures of the private sector is also a textbook construct that few if any real-world government agencies could replicate. In sum, since both real-world markets and real-world governments exhibit varying degrees of imperfection, the actual policy debate concerning regulation—that is, whether to regulate, how to regulate, the breadth of regulation, and so forth—must always involve choices among imperfect markets *and* imperfect governments.

Subject to this caveat, this listing of the sources of market failure can be linked to the types of regulation discussed in the previous section. The problems of market power and of economies of scale may be best treated through economic regulation;[28] externalities, public goods, and individuals' lack of awareness of their own best inter-

---

27. See Lipsey and Lancaster (1956–1957).

28. Government ownership and taxes and subsidies are other possible tools of intervention.

ests may be best approached through H-S-E regulation;[29] the problems of incomplete information and asymmetric information may be best approached through some combination of H-S-E and information regulation; and problems of "second best" are, in principle, the domain of any form of regulation.

Government Failure. Though government regulation can in principle improve the efficiency of imperfect markets, governments too can fail to deliver their promised outcomes, and their efforts at intervention can cause the efficiency of markets to deteriorate rather than increase.[30] This government failure can occur for a number of reasons:

Difficulty in formulating clear and implementable goals. Without the specific profit goal that motivates most private enterprises, a government agency may well be buffeted by diffuse goals (for example, to improve the economy's efficiency; to improve the economy's income or wealth distribution; to avoid economic disruptions; to treat individuals fairly) that are likely to be conflicting and difficult to translate for specific implementation. Overarching goals (such as "serving the people") may be even more subjective and open to conflicting interpretations and haphazard implementation.

Weak (or absent) incentives. Again, without profit incentives or the threat of bankruptcy, the diffuse goals of a government agency may make difficult the development of incentives to motivate government employees to work toward those goals. Also, social values concerning income distribution and greater equality of incomes are more likely to hold sway in the public sector, making links between government employees' job performances and their wages (with the likely consequence of wage differentials) more difficult to implement. Further, agency personnel may act in ways that enhance the importance and security of their own jobs rather than pursuing the larger public interest that is supposed to be the mission of their agency.

Difficulties of management. To be effective, organizations have to be well managed. With diffuse goals, government agencies are likely to be more difficult to manage than are organizations with more specific goals. And in any event, good management is a relatively scarce

---

29. Again, taxes (effluent fees) and subsidies are other possible tools for dealing with externalities and public goods. The creation and enforcement of property rights in "intellectual property" (such as patents, copyrights, and trademarks) is yet another way of dealing with the public goods problems that arise in the context of the creation of ideas and information.

30. See Wolf (1989) and White (1994).

skill that usually commands premium wages in an economy. The egalitarian ethos that makes performance-linked pay difficult to implement in government agencies also causes a compression in the government wage scale, so that low-skill jobs are usually overpaid (as compared with their private market counterparts) and high-skill jobs are underpaid. As a consequence, governments frequently have difficulty in attracting and retaining highly skilled individuals, including managers, and government effectiveness suffers.[31]

Inadequate information. Government agencies may be no better at acquiring and using information than private-sector entities.[32] Indeed, the previously described problems of incentives and management would argue that government agencies may well have substantial difficulties in this respect. But with inadequate information, government agencies are likely to be plagued by the same types of problems and inefficiencies that were raised as potential market failures for private-sector entities. Regulatory controls based on poor information could well be costly; government regulators are likely to face asymmetric information problems vis-à-vis their regulated entities.[33]

Rent-seeking behavior. In an economy of gain-seeking individuals, those who are significantly affected by government action are unlikely to remain passive.[34] Instead, they are likely to try to influence governmental processes to achieve outcomes that are favorable to themselves (*rent seeking*) and will find worthwhile the expenditure of considerable resources (ranging from outright bribery and corruption to more subtle lobbying and promises of electoral support) in efforts to twist government policy and actions in their favor. Even if these rent-seeking individuals and groups do not succeed in affecting poli-

---

31. Government agencies may be able to attract some highly skilled individuals who hope to acquire the specific skills related to government operation and then leave to use those skills in the private sector. For example, the U.S. government has been able to attract young lawyers, even though its entry-level pay scale has been below the levels of the private-sector alternatives. But the flow of skilled human resources at senior levels is usually one-way—from government to the private sector—with the exception of short-term political appointments. The exceptions to this pattern are individuals who strongly believe that government service has an important intrinsic value and are willing to enter and remain in government service despite unfavorable pay differentials vis-à-vis the private sector.

32. For overviews and further discussion, see Stiglitz (1988, 1990).

33. For an overview, see Baron (1989).

34. See Krueger (1974) and, for an overview, Noll (1989).

cies (such as capturing an agency or a legislature, as is discussed below), their efforts may well use up substantial real resources.

Rent-creating capture. Comparatively small groups of individuals who are potentially affected a great deal by government actions will have the most to gain from organizing themselves to influence government policy—to "capture" a regulatory agency or even a legislature—in their favor.[35] Their success in achieving *rent-creating* policies—for example, regulatory protection—is likely to be at the expense of the general public. The latter, with each individual suffering only a small loss as a consequence of the altered policies, finds the organizational costs of trying to oppose the changes to be too high. Consequently, rent-creating "special interest" regulatory measures and outcomes are likely to prevail, at the expense of the general population and of efficiency in the economy.

Pursuit of income redistribution. A society may well decide that it is dissatisfied with the income distribution among individuals that would arise as a consequence of the workings of markets, whether those markets are operating perfectly or imperfectly. Government action is the vehicle for redistribution, and regulation can be an important means of implicitly affecting the distribution of income, although taxes and subsidies are more common and more direct.[36] But these actions surely create inefficiencies, even if they are successful at redistributing income.[37] Further, the greater is the perceived legitimacy of government as a redistributive force, the greater is the potential for the rent-seeking behavior and rent-creating capture discussed above.

Regulatory efforts to achieve "fair" outcomes—as is true of much regulation in the securities area—would fall into this same general category. Although the regulation may apparently be aimed at correcting specific imperfections—for example, informational deficiencies or asymmetries, or market-power problems—the inclusion of fairness as a goal will usually imply some explicit or implicit notions of income redistribution, as compared with what an unregulated market would yield.

A Stronger Caveat. The combination of rent-seeking and rent-creating behavior and social concerns encompassing income distribution and

---

35. See Stigler (1971), Posner (1974), Peltzman (1976), and, for an overview, Noll (1989).
36. See Posner (1971).
37. See Okun (1975).

"fairness" can create potent regulatory forces that impede the efficient functioning of markets. The American regulatory landscape is littered with instances in which government agencies have practiced extensive *economic* regulation with the proffered justification of restricting the exercise of market power but with the reality of protecting and enhancing it. Examples at the federal level include airlines, rail transportation, trucking, banking, stock brokerage commissions, long-distance telephone service, and broadcasting. Examples at the state and local levels include trucking, banking, insurance, long-distance and local telephone service, and taxicabs.[38] For the purposes of this chapter, it is especially worth noting that the major instances of state and federal economic regulation of banking—restrictions on branching, restrictions on entry, ceilings on the interest rates that can be paid on deposits, and restrictions on the nonbanking activities that can be pursued by bank holding companies—have protected market power and impeded competition, rather than the reverse. And other economic regulatory measures, such as ceilings on the interest rates that can be charged on loans, have discouraged competitive banks from making loans during inflationary periods and, again, have impeded the efficient functioning of these markets. Similarly, state regulation of some lines of insurance has protected market power in some instances and often prevented the efficient workings of insurance markets.

Further, the regulatory goal of cross-subsidy—achieving income redistribution by keeping prices paid by some users above long-run marginal costs so as to be able to use the surplus to keep the prices paid by other users below long-run marginal costs—has been an additional force for the employment of the tools of economic regulation in ways that protect and enhance market power. If prices are to be kept above long-run marginal costs, entrants must be prevented from "cream-skimming" or "cherry-picking" these supraprofitable markets, and market incumbents must also be protected from "excessive" competition among themselves in these markets; hence, these regulatory regimes must prevent entry and restrict competition among incumbents. Many of the perverse examples of economic regulation that were just cited have involved, at least in part, efforts to achieve cross-subsidy. In banking, the Community Reinvestment Act's mandate that banks "serve the needs" of their local communities represents the pursuit of cross-subsidy.[39] Similar community must-serve

---

38. Discussion and examples can be found in Philips (1975), Weiss and Klass (1981, 1986), and Joskow and Rose (1989).

39. For further discussion, see White (1993a).

requirements imposed on insurance companies also represent the regulatory pursuit of cross-subsidy.

At first glance, H-S-E regulation would seem less susceptible to the forms of abuse and perverse application just described; but there are "winners" and "losers" arising from virtually every H-S-E regulatory action. The combination of less-than-omniscient regulatory bodies with rent-seeking and rent-creating behavior, as well as the importance of fairness as a social goal, can lead to regulatory efforts and outcomes that involve substantial market distortions and inefficiencies.[40] The mantle of H-S-E goals can also serve to cloak protectionist and exclusionary measures, such as the Glass-Steagall Act's barrier between commercial banking and investment banking and the Bank Holding Company Acts' exclusion of banks from most forms of insurance.

Further, the costs of regulation can have disproportionate effects on some types of firms as compared with others; for example, compliance with H-S-E regulation often entails substantial fixed costs, which favor larger firms (which can spread these costs over larger volumes of output) over smaller firms.[41] If the form and extent of the regulation are otherwise appropriate, then these are just the legitimate social costs of doing business, which may have the same kind of uneven effects that the purchase of a necessary but expensive piece of equipment may have.[42] But if the type or extent of regulation is inappropriate *and* it has an uneven impact (disfavoring smaller or newer firms), protectionism in outcome—and possibly in intent—is an added feature of such regulation.[43]

Information regulation almost always has costs as well as benefits and thus is susceptible to the same problem of the potential inappropriateness of types and levels as was just described for H-S-E regulation. Though information regulation is less likely to be explicitly exclusionary, the combination of inappropriate levels and large fixed costs is likely to have implicit exclusionary effects on smaller firms.

In sum, the real-world imperfections of government have yielded

---

40. For examples and further discussion, see White (1981), Gruenspecht and Lave (1989), and Viscusi (1994).

41. This disproportionate impact on small firms is exacerbated when H-S-E regulation takes the form of "design standards" (a specific process or type of equipment is mandated) rather than "performance standards" (a specific result or performance is required). The latter type of standard would give smaller firms greater flexibility in meeting a given requirement.

42. Again, the inflexibility of design standards would exacerbate the impact.

43. For a discussion, see White (1993b) and the references cited there.

numerous instances of the regulatory process's being used for abusive purposes and reaching inefficient outcomes; the regulation of financial services has not been an exception. Indeed, the deregulation movement of the late 1970s and the 1980s was a reaction to these abusive purposes and inefficient outcomes, especially in the economic regulation areas.[44] These abuses need not lead to the conclusion that all governmental regulation should be forsaken. But they do point toward constant caution in embracing new regulation—national or international—and toward the value of frequent reassessments of the motives, methods, and outcomes of existing regulatory regimes.

Competition versus Harmonization

The process of competition among firms can be analyzed as occurring within the confines of a market; indeed, one useful definition of a market is the collection of sellers who are in effective competition with each other.[45] This market may be embodied in a formal structure, with a physical representation and legal ownership framework, as is true for securities exchanges; or the market may simply be a group of firms that are effectively competing with each other.

The Widening Scope of Competition. As the costs of transacting over longer distances fall (because of improvements in the technologies of transportation, telecommunications, or data processing), markets widen. Buyers and sellers who are located farther apart can now more easily transact with each other. Also, if changes in production or product technologies allow incumbent firms more easily to produce and sell a wider array of products or allow new opportunities for entrants, markets are again widened: buyers face more sellers who are competing for the former's purchases.

In the absence of formal market structures, the process of market widening is fully described by the larger numbers of sellers or buyers who are encompassed. To the extent that groups of firms initially believe that they constitute a local market and then find themselves enmeshed in a larger market, the description below of wider competition among formal market structures, such as exchanges, may apply

---

44. See, for example, Weiss and Klass (1986), Joskow and Rose (1989), White (1993b, 1996), Winston (1993), and Joskow and Noll (1994).

45. Indeed, this is approximately the market definition approach underlying the Merger Guidelines that guide U.S. merger antitrust policy. See U.S. Department of Justice and FTC (1992) and, for discussion, Kwoka and White (1994).

as well. A local trade association—say, a state association of bankers—may be the vehicle through which the concerns of the local group are expressed.

But where formal market structures are present, there is an additional element: the wider markets mean that the formal market structures (such as securities exchanges) themselves are in competition with each other, for sellers as well as buyers.[46] In essence, with improved technology both buyers and sellers can evade (or arbitrage) any higher costs of transacting in a local market by conducting their transactions in a more distant market—where distance may represent either geographic mileage or the extent of product dissimilarity.

Financial services markets in the United States have experienced substantial widening and the concomitant intensified competition in the past few decades. Banks are increasingly competing with each other's branches and subsidiaries over greater geographic distances, with other intermediating lenders (for example, insurance companies, industrial finance companies, consumer finance companies), with providers of deposit-like products (such as money market mutual funds), and with the facilitators of direct securities issuances (commercial paper, junk bonds, securitized residential mortgages). Securities exchanges have experienced similar market expansions. Geographically separated stock exchanges have increasingly competed among themselves (and with the less formally organized NASDAQ market system) for members, for listings, and for order flow. The stock exchanges have increasingly competed with the exchanges that trade other (but somewhat similar) kinds of instruments (such as financial options and futures). All exchanges are increasingly competing with over-the-counter (OTC) transactions in stocks and in customized swaps, options, and futures. And in the 1990s the U.S. financial markets and exchanges are facing increased international competition, as are the markets and exchanges located in other countries.[47]

---

46. See Bradley (1992).

47. A recent example of competition among exchanges is provided by the decision of the London Metal Exchange (LME) to open copper warehouses in the United States, thereby improving the LME's competitive position in copper trading vis-à-vis the New York Mercantile Exchange (NYME); see McGee (1994). It is also worth noting that the globalization of markets has displayed a pattern that is quite consistent with the predictions of the asymmetric information paradigm. A recent overview (Bodner 1990) describes the process of globalization as most advanced for foreign exchange, next for government obligations, corporations' debt (bonds) in third place, and corporate equity markets as being the least globalized. This ranking is consistent with the transparency and simplicity of the various types of instruments and the infor-

A parallel process applies to regulatory regimes: if a regulatory agency has responsibility for local markets or exchanges, the widening of markets represents a potential erosion of its authority. Buyers or sellers can more easily evade the agency's regulatory strictures (if they are burdensome) by transacting in an out-of-jurisdiction market or exchange. Previously separate and autonomous regulatory regimes are increasingly conscious of each other's jurisdictions and potential for snaring transaction volumes by reducing their regulatory burden. To the extent that regulatory agencies are concerned about avoiding the loss of transactions from their jurisdictions—because of concern as to the possible consequences for buyers or sellers within their jurisdictions of such out-of-jurisdiction transactions,[48] or because of worries by agency personnel that reduced within-jurisdiction volumes might bring into question the size of their agency and perhaps even the justification for their agency—they are thereby implicitly or explicitly in competition with each other.

Again, the American experience is instructive. Since 1863 U.S. banking regulation has been characterized by a "dual banking system."[49] Both the federal government and the individual state governments have the ability to charter and regulate commercial banks. (The same dualism has characterized the regulation of savings and loan institutions since 1932.) Since a bank can usually switch easily between a federal charter (and primary regulation) and a state charter for the state in which the bank is headquartered,[50] the federal and state regulatory regimes have been in effective bilateral competition.[51] (Periodically, however, the Congress has imposed federal harmonization by passing laws that impose federal requirements on state-chartered banks.)[52] Further, since the late 1970s banks have been

---

mation disadvantage that nonnational transactors would experience relative to national entities.

48. For example, the regulators may be concerned that within-jurisdiction sellers are unduly losing sales or that within-jurisdiction buyers are not being adequately protected.

49. See Scott (1977), Bloch (1985), Isaac (1994), and Coffee (1995).

50. A very recent example is Continental [Illinois] Bank's decision to switch from a federal charter to an Illinois charter. See Klinkerman (1993).

51. For a recent discussion, see Isaac (1994).

52. These landmark events would include the Banking Acts of 1933 and 1935, the Bank Holding Company Acts of 1956 and 1970, the Community Reinvestment Act of 1977, the Depository Institutions Deregulation and Monetary Control Act of 1980, the Garn-St Germain Act of 1982, the Financial Institutions Reform, Recovery, and Enforcement Act of 1989, the Federal Deposit Insurance Corporation Improvements Act of 1991, and the Riegle-Neal Interstate Banking and Branching Act of 1994.

technologically capable of offering their customers some services (such as credit cards and some limited insurance services) from remote locations, outside their headquarters state. This technological capability has brought state regulatory regimes into competition with each other. And in the 1980s and 1990s, foreign-based banks expanded their operations in the United States, and large U.S. banks have been competing for large corporate customers, at home and abroad, with other large foreign-based banks. The U.S. regulatory regime for banks is now in competition with other national regulatory regimes.

A somewhat similar story has applied to securities regulation. So long as the widening of securities markets remained within the United States and was largely confined to equity instruments, the Securities and Exchange Commission (SEC) did not feel seriously threatened, although it clearly felt more comfortable dealing with the New York Stock Exchange (NYSE) and its member firms and was somewhat worried about its weakened control over over-the-counter (OTC) and off-floor transactions. With the rise of the financial options and futures markets in the early 1970s—largely in Chicago, away from the SEC's traditional eastern seaboard focus—and the establishment of the Commodities Futures Trading Commission (CFTC) to regulate some of these markets,[53] however, the SEC faced more serious challenges to its authority and jurisdiction. Its two decades of coexistence with the CFTC have been marked by alternating periods of open political battles for jurisdiction, uneasy political truces, and sporadic efforts at harmonization.[54] And both agencies now face international competition in the 1990s—as do the national regulatory agencies of other countries.[55]

Two current regulatory issues typify U.S. regulators' concern about international competition. First, in banking, different national regulatory requirements, especially capital requirements, are likely to affect the ability of nationally headquartered banks to compete internationally. Further, the failure of one large bank that is involved extensively in international transactions may have major ramifications

---

53. The CFTC was also given regulatory authority over the agricultural and mineral commodities futures markets. The former markets had been regulated by the U.S. Department of Agriculture; the latter had been largely unregulated.

54. See, for example, Kane (1986), Johnson (1992) and Coffee (1995).

55. The LME competition with the NYME is again instructive. In response to the LME's competitive thrust, the chairman of the NYME indicated that he planned to meet with the chairman of the CFTC "to discuss regulatory changes that would help [NYME] confront the LME's challenge" (McGee, 1994).

across national borders. To what extent should U.S. regulators pursue and cooperate with international efforts at harmonizing capital requirements? How should the local (U.S.) activities of foreign-headquartered banks be regulated? Should these banks be allowed to operate through branches, or should they be required to establish separately capitalized subsidiaries?

Second, in securities, should the SEC maintain its requirements that all companies whose equity shares are listed for trading in the United States (on an exchange or in other markets) must report their financial information according to U.S. GAAP? Will unyielding insistence on this requirement cause non-U.S. companies (for whom a restatement of their financial information to conform with U.S. GAAP is an extra cost) to decline to list their shares for trading in the United States, thereby disadvantaging U.S. exchanges and market makers? But would relaxation of the GAAP reporting requirements for all firms mean that U.S. investors would be less well informed and protected? If the SEC relaxed the GAAP reporting requirements only for non-U.S. firms, would U.S. firms be somehow disadvantaged? And would U.S. investors in these non-U.S. companies' shares thereby be at an information disadvantage because of the less complete information that they would receive? But, if the SEC maintains its strict GAAP requirements, will U.S. investors simply evade the SEC's efforts to protect them by purchasing these non-U.S. companies' shares through markets or exchanges abroad, albeit with larger transaction costs?[56]

Some Generic Answers. We can now restate the questions that have motivated this chapter. In an environment of increasing global competition in financial services, when (if ever) is international harmonization of national securities regulation likely to improve the efficiency of financial services markets? Conversely, when (if ever) is an absence of international harmonization, and thus a process of implicit or explicit competition among national regulatory regimes, likely to improve the efficiency of financial services markets?

The framework of the previous section provides a basis for generic answers to these questions.[57] For international harmonization

---

56. For further discussion see Edwards (1992), Freund (1993a, 1993b), Shapiro (1993), and Torres (1993).

57. A somewhat similar framework was adopted by White (1986) in addressing the question of competition among states to attract industry and by Bebchuk (1992) to address and review the literature on the competition among states to be the state of incorporation for U.S. companies. See also Steil (1992, 1993), Key and Scott (1991, 1992), Benston (1992a, 1992b), and Coffee (1995).

to be potentially worthwhile there must be some form of market failure (such as market power or externality) that transcends national boundaries and for which individual national regulatory efforts are somehow inadequate. But even in such instances the dangers of internationally harmonized government failure should lead to caution in endorsing a harmonization approach.

The application of these principles to financial services leads to the following general approach to the international harmonization questions:

Pro-harmonization. The conditions under which international harmonization of a *specific* regulatory provision could improve the efficiency of financial services markets would be one or more of the following:

• The specific national regulatory provision is efficiently addressing a genuine market failure condition and evasive transactions abroad would somehow undermine that effort.

• The process of harmonization itself may be a vehicle for *relaxing* the stringency of protectionist national regulations that have created pockets of market power.

• The process of harmonization itself may be a means of simplifying and making more uniform a diverse set of different national rules and procedures, with the consequence of lowering the transaction costs for the financial services firms and users who try to transact on a multinational basis.

There is a separate question as to whether harmonization, even if desirable, can succeed in an environment of international competition. We will return to this question below.

Pro-competition. The conditions under which international competition among specific regulatory provisions could improve the efficiency of financial services markets would be one or both of the following:

• The regulatory provision is not efficiently addressing a genuine market failure but is instead the product of one or more of the government failure conditions and is thereby a force for decreased efficiency. Evasive transactions abroad are thus a proefficiency response (albeit an unnecessarily costly one) to the regulation; harmonization (to the extent it succeeds) would only buttress the national effort at inefficiency. By contrast, international competition of regulatory regimes would encourage the migration of financial transactions and services away from the locus of the inefficient regulation and would thereby increase global financial efficiency.

• The forced uniformity that harmonization would bring would mean too great a loss of diversity and of valuable adaptations to local (national) conditions. Also, even if uniformity at the proper regulatory standard would be better (for example, because of cost savings) than local diversity, the risk that a forced harmonization would occur at an inappropriate regulatory standard (because of the foibles of government failure) is too great.

In this author's judgment, competition—whether among firms, among markets and exchanges, or among national regulatory regimes—ought to be the "default option"; that is, in the absence of a strong showing that there is a substantial market failure and that the problems of government failure can be overcome so as to create a reasonable likelihood that government intervention will improve outcomes, the competitive outcome should prevail. For the competition-versus-harmonization controversy, this position would imply that those who favor the international harmonization of specific national regulatory provisions should bear a substantial burden of making a convincing case. As is discussed below, there do seem to be specific instances where international harmonization may well be desirable; but the presumption should be in favor of competition, and a strong affirmative case for harmonization must be made in these specific instances.

Some Specific Examples. Most of the discussions of international harmonization of national regulation have been at a broad level of generality and vagueness, and it is often difficult to determine exactly what regulatory provisions are candidates for harmonization. No one suggests that the entire repertory of U.S. laws and regulations that govern banking or that are the province of the SEC and the CFTC should be subject to international harmonization. But the specific regulatory provisions that might be the subject of harmonization are often unstated.

Accordingly, the use of the regulatory classification system outlined in an earlier section is a reasonable way to proceed in examining some specific areas where harmonization might be worthwhile and others where harmonization is likely instead to be yet another instance of government failures' dominating and worsening the market outcome.

Economic regulation. As was discussed in the previous section, economic regulation in principle can be a means of correcting the problems of market power. Where it is doing so effectively, the process of harmonization seems unnecessary; indeed, the widening of markets and of competition is likely to aid the process of limiting market power.

But, as was also discussed above, economic regulation in practice has frequently been the means by which market power has been protected and enhanced, often with the goal of preserving cross-subsidy. In this context, international competition is a threat to national regulation, and harmonization could be a vehicle for buttressing these anticompetitive national regulatory provisions and worsening market outcomes. There are at least three examples outside the field of financial services where an international coordinating and harmonizing organization has substantially reinforced market power and restricted competition: the International Air Transport Association (IATA) in the field of airlines, the United Nations Conference on Trade and Development (UNCTAD) for ocean shipping, and the International Telecommunication Union (ITU) for telecommunications.[58] These are cautionary counter-examples for anyone who might advocate international harmonization of national economic regulation.

Nevertheless, it is possible that harmonization could serve as a vehicle for *decreasing* the levels of national regulatory protectionism (local market power) and subsidy. The General Agreement on Tariffs and Trade (GATT) is a useful example here. Under the partial guise of multilateral harmonization, the GATT has succeeded in greatly reducing the levels of international trade protectionism. Unfortunately, until recently, trade in services was excluded from the GATT negotiations; and even with the inclusion of services in the recently completed Uruguay Round of negotiations, the final agreement was largely silent with respect to any specific dismantling of protectionist barriers in financial services. But future GATT (or International Trade Organization) negotiations may well succeed in lowering these barriers.

Further, it is possible that regional trade agreements may be the means for reducing protectionist barriers in financial services. The European Union and the North American Free Trade Agreement (NAFTA) are positive examples.

In addition, the International Organization of Securities Commissions (IOSCO) or the International Association of Insurance Supervisors (IAIS) could be the vehicles for mutual reductions in the

---

58. See, respectively, Kasper (1988), White (1988), and Aronson and Cowhey (1988).

restrictive national regulatory treatments of nonnational financial services providers—under the guise of harmonization. The results could be beneficial indeed.

Unfortunately, there is also the possibility that such efforts could be transformed into a defense and strengthening of protectionism; the IATA, UNCTAD, and ITU counter-examples should be remembered for their cautionary value. Further, the American regulatory experience has yielded numerous instances in which regulatory bodies whose initial mandate was to limit market power were transformed over time into defenders and protectors of market power. Nevertheless, the value of decreased protectionism through harmonization here could be great, and any vehicle through which it could be pursued should be encouraged. In addition, the value of some forms of harmonization in reducing transaction costs for financial services firms that want to offer their products and services in multiple jurisdictions could be substantial, and this too would support some cautions and limited efforts at harmonization. (Some caveats to the reduced-transaction-costs arguments, however, will be offered below.)

H-S-E regulation. At first glance, the globalization of financial transactions would seem likely to extend to international markets the externalities and spillover effects that motivate some forms of national H-S-E regulation and thus would seem to justify harmonization to help control these effects. Upon closer examination, however, the argument is more complicated. We will explore specifically the issues of systemic risk and price-and-market relationships.

Systemic risk. Concerns about market disruptions linked to the "systemic risk" caused by the failure of one or more financial services firms—a negative externality—is a dominant concern of national regulators. Much of the panoply of national safety-and-soundness (prudential) regulation of commercial banks and insurance companies (for example, the minimum capital requirements, limitations on suitable investments, and extensive examination and supervision procedures) and the minimum capital requirements and other safety requirements for securities firms are motivated by this regulatory concern about the consequences of insolvency and failure.

Before asking whether these national concerns are a legitimate basis for seeking international harmonization, it is worth considering the reasons why a firm's insolvency and failure can have negative externality effects on financial markets. Two alternative scenarios of systemic risk are usually offered. The first might be termed the scenario of "cascading failures": the insolvency failure of one large financial firm (such as a large commercial bank, securities firm, or reinsurer) would rapidly lead to a series of other failures, as firms that were substantial creditors of the initial firm are thereby thrown into insolvency, with consequent effects on yet more firms.[59] This was one of the scenarios that motivated U.S. bank regulators to keep an insolvent Continental Illinois Bank open in 1984, rather than closing and liquidating it; and it is a scenario that is often offered in discussions surrounding the risks of the operations of the large interbank funds–transfer systems, such as FedWire and the Clearing House Interbank Payment System (CHIPS).[60] It is instructive, though, that the failures of Drexel Burnham Lambert in 1990 and of the Bank for Credit and Commerce International (BCCI) in 1991 did not have any serious cascading consequences.

The second scenario of systemic risk is the "depositor runs" phenomenon described in the previous section. The fear of an insolvency failure (real or imagined) of a large institution causes depositors to run (withdraw their deposits in the form of cash) on the institution and on other institutions that they fear might be in similar straits. The anticipation of such depositor runs, which could (at a minimum) impair otherwise nonfearful depositors' timely access to the liquidity of their deposits and could even lead to the premature closing and liquidation of an otherwise solvent bank, may itself spark runs. As was noted above, a similar scenario might apply to life insurance policy holders.

Closer examination of the first scenario reveals the heart of that version of the problem: the asymmetric information ("moral hazard") problems related to financial institutions' extending sizable amounts of credit to each other for short-term periods, often as short as a few hours within a trading day. The primary responsibility for correction of this problem should be on the institution that is extending the credit. Regulatory requirements of adequate capital levels, so that the firm can better withstand loan losses of any kind, are vital, as are limits on its loan exposure to any borrower. If virtually all of a firm's exposure occurs through its transactions with other members of an exchange, the exchange may be an appropriate vehicle for ensuring payment; but the exchange similarly must be adequately capitalized and must have a mechanism for limiting exposure.

U.S. banking regulations already encompass limits on a commer-

---

59. The "cascading failure" scenario could be exacerbated by the "depositor run" scenario described below.

60. See Sprague (1986), Humphrey (1986), Dudley (1986), and the discussions in England (1991) and in the references cited in footnote 1.

cial bank's exposure on commercial loans to any single borrower. The concept underlying these limits is a sensible one, and it should be broadened to include *all* extensions of credit for *any* length of time by any type of financial institution where a cascading systemic risk problem may be present. Further, the logic of this position leads quickly and sensibly to the conclusion that minimum capital requirements for financial institutions (banks, insurance companies, or securities firms or exchanges) should be applicable on a continuous (real time) basis, rather than the periodic "snapshot" (such as the end of a calendar quarter) basis that currently applies. A financial institution's exposure to default by others is on a continuous time basis, not just at discrete time intervals; the minimum capital requirements that protect the institution's liability holders should therefore be *binding* on a continuous time basis.

With these changes, national regulatory provisions should be adequate to prevent cascading consequences from institutional failures even in a world of major international interinstitutional financial flows. So long as national regulatory agencies can ensure that their home country institutions have adequate capital on a continuous basis and are not unduly exposed to default by any borrower on a continuous basis, systemic risk can be contained nationally. Harmonization is not needed.

As was noted earlier, the depositor runs version of the systemic risk problem is a genuine negative externality problem, compounded by asymmetric information. Each depositor's act of withdrawing cash increases the probability that other depositors will be unable to exercise their option to withdraw cash, thereby inducing the latter to move even earlier. It is a problem of potential contagion.

At the national level for commercial banks, a combination of a lender of last resort, a deposit insurer, and a strong safety-and-soundness regulator that relies heavily on economic incentives (such as risk-based minimum capital requirements that are derived from a market value accounting system, the use of subordinated debt as a required component of capital, and risk-based deposit insurance premiums) should be adequate to deal with the problem.[61] There are problems of how to deal with the local subsidiary and branch operations of a bank that is headquartered abroad and offers deposit services to local residents; but these can probably be handled adequately through cooperation and information exchanges among national regulators, although mutual (reciprocal) confidence in national safety-

---

61. See, for example, White (1991, 1992).

and-soundness regulatory regimes will clearly be necessary.[62] Similarly for insurance companies and securities firms, some form of guarantee or insurance arrangement for customers and sensible safety-and-soundness regulation (again, encompassing economic incentives) should be adequate, with some international cooperation necessary for dealing with overseas branches.

In principle the problem of depositor runs could extend across national boundaries; in practice the less sophisticated (more poorly informed) depositors, insurance policy holders, or securities customers who would be the most likely "stampeders" would be unlikely to be major transactors with banks, insurance companies, and securities firms located outside a country. The transnational transactors are likely to be more sophisticated (or to have more sophisticated agents) and to be more knowledgeable; fear-driven contagion effects seem less likely. Again, it appears that national regulatory efforts should be adequate, and international harmonization is not necessary. In this respect it is worth noting again that the 1991 failure of BCCI did not exhibit large-scale contagion effects, and neither did the 1990 failure of Drexel.[63]

Is there any value to the harmonization achieved by the Basel Accord on minimum capital levels for commercial banks or by IOSCO's efforts for a similar agreement on capital standards for securities firms? Despite the previous conclusions, there is positive value from these harmonization efforts—but the rationale in support of the efforts is more subtle than the two systemic risk arguments that have just been rejected. The value of these harmonization arrangements is primarily in limiting the implicit subsidy that most governments seem prepared to provide to their major financial institutions.[64]

---

62. See Key and Scott (1991, 1992).

63. It is worth noting, however, that the failure of the BCCI did spawn some depositor runs on small, immigrant-owned banks in England, which were damped by the provision of liquidity by the Bank of England. See George (1994).

64. One should ask why it is in the interests of other countries' residents to prevent any given country's government from subsidizing its own (resident) banks; after all, consumers in importing countries should generally applaud when the governments of exporting countries subsidize their exports. There are two answers. First, if other countries' banks are more efficient than the subsidized banks, the subsidy will discourage the more efficient banks from exporting their services to the subsidizing country and will also disadvantage them in competition in third markets; the subsidy is inflicting genuine (Pareto deteriorating) harm on the countries with the more efficient banks. Second, the other countries' governments may experience pressures (see the discussion of government failure) to respond with their own subsidies.

This rationale can most clearly be seen for the case of commercial banks. With or without the presence of explicit deposit insurance, most governments appear unwilling to force depositors to absorb the losses that would otherwise fall on them when major home-country banks become insolvent.[65] Though governments may be vague ex ante about their likely reactions, their ex post behavior has been consistent with this statement.[66] In essence, governments are absorbing the losses of these insolvent institutions and are thereby subsidizing risk taking by banks. International competition among banks (and their regulatory regimes) places extra pressures on them to try to reduce their direct funding costs by reducing their capital levels. Competitive regulatory regimes accede, since they are reluctant to put the banks within their jurisdiction at a cost disadvantage. But with lower capital levels, banks are more susceptible to failure and have greater incentives to engage in riskier behaviors, thereby raising the likelihood of failure and the level of subsidy.

The Basel Accord, by establishing a uniform set of minimum capital standards, may make this competitive regulatory behavior more difficult and thus may serve to limit the competitive subsidy process.[67]

To the extent that governments would not be willing to have the creditors of securities firms or insurance policy holders absorb the losses from failures of those firms, the same argument would apply to IOSCO's efforts to develop harmonized capital standards for

---

65. The failure of BCCI, with substantial losses to depositors, is an exception, but it is an explainable one. No country considered BCCI to be its responsibility, and the British government, which might have been the most concerned, was unlikely to be especially responsive to the political pressures of the depositor groups (immigrants from African and Asian Commonwealth countries) who were most affected.

66. For example, in late 1993 and early 1994, the governments of Spain, France, Japan, and Venezuela separately indicated that they would absorb specific bank losses in their countries, so as to avoid imposing losses on liability holders.

67. For a study that reaches quite a different conclusion, see Scott and Iwakara (1994). Also, the Basel Accord may have a secondary effect in reducing the problems of cascading failures or depositor runs. Although the Basel Accord points in the right direction, however, it is substantially flawed: Its broad risk categories have no obvious empirical foundation; they ignore portfolio considerations; they ignore interest-rate risk; and they are based on a cost-based historical book value accounting framework rather than a market value accounting framework. Also, as is discussed in the text below, it may be easy for countries to "cheat" on the Accord if they choose to do so.

securities firms or to any efforts that might develop to harmonize insurance company capital requirements.

Securities prices and markets. A frequent concern by securities market makers and exchanges is that "outside firms" will "free ride" on the information—especially the price information—generated by the market. The outsider will thereby benefit and divert transactions away from the exchange. An additional concern is that such diversions will reduce the transaction volumes in the primary market, with consequent reductions in its liquidity and increases in its volatility. Finally, there are concerns that some market makers or exchanges may be willing to provide less transparency to transactions and will thereby attract the transactions of those who gain from reduced transparency. The competition among markets (and regulatory regimes) for this order flow may well lead to securities markets that generally have less transparency.

These concerns about the relationships among markets have been the basis for calls for greater international harmonization of regulatory provisions that would solve or ameliorate these problems. Again, though, closer examination is warranted.

It is clear that the information yielded by a market, including its level of transparency, is a public good in the sense defined above, and public goods can generate the problems described. But less drastic measures may be able to ameliorate the problem.

With respect to the price information provided by markets, the relevant market maker or exchange could be assigned the property rights to the market's information. This property rights approach, which is similar to the way that other problems related to the creation and dissemination of information (intellectual property) in market-oriented economies are handled, would reduce free riding but need not unduly discourage the possible development of new forms of market making.[68] Further, it would be worthwhile for the exchanges themselves to investigate how their costs relate to the services that they provide and whether they are pricing those services appropriately. For example, the value of a dealer or market maker's capital is to serve as a buffer during adverse circumstances (for example, unexpectedly volatile conditions). During favorable times the market maker's capital is redundant; during adverse times it is vital. In essence, the market maker's costs of making an orderly market are lower during favorable times and higher during adverse times. The market maker's prices, or spreads, for its services should reflect those

---

68. See, for example, Bronfman and Ordahl (1993).

differential costs. To try to maintain uniform spreads across good times and bad is to maintain a form of cross-subsidy—which, as was noted above, will invite entry and cherry-picking.

The rapid improvements in telecommunications and data processing that have caused the apparent fragmentation of local markets have also improved the ability of transactors to arbitrage across these local markets, widening and deepening the market. Fragmentation may well be more of an illusion than a reality.

Finally, transparency is a problem that probably has no easy solution. Though all transactors would like to be the recipients of the information that greater transparency would yield, larger transactors are reluctant to provide the necessary information about their own actions and positions. If required to do so by a market, they will try to find another forum where they are not so required—either another formal market, or informal (and less well reported) transactions among themselves. Paradoxically, an insistence on too great a level of transparency could reduce the actual levels of transparency achieved.

International harmonization of national transparency requirements might prevent a competitive regulatory race to the bottom, but it might instead simply drive large transactors away from organized markets and result in even less information's being generated. The dangers of the latter outcome seem great enough that harmonization should only be attempted gingerly, or not at all.

Information regulation. The needs of national securities regulators to enforce regulations that are information-intensive—for example, restrictions on insider trading or on front running—can probably be satisfied through cooperation and information exchanges among regulatory regimes. Harmonization is not necessary.

For information regulation itself, however, the issues are more complex. The SEC's dilemma with respect to financial reporting by non-U.S. firms, mentioned earlier in this section, is a good illustration. If U.S. investors persist in investing in the non-U.S. companies, there is little the SEC can do. It might make the investors' efforts a bit more difficult by refusing to allow any securities firm located in the United States to act as an agent for investors in these transactions. But if the U.S. investors persist and simply transact with agents abroad, then even more financial services will have been diverted from U.S. providers.[69]

---

69. In principle, the SEC could go even further and try to forbid U.S. investors from even owning the securities of firms that do not report according to U.S. GAAP. In practice, this would be a system of capital controls that is unlikely to be politically acceptable in the United States or in many other countries.

The SEC is trying another strategy. It is allowing these firms' securities to be sold in the United States without a restatement of their financial results to U.S. GAAP, but limiting the purchases of these securities to institutions: in essence, these securities are being treated as private placements.[70] Does this system of dual listing mean that U.S. firms are at a disadvantage? This would be true only if U.S. investors do not find the greater information provided by U.S. GAAP to be worth the extra costs to the U.S. firms of conforming to GAAP, or if the SEC's reporting requirements are largely designed to remedy a genuine "widows and orphans" type of market failure discussed in the previous section.

Ultimately, though, because other countries are unlikely to harmonize their accounting systems to U.S. GAAP (just so the U.S. markets could gain more listings?), the SEC may have to ask difficult questions as to whether its stringent reporting requirements for U.S. firms are necessary. This is especially true in light of the evidence offered in a recent study that indicates that the lesser reporting requirements of other countries' securities regulators may be adequate to prevent small investors from being at a disadvantage vis-à-vis larger (and possibly more knowledgeable) investors.[71]

The eventual harmonization of reporting requirements across the countries with major financial markets could well be worthwhile.[72] The major advantage would be a savings in transaction costs, since investors (and accountants) would need to learn and become familiar with only one set of accounting rules and their applications. (As a thought experiment, it is intriguing to imagine the transaction costs that would be present if each securities regulator in the fifty U.S. states had its own version of GAAP and required companies operating in that state to report their financial results in terms of that state's GAAP.) In essence, the accounting frameworks of these countries would become fully compatible with each other;[73] equivalently, there are economies of scale that can be achieved from the international harmonization of national accounting frameworks.[74] There are, how-

70. See Seidman (1991), Kokkalenios (1992), Schimkat (1992), and Torres (1993).

71. See Baumol and Malkiel (1992).

72. For a discussion, see Choi and Levich (1990) and Choi (1994).

73. For discussions of compatibility, see Braunstein and White (1985) and Economides and White (1994) and the references cited in the latter paper.

74. In this sense there is a parallel between the economies of scale (lower transaction costs) that can be achieved with broader securities markets and the economies of scale (lower "translation" costs) that can be achieved with broader (internationally harmonized) accounting frameworks. And, just as "customized" or niche market making may benefit some transactors but di-

ever, potential costs. One danger is that diversity and the suitability of local accounting frameworks to local circumstances, and the opportunities for local experimentation within those frameworks, would be lost. Further, even though harmonization on a single accounting system might be worthwhile if the "right" system were chosen, the process of harmonization might result in the choice of some other framework, yielding a worse outcome than the current (albeit imperfect) pattern of diversity.

An analogy may prove useful here. A compatible nationwide system of railroads with a uniform rail gauge has great value in reducing the transaction costs that would otherwise occur in trans-loading freight between incompatible rail systems. But different rail gauges might be best suited to different geographic terrains or different types of freight, and the advantages of this diversity are lost when uniformity is achieved. Also, if uniformity were somehow achieved with only an excessively narrow or excessively broad gauge, the outcome of uniformity (in terms of the costs of hauling freight) might be worse than the nonuniform system.

There is no automatic answer to the question of whether the uniformity of a single accounting framework across all countries would be superior to the current pattern of different national systems.[75] But the possibility that harmonization could yield gains is real and worth further exploration.

Is Harmonization Feasible? A final question worth considering is whether agreements among countries to harmonize and limit competition among their regulatory regimes are feasible, or whether the perceived private advantages of competition and the competitive instincts of the countries would be too strong. In the latter case, they would be tempted to cheat on any harmonization agreement, and such agreements might soon unravel.

Any harmonization arrangement is likely to have multiple facets and multiple unspecified details that could leave plenty of room for

---

minish the volume of transactions in the principal market (thereby raising transaction costs for the transactors in the principal market), customized accounting frameworks may better suit some securities issuers or some investors but raise the transaction costs for others (who must devote more resources and effort to "translating" the customized financial information to the more common framework).

75. In essence, the choice between a single system and the current diverse system is similar to asking whether a system of monopolistic competition in equilibrium provides too many or too few varieties. The answer, as shown by Spence (1976) and Dixit and Stiglitz (1977), is that "it all depends."

competitive maneuvering. For example, the Basel Accord on minimum capital levels for commercial banks only specifies the broad categories and risk weights but leaves many definitions and details unspecified; most important, it is silent on the details of the accounting system that should be the basis for the calculation of capital levels. This flexibility gives national regulatory regimes wide room for competitive manipulation, and over time the erosion of the accord could be substantial.[76]

In sum, any international harmonization arrangement that is designed to dampen competition among national regulatory regimes must face the same problem that confronts all cartel arrangements: how to prevent cheating by cartel members, which can cause the arrangement to unravel. Strong economic, political, and moral commitments by member countries will be necessary to make these arrangements work.

Conclusion

The increasing globalization of financial services will put a strain on many facets of national regulation. It is a natural reaction for national regulators to try to reduce this strain by attempting to harmonize key regulatory provisions through international agreements.

In many instances such efforts pose substantial dangers to the efficient operation of financial services markets. Much national regulation of these markets is protectionist and inefficient in outcome (and often in intent and spirit as well), and international harmonization could well buttress such inefficient regulatory outcomes. But there are cases where harmonization could improve the efficiency of financial markets: harmonization can serve as a guise for *reducing* national protectionist provisions; harmonization can limit the tendency of national governments to subsidize their domestic financial services firms; and harmonization can reduce transaction costs.

An important task for public policy, national and international, in the 1990s and after will be to encourage competition in financial services generally—among firms, markets, exchanges, *and* regulators—so as to achieve greater global efficiencies in these markets, while focusing international harmonization on those limited instances where positive results from harmonization could emerge and would indeed improve the efficiency of these markets.

---

76. See, for example, Scott and Iwahara (1994).

References

Aronson, Jonathan D. *The Rise of Global Telecommunication Networks.* Washington, D.C.: AEI Press, forthcoming.

Aronson, Jonathan D., and Peter F. Cowhey. *When Countries Talk: International Trade in Telecommunications Services.* Cambridge, Mass.: Ballinger, 1988.

Baron, David P. "Design of Regulatory Mechanisms and Institutions." In Richard Schmalensee and Robert D. Willig, eds., *Handbook of Industrial Organization*, vol. 2. Amsterdam: North Holland, 1989, ch. 24.

Baumol, William J., and Alvin K. Klevorick. "Input Choices and Rate-of-Return Regulation: An Overview of the Discussion." *Bell Journal of Economics and Management Science,* 1 (Autumn 1970), pp. 162–90.

Baumol, William J., and Burton G. Malkiel. "Redundant Regulation of Foreign Security Trading and U.S. Competitiveness." In Kenneth Lehn and Robert W. Kamphius, Jr., eds., *Modernizing U.S. Securities Regulation: Economic and Legal Perspectives.* Homewood, Ill.: Business One Irwin, 1992, pp. 39–55.

Bebchuk, Lucian Arye. "Federalism and the Corporation: The Desirable Limits on State Competition in Corporate Law." *Harvard Law Review,* 105 (1992), pp. 1472–1510.

Benston, George J. "Competition versus Competitive Equality in International Financial Markets." In Franklin R. Edwards and Hugh T. Patrick, eds., *Regulating International Financial Markets: Issues and Policies.* Boston: Kluwer, 1992a, pp. 277–90.

———. "International Regulatory Coordination of Banking." In John Figleton, ed., *The Internationalization of Capital Markets and the Regulatory Response.* London: Graham & Trotman, 1992b, pp. 197–210.

Berger, Allen N., and Timothy H. Hannan. "The Price-Concentration Relationship in Banking." *Review of Economics and Statistics,* 71, (May 1989), pp. 291–99.

———. "The Price-Concentration Relationship in Banking: A Reply." *Review of Economics and Statistics,* 74 (May 1992), pp. 376–79.

Berger, Allen N., William C. Hunter, and Stephen G. Timme. "The Efficiency of Financial Institutions: A Review and Preview of Research Past, Present, and Future." *Journal of Banking and Finance,* 17 (April 1993), pp. 221–50.

Bloch, Ernest. "Multiple Regulators: Their Constituencies and Policies." In Yakov Amihud, Thomas S. Y. Ho, and Robert A. Schwartz, eds., *Market Making and the Changing Structure of the Securities Industry.* Lexington, Mass.: Heath, 1985, pp. 155–82.

Bodner, David E. "The Global Markets: Where Do We Stand?" In Hans R. Stoll, ed., *International Finance and Financial Policy.* New York: Quorum, 1990, pp. 201–6.

Bradley, Caroline. "The Market for Markets: Competition between Investment Exchanges." In John Fingleton, ed., *The Internationalization of Capital Markets and the Regulatory Response*. London: Graham and Trotman, 1992, pp. 183–96.

Braunstein, Yale, and Lawrence White. "Setting Technical Compatibility Standards: An Economic Analysis." *The Antitrust Bulletin*, 30 (Summer 1985), pp. 337–55.

Braeutigam, Ronald R. "Optimal Policies for Natural Monopolies." In Richard Schmalensee and Robert D. Willig, eds. *Handbook of Industrial Organization*, vol. 2. Amsterdam: North Holland, 1989, chap. 23.

Breeden, Richard C. "Reconciling National and International Concerns in the Regulation of Global Capital Markets." In John Figleton, ed., *The Internationalization of Capital Markets and the Regulatory Response*. London: Graham & Trotman, 1992, pp. 27–32.

Bronfman, Corinne, and James A. Overdahl. "Would the Invisible Hand Produce Transparent Markets?" Mimeo, 1993.

Choi, Frederick D. S. "International Accounting Standards: A Capital Markets Perspective." *Accounting and Business Review*, 1 (January 1994), pp. 1–27.

Choi, Frederick D. S., and Richard L. Levich. *The Capital Market Effects of International Accounting Diversity*. Homewood, Ill.: Dow Jones-Irwin, 1990.

Coffee, John C., Jr. "Competition versus Consolidation: The Significance of Organizational Structure in Financial and Securities Regulation." *Business Lawyer*, 50 (February 1995), pp. 1–38.

Dermine, Jean. "International Trade in Banking." Chapter 3 in this volume.

Diamond, Douglas W., and Philip H. Dyburg. "Bank Runs, Deposit Insurance, and Liquidity." *Journal of Political Economy*, 91 (June 1983), pp. 401–19.

Dixit, Avinash K., and Joseph E. Stiglitz. "Monopolistic Competition and Optimum Product Diversity." *American Economic Review*, 67 (June 1977), pp. 297–308.

Doty, James R. "The Role of the Securities and Exchange Commission in an International Marketplace." *Fordham Law Review*, 60 (May 1992), pp. S77–S90.

Dudley, William C. "Controlling Risk in Large-Dollar Wire Transfer Systems." In Anthony Saunders and Lawrence J. White, eds., *Technology and the Regulation of Financial Markets: Securities, Futures, and Banking*. Lexington, Mass.: Heath, 1986, pp. 121–36.

Economides, Nicholas, and Lawrence J. White. "Networks and Compatibility: Implications for Antitrust." *European Economic Review*, 38 (April 1994), pp. 651–62.

Edwards, Franklin R. "Listing of Foreign Securities on U.S. Exchanges." In Kenneth Lehn and Robert W. Kamphius, Jr., eds., *Modernizing U.S. Securities Regulation: Economic and Legal Perspectives.* Homewood, Ill.: Business One Irwin, 1992, pp. 57–76.

Edwards, Franklin R., and Hugh T. Patrick, eds. *Regulating International Financial Markets: Issues and Policies.* Boston: Kluwer, 1992.

England, Catherine, ed. *Governing Banking's Future: Markets vs. Regulation.* Boston: Kluwer, 1991.

Fingleton, John, ed. *The Internationalization of Capital Markets and the Regulatory Response.* London: Graham & Trotman, 1992.

Freund, William C. "That Trade Obstacle, the SEC." *Wall Street Journal,* August 27, 1993a.

———. "Two SEC Rules in an Era of Transnational Equities Trading." New York University Salomon Center's Conference on Global Equity Markets: Technological, Competitive, and Regulatory Challenges, October 21–23, 1993b.

George, Eddy. "The Pursuit of Financial Stability." *Bank of England Quarterly Bulletin* (February 1994), pp. 60–66.

Gilbert, Alton. "Studies of Bank Market Structure and Competition: A Review and Evaluation." *Journal of Money, Credit, and Banking,* 16 (November 1984), pp. 617–44.

Gruenspecht, Howard K., and Lester B. Lave. "The Economics of Health, Safety, and Environmental Regulation." In Richard Schmalensee and Robert D. Willig, eds., *Handbook of Industrial Organization,* vol. 2. Amsterdam: North Holland, 1989, ch. 26.

Grundfest, Joseph A. "Internationalization of the World's Securities Markets: Economic Causes and Regulatory Consequences." *Journal of Financial Services Research,* 4 (December 1990), pp. 349–78.

Guy, Paul. "Regulatory Harmonization to Achieve Effective International Competition." In Franklin R. Edwards and Hugh T. Patrick, eds., *Regulating International Financial Markets: Issues and Policies.* Boston: Kluwer, 1992, pp. 291–98.

Hannan, Timothy H. "Bank Commercial Loan Markets and the Role of Market Structure: Evidence from Surveys of Commercial Lending." *Journal of Banking and Finance,* 15 (February 1991), pp. 133–49.

Humphrey, David B. "Payments Finality and Risk of Settlement Failure." In Anthony Saunders and Lawrence J. White, eds., *Technology and the Regulation of Financial Markets: Securities, Futures, and Banking.* Lexington, Mass.: Heath, 1986, pp. 97–120.

Isaac, William. "Miracle of the Marketplace Applies to Regulators, Too." *American Banker,* December 15, 1994, p. 5.

Johnson, Phillip McBride. "Reflections on the CFTC-SEC Jurisdictional Dispute." In Franklin R. Edwards and Hugh T. Patrick, eds., *Regulating International Financial Markets: Issues and Policies.* Boston: Kluwer, 1992, pp. 143–50.

Joskow, Paul L., and Roger G. Noll. "Economic Regulation: Deregulation and Regulatory Reform during the 1980s." In Martin Feldstein, ed., *American Economic Policy in the 1980s*. Chicago: University of Chicago Press, 1994, pp. 367–440.

Joskow, Paul L., and Nancy L. Rose. "The Effects of Economic Regulation." In Richard Schmalensee and Robert D. Willig, eds., *Handbook of Industrial Organization*, vol. 2. Amsterdam: North Holland, 1989, ch. 25.

Kane, Edward J. "Technology and the Regulation of Financial Markets." In Anthony Saunders and Lawrence J. White, eds., *Technology and the Regulation of Financial Markets: Securities, Futures, and Banking*. Lexington, Mass.: Heath, 1986, pp. 187–94.

———. "Tension between Competition and Coordination in International Financial Regulation." In Catherine England, ed., *Governing Banking's Future: Markets vs. Regulation*. Boston: Kluwer, 1991, pp. 33–48.

———. "Government Officials as a Source of Systemic Risk in International Financial Markets." In Franklin R. Edwards and Hugh T. Patrick, eds., *Regulating International Financial Markets: Issues and Policies*. Boston: Kluwer, 1992, pp. 257–66.

Karmel, Roberta S. *National Treatment, Harmonization and Mutual Recognition—The Search for Principles for the Regulation of Global Equity Markets*. Capital Markets Forum Discussion Paper no. 3, London: 1993.

Kasper, Daniel M. *Deregulation and Globalization: Liberalizing International Trade in Air Services*. Cambridge, Mass.: Ballinger, 1988.

Klinkerman, Steve. "Continental Files to Do U.S.-State Charter Flip." *American Banker*, November 22, 1993, p. 1.

Key, Sydney J., and Hal S. Scott. *International Trade in Banking Services: A Conceptual Framework*. Occasional Paper no. 35, Group of Thirty, Washington, D.C.: 1991.

———. "International Trade in Banking Services: A Conceptual Framework." In John Fingleton, ed., *The Internationalization of Capital Markets and the Regulatory Response*. London: Graham & Trotman, 1992, pp. 35–68.

Kokkalenios, Vickie. "Increasing United States Investment in Foreign Securities: An Evaluation of SEC Rule 144A." *Fordham Law Review*, 60 (May 1992), pp. S174–S202.

Kopke, Richard W., and Richard E. Randall, eds. *The Financial Condition and Regulation of Insurance Companies*. Conference Series no. 35, Federal Reserve Bank of Boston, June 1991.

Kosters, Marvin H., and Allan H. Meltzer. "Special Issue: International Competitiveness in Financial Services." *Journal of Financial Services Research*, 4 (December 1990), pp. 259–511.

Krueger, Anne O. "The Political Economy of the Rent-Seeking Society." *American Economic Review*, 66 (June 1974), pp. 291–303.

Kwoka, John E., Jr., and Lawrence J. White, eds. *The Antitrust Revolution: The Role of Economics*. New York: HarperCollins, 1994.

Levine, Ross. "Foreign Banks, Financial Development, and Economic Growth." Chapter 6 in this volume.

Lipsey, R. G., and K. Lancaster. "The General Theory of the Second Best." *Review of Economic Studies*, 24 (1956–1957), pp. 11–32.

McGee, Suzanne. "Plan by LME to Open U.S. Copper Warehouses Alarms Some Who Fear End of Comex Contract." *Wall Street Journal*, November 11, 1994.

Noll, Roger G. "Economic Perspectives on the Politics of Regulation." In Richard Schmalensee and Robert D. Willig, eds., *Handbook of Industrial Organization*, vol. 2. Amsterdam: North Holland, 1989, ch. 22.

Okun, Arthur. *Equality and Efficiency: The Big Trade-off*. Washington, D.C.: Brookings Institution, 1975.

Peltzman, Sam. "Toward a More General Theory of Regulation." *Journal of Law & Economics*, 19 (August 1976), pp. 211–40.

Phillips, Almarin. *Promoting Competition in Regulated Markets*. Washington, D.C.: Brookings Institution, 1975.

Posner, Richard A. "Taxation by Regulation." *Bell Journal of Economics and Management Science*, 2 (Spring 1971), pp. 22–50.

———. "Theories of Economic Regulation." *Bell Journal of Economics and Management Science*, 5 (Autumn 1974), pp. 335–58.

Postlewaite, Andrew, and Xavier Vives. "Bank Runs as an Equilibrium Phenomenon." *Journal of Political Economy*, 95 (June 1987), pp. 485–91.

Pugel, Thomas, and Anthony Saunders. "An Investigation of the U.S. Property-Casualty Insurance Industry." Mimeo, 1992.

Quinn, Brian. "Regulating Global Financial Markets: Problems and Solutions." In Franklin R. Edwards and Hugh T. Patrick, eds., *Regulating International Financial Markets: Issues and Policies*. Boston: Kluwer, 1992, pp. 299–306.

Schimkat, Harold. "The SEC's Proposed Regulation of Foreign Securities Issued in the United States." *Fordham Law Review*, 60 (May 1992), pp. S203–S226.

Scott, Kenneth E. "The Dual Banking System: A Model of Competition in Regulation." *Stanford Law Review*, 30 (1977), pp. 1–50.

Scott, Hal S., and Shinsaku Iwahara. *In Search of a Level Playing Field: The Implementation of the Basel Capital Accord in Japan and the United States*. Occasional Paper no. 46, Group of Thirty, Washington, D.C.: 1994.

Seidman, Lawrence R. "SEC Rule 144A: The Rule Heard Round the Globe—Or the Sounds of Silence?" *Business Lawyer*, 47 (1991), pp. 333–54.

Shapiro, Mary L. "The SEC's Open-Door Policy." *Wall Street Journal,* September 23, 1993.

Siegel, Daniel R., ed. *Innovation and Technology in the Markets: A Reordering of the World's Capital Market System.* Chicago: Probus, 1990.

Skipper, Harold D., Jr. "International Trade in Insurance." Chapter 5 in this volume.

Spence, A. Michael. "Product Selection, Fixed Costs, and Monopolistic Competition." *Review of Economic Studies,* 43 (June 1973), pp. 217–35.

Sprague, Irwin H. *Bailout: An Insider's Account of Bank Failures and Rescues.* New York: Basic Books, 1986.

Stansell, Stanley R., ed. *International Financial Market Integration.* Cambridge, Mass.: Blackwell, 1993.

Steil, Benn. "Regulatory Foundations for Global Capital Markets." In Robert O'Brien, ed., *Finance and the International Economy: 6.* Oxford: Oxford University Press, 1992, pp. 63–76.

———. "Competition, Integration, and Regulation in EC Capital Markets." Special Paper, Royal Institute of International Affairs: London, 1993.

Stigler, George, J. "The Theory of Regulation." *Bell Journal of Economics and Management Science,* 2 (Spring 1971), pp. 3–21.

Stiglitz, Joseph E. "Economic Organization, Information, and Development." In Hollis Chenery and T. N. Srinivasan, eds., *Handbook of Development Economics,* vol. 1. Amsterdam: North Holland, 1988, ch. 5.

———. "Imperfect Information in the Product Market." In Richard Schmalensee and Robert D. Willig, eds., *Handbook of Industrial Organization,* vol. 1. Amsterdam: North Holland, 1989, ch. 13.

———. "Development Strategies: The Roles of the State and the Private Sector." In *Proceedings of the World Bank Annual Conference on Development Economics,* 1990, pp. 430–33.

Stoll, Hans R., ed. *International Finance and Financial Policy.* New York: Quorum, 1990.

Torres, Craig. "Latin American Firms Break with Past, Scramble to Be Listed on U.S. Exchanges." *Wall Street Journal,* September 28, 1993.

U.S. Department of Justice and Federal Trade Commission. *Horizontal Merger Guidelines,* 1992.

Viscusi, W. Kip. "Health and Safety Regulation: The Mis-Specified Agenda: The 1980s Reform of Health, Safety, and Environmental Regulation." In Martin Feldstein, ed., *American Economic Policy in the 1980s.* Chicago: University of Chicago Press, 1994, pp. 453–504.

Walker, David. "Major Issues Relevant for Regulatory Response to the Internationalization of Capital Markets." In John Fingleton, ed.,

The Internationalization of Capital Markets and the Regulatory Response. London: Graham & Trotman, 1992, pp. 21–26.

Walter, Ingo. "Global Competition and Market Access in the Securities Industry." Chapter 4 in this volume.

Weiss, Leonard W. *Concentration and Price.* Cambridge, Mass.: MIT Press, 1989.

Weiss, Leonard W., and Michael W. Klass, eds. *Case Studies in Regulation: Revolution and Reform.* Boston: Little, Brown, 1981.

———. *Regulatory Reform: What Actually Happened.* Boston: Little, Brown, 1986.

White, Lawrence J. *Reforming Regulation: Processes and Problems.* Englewood Cliffs, N.J.: Prentice-Hall, 1981.

———. "The Title Insurance Industry, Reverse Competition, and Controlled Business—A Different View." *Journal of Risk and Insurance,* 51 (Summer 1984), pp. 308–19.

———. "Should Competition to Attract New Investment Be Restricted?" *New York Affairs,* 9 (no. 3, 1986), pp. 6–18.

———. *International Trade in Ocean Shipping Services: The U.S. and the World.* Cambridge, Mass.: Ballinger. 1988.

———. *The S&L Debacle: Public Policy Lessons for Bank and Thrift Regulation.* New York: Oxford, 1991.

———. "What Should Banks *Really* Do?" *Contemporary Policy Issues,* 10 (July 1992), pp. 104–12.

———. "The Community Reinvestment Act: Good Intentions Headed in the Wrong Direction." *Fordham Urban Law Journal,* 20 (Winter 1993), pp. 281–92.

———. "Competition Policy in the United States: An Overview." *Oxford Review of Economic Policy,* 9 (Summer 1993b), pp. 133–53.

———. "Market Failures, Government Failures, and Economic Development." Stern School of Business, New York University, Working Paper #EC-94-02: January 1994.

———. "International Regulation of Securities Markets: Competition or Harmonization?" In A. Lo, ed., *The Industrial Organization of Securities Markets.* Chicago: University of Chicago Press, 1995.

———. "Government-Business Relationships in the United States in the 1980s." In Martin Feldstein and Ytaka Kosai, eds., *U.S.-Japan Economic Forum,* vol. 2. Chicago: University of Chicago Press, 1996.

Winston, Clifford. "Economic Deregulation: Days of Reckoning for Microeconomists." *Journal of Economic Literature* 31, (September 1993), pp. 1263–89.

Wolf, C., Jr. *Markets or Governments: Choosing between Imperfect Alternatives.* Cambridge, Mass.: MIT Press, 1989.

Worth, Nancy. "Harmonization of Capital Adequacy Rules for International Banks and Securities Firms." *North Carolina Journal of International Law & Commercial Regulation,* 18 (Fall 1992), pp. 134–71.

3

International Trade in Banking

Jean Dermine

This chapter develops an economic analysis to guide the legal framework governing international trade in banking services. This is timely because, in response to the GATT Uruguay Round concluded in April 1994, further negotiations on the liberalization of the financial services sector began in 1995. Close attention is paid to the capability of the national treatment principle to deal with banking, to reciprocity clauses, and to the eventual need for an additional harmonization of national regulations.

The internationalization of corporate clients, progress in information technology, and financial innovations have led to the substantial growth and globalization of the financial services industry. At the insistence of the United States, and despite strong opposition from developing countries, financial services have been included in the Uruguay Round of the GATT negotiation. The Round concluded in Marrakesh in April 1994 recognizes the obligation to give equal access to all trading partners (most favored nation treatment). Financial services are excluded from the agreement, however, because the commitments by some countries to liberalize their financial markets were deemed inadequate. Further negotiations to liberalize the financial services sector began in 1995. More rapid success for financial market integration has been observed at regional levels. In 1992 the European

The author acknowledges helpful discussion with O. Cadot and comments from L. White.

Commission finalized the framework governing the provision of financial services in the European Union, while Canada, Mexico, and the United States have adopted the North American Free Trade Agreement (NAFTA). Barriers to trade in financial services are unique because they originate not from tariffs or quotas, as they do in manufacturing, but from disparate sets of national prudential and macroeconomic regulations that have been developed over time. Any agreement on trade in financial services raises immediately the policy issues of prudential regulation and supervision, the allocation of responsibilities among national supervisors, and the eventual need for further harmonization of regulations.

The objective of this chapter is to develop an economic analysis to guide the legal framework governing international trade in banking services. Since the ultimate objective of most trade negotiations is the adoption of the national treatment principle, according to which foreign and domestic firms operating in one particular country are subject to similar rules, this chapter pays close attention to the capability of national treatment to deal with banking, to the eventual need for reciprocity clauses, and to an additional harmonization of national regulations.[1]

This chapter first documents the business of banking, its core services, its main types of regulations, and the relative importance of the sector in international trade. It then reviews the literature on the potential market failures in banking services, the eventual need for public interventions, and the implications for the design of a legal framework governing international trade in banking services. In the third part of the chapter I discuss the capability of the national treatment principle to deal with trade in financial services, the issue of reciprocity, and the potential existence of nondiscriminatory barriers. Finally, I summarize the experience of the European Union with the integration of fifteen banking markets. This experience provides a unique example of advanced financial integration from which standing issues can be identified.

The six main conclusions of the chapter are as follows:

• A sensible discussion of the legal framework governing international trade in banking services must start with an understanding of the potential market failures leading to public interventions and

---

1. The literature on international trade in financial services includes, among others, Dale (1984), Herring (1993), Herring and Litan (1993), Hultman (1992), Key (1993), Key and Scott (1992), Pecchioli (1987), and Walter (1985, 1988).

regulations. The economics literature has identified three potential sources of market failure calling for public interventions: imperfect information, bank runs and the related fear of systemic crisis, and implicit subsidies that can distort international trade. Each of these sources demands its own regulatory and supervisory responses.

• As long as national authorities are responsible for the stability of their own markets, I fully support the recommendations of the Basel committee and the General Agreement on Trade in Services (GATS) on banking supervision, which allocate to national authorities the prudential supervision of firms operating in their own markets. In practice, this often implies collaboration between the home- and host-country supervisors.

• As far as the protection of investors is concerned, it is for each country to choose the level of protection for the uninformed investor. Moreover, I recommend that insured bank deposits be made first-order claim. This would reinforce private incentives for bank monitoring, since uninsured deposits, being second-order claims, would be more at risk in the event of a bank failure.

• As domestic regulators will be responsible for controlling the ownership of banks (public or private), the degree of market power in their domestic market, and the public policies for bailing out, countries must ensure that banks do not exploit domestic rents to subsidize their international activities. Moreover, in this context of fair trade, harmonization of banking regulations is necessary only in the case of an identified public subsidy that confers a competitive advantage.

• As concerns national treatment and reciprocity, I argue that, although the national treatment principle governing international trade seems adequate in many aspects, there can be cases where differences between domestic and foreign regulations limit de facto entry in banking markets. Since entry (direct investment) is essential to deliver many financial services, it would seem that negotiations on reciprocity are warranted in those cases where entry is restricted de facto by differences among national regulations.

• Finally, European banking integration presents a useful case of advanced integration from which standing issues can be identified. In particular, taxation of income on capital becomes increasingly difficult. The economic benefits expected from integration of banking markets should not be reversed by tax inefficiencies. Substantial work must be done to counter inefficient competitive efforts to reduce taxation of income on capital.

The Banking Industry

A description of the core services offered by banks is followed by a brief description of the regulatory regimes, and then of the relative importance of the banking sector in international trade.

The Nature of Banking Services. Although banking services are often interrelated, it is convenient to distinguish five categories: underwriting and placement, portfolio management, screening and monitoring, payment (transmission) mechanism, and risk management.

Underwriting and placement. Underwriting and placement is a function that helps borrowers (private or public) to meet the investment needs of savers by structuring the type of securities that meets their risk-return requirement. In this function, the underwriter is involved not only in designing the security, but also in the valuation of assets and pricing of securities to ensure that the terms of the issue are competitive. In a purely underwriting-and-placement service, it is assumed that the return and risk of the securities can be properly measured, so that these instruments are liquid and easily tradable on securities markets. With the underwriting-placement service, the end-investor directly holds the claims on deficit units.

Portfolio management. At low cost, investors can acquire a diversified portfolio of liabilities issued by deficit spending units. The pure case is the mutual fund (unit trust in the United Kingdom, or Société d'Investissement à Capital Variable [SICAV] in France and Luxembourg), which supplies a diversified portfolio to the holders of its shares. The income derived from the financial assets is paid to the holders of the shares minus a management fee paid to the fund manager. The reasons for the existence of these funds are twofold. First, they reduce the divisional cost incurred in issuing securities. Second, the investor may wish to delegate the assessment of economic prospects and fund management to specialists.

Screening and monitoring. Private information held by borrowers results in contracting problems because it is costly to assess the solvency of borrowers and to monitor their actions after financing has taken place. Sometimes bank loans emerge as a preferred mode of financing.[2] This third service is related to the first one—underwriting. I take it as a separate service because it corresponds to those cases where severe information problems make it difficult to issue financial claims traded on securities markets. An implication of the screening and monitoring function of banks is that loans are likely to be illiquid, not easily tradable on financial markets. One should note, however,

---

2. Diamond (1984).

that the distinction between liquid bonds and illiquid loans is not a sharp one. Indeed, financial technology allows banks to transform a pool of loans into tradable securities (the process of securitization).

Payment mechanism. A fourth function performed by banks is the management of the payment system—that is, to facilitate and keep track of transfers of wealth among individuals. This bookkeeping activity of banks is realized by debiting and crediting accounts. Although the payment system is limited by regulation to a specific type of deposit (demand deposit), it could be achieved by crediting or debiting any type of liquid assets. The so-called cash management or sweep account that automatically transfers money to special funds is a perfect illustration of the possibility to extend the payment system to other assets.

Risk-sharing services. An increasingly important function of financial markets is to facilitate insurance, or risk taking. Several examples can be given. First, financial institutions not only supply diversified assets but also efficiently organize the distribution of the risky income earned on the asset pool. The debtholders receive a fixed payment, while the shareholders receive the residual income. Other insurance services would include liquidity insurance (option for the deposit holder to withdraw quickly at face value), interest-rate insurance (floating rate lending with various ceilings on interest rates), or inflation insurance, with the supply of indexed contracts. Financial contracts such as forward-rate agreements, options, or swaps are called *contingent* or *derivatives* claims, in the sense that, like an insurance contract, the payment is linked to the occurrence of a particular event, such as movements in currency, interest rates, commodity prices, or stock indexes.

To illustrate the growth and relative importance of the financial service sector, I provide in table 3–1 some data on the share of the labor force employed in financial services in various countries. The share of the labor force occupied in banking, insurance, or real estate has grown substantially over the past ten years, reaching more than 10 percent in the United Kingdom, the United States, and Switzerland. Over the past ten years, the share of the labor force occupied in financial services has grown on average by 40 percent.

Banking Regulations. Historically, the banking industry has been one of the most heavily regulated. This is attributable to at least four causes: the macromonetary management of the economy, the protection of depositors, nationalism, and regulatory capture by incumbents. In several foreign countries, for instance, the banking sector

TABLE 3–1

PERCENTAGE OF LABOR FORCE IN BANKING, INSURANCE,
OR REAL ESTATE IN SELECTED OECD COUNTRIES, 1980 AND 1989

Country	1980	1989
Belgium	6.2	8.6
France	7.5	9.6
Germany	N.A.	7.9
Switzerland	N.A.	10.5
United Kingdom	8.2	12.7
United States	8.4	11.3
Japan	5.7	7.8

N.A. = Not available
SOURCE: OECD (1991).

was compartmentalized. In Japan, banks were divided into three main groups: the city banks with national branch networks specialized in short-term loan funding and consumer- and corporate-deposit gathering; the long-term credit banks specialized in long-term finance; and the trust banks, with special rights, in managing pension funds. In many countries, savings banks were constrained to lend mostly to the mortgage sector. The rationale for the compartmentalization of the financial service sector was the perceived need to facilitate the channeling of funds to specific investment needs.

Another form of compartmentalization has been the separation of the banking business (deposit and lending) from the securities activities (bond or equity underwriting and trading) in the United States and Japan. This form of regulation was motivated by the wish to protect depositors and create safer banks. The Glass-Steagall Act of 1933 has limited the underwriting activities of U.S. banks since it was enacted. After World War II, the United States imposed on Japan the main features of Glass-Steagall.[3] It must be noted that the separation of banking from securities activities has not existed in Europe, where the universal banking model has allowed banks to operate in both markets.

As is discussed below, the economic rationale for compartmentalization is being questioned, and the universal banking model is being adopted in an increasingly large number of countries. Finally, nationalism or regulatory capture by incumbents has led many countries to limit the control of local banks by foreign shareholders. Table 3–2 illustrates the restrictions on the individual foreign ownership of banks in several countries.

---

3. See the discussion in chapter 4, by Ingo Walter.

TABLE 3-2
PERCENTAGE OF BANK OWNERSHIP ALLOWED TO FOREIGN INVESTORS IN
SELECTED COUNTRIES, 1992

Country	Allowable Foreign Ownership
Australia	< 10
Brazil	< 50
Canada	< 25
Italy	< 3
Japan	No
Korea	<10
Malaysia	<20
Mexico	< 30 of voting rights
Singapore	< 5

SOURCE: European Commission (1992).

International Banking. To complete this brief description of the banking sector, I document its relative importance in international trade. Table 3–3 reports the results of a recent study by the OECD (1993).

The figures that refer to the share of fees and commissions in trade (excluding interest revenues) show sharp differences across countries. France and the United States lead, with shares of 5.7 percent and 4.7 percent of goods and services exports linked to commissions and fees.

International trade in financial services can be described not only by commissions and fees received from or paid to nonresidents, but also by the magnitude of cross-border interbank claims. This is documented in table 3–4.

Between 1983 and 1994, the international interbank claims within the Bank of International Settlements (BIS) reporting area grew at a compounded annual average rate of 12 percent. The evolution of cross-border interbank activity vis-à-vis Japan differed considerably from that between other centers. Between 1983 and 1994, interbank business involving Japan expanded at an annual average rate of 21 percent, whereas business between other centers expanded at a lower rate. Reflecting the above developments, the nationality distribution of banks' exposures in the international market changed rapidly in the course of the 1980s. As documented in table 3–5, Japanese as well as continental European banks saw a large increase between 1983 and 1993. Among the factors contributing to this growth was the lifting of foreign exchange controls (notably in France, Italy, and Sweden), the prospects for the European internal market, and the growth in Japanese foreign trade and direct investment. Difficulties in meeting the

55

TABLE 3–3

TRADE IN FINANCIAL SERVICES IN SELECTED OECD COUNTRIES, 1988 AND 1991

(percent)

Country	1988	1991
Belgium		
Exports	1.17	2.60
Imports	0.74	1.70
France		
Exports	1.50	5.70
Imports	1.70	6.30
Germany		
Exports	0.74	0.96
Imports	0.12	0.33
Switzerland		
Exports	3.00	3.80
Imports	N.A.	N.A.
United Kingdom		
Exports	2.40	3.20
Imports	0.09	0.20
United States		
Exports	3.80	4.70
Imports	1.70	2.30
Japan		
Exports	N.A.	N.A.
Imports	N.A.	N.A.

N.A. = Not available.
NOTES: The data include commissions and fees received or paid related to the following transactions: foreign exchange, international payments, management of cash balances, factoring, operations in securities, asset management, fiduciary funds, guarantees and endorsements, financial leasing, counseling on takeovers or mergers, participation in barter arrangements.
SOURCE: OECD (1993).

8 percent capital regulation, however, have forced Japanese banks to reduce their assets since 1991.

As to the relative position of individual banks documented in table 3–6, the Japanese banks have taken a leading position in terms of asset size. At the end of 1994, eight of the ten largest banks in the world were Japanese; none were American. This last observation reflects in part the appreciation of the yen and the increasing use of off-balance sheet transactions by American institutions. In this re-

TABLE 3–4

THE INTERBANK MARKET WITHIN THE BIS REPORTING AREA, 1983 AND 1994

(billions of $U.S.)

Interbank Claims	1983	1994
Cross-border interbank claims	1194.8	4363.0
Between Japan and other BIS inside- area countries	162.3	1320.0
Between the United States and other BIS inside-area countries, except Japan	393.1	856.0
Between European countries	341.7	1645.0
Other inside-area countries	297.7	542.0
Local foreign currency interbank claims	285.7	685.0
Total international interbank claims	1480.5	5048.0

NOTE: BIS inside-area countries include: Group of Ten, Luxembourg, Austria, Denmark, Finland, Ireland, Norway, Spain, the Bahamas, Bahrain, Cayman Island, Hong Kong, the Netherlands Antilles, Singapore, and branches of U.S. banks in Panama.
SOURCE: BIS (1992, 1995).

TABLE 3–5

INTERNATIONAL BANK ASSETS BY NATIONALITY OF BANKS IN SELECTED

OECD COUNTRIES, 1983, 1991, AND 1993

(billions of $U.S.)

Country	1983	1991	1993
Belgium	38.2	135.1	142.7
France	191.4	565.4	642.0
Germany	144.5	640.4	749.0
Switzerland	79.9	408.9	379.2
United Kingdom	178.8	282.1	324.0
United States	605.5	650.7	678.0
Japan	456.9	1935.1	1628.0

SOURCE: BIS (1992, 1995).

spect, as is documented in tables 3–7 and 3–8, it is remarkable to observe that more than 50 percent of open positions on the option or financial futures markets involve foreign institutions, both in Chicago (CME-IMM) and in Paris (MATIF).

Although figures reflect growth in the financial sector and globalization, they should not hide the fact that in several markets, particularly in commercial banking, the penetration of foreign institutions is rather

TABLE 3–6
ASSETS AND MARKET VALUE OF EQUITY OF
SELECTED INTERNATIONAL BANKS, 1994
(billions of $U.S.)

Bank	Assets	Market Value of Equity
Fuji Bank (J)	507.0	58.0
Dai-Ichi Kangyo (J)	506.5	55.9
Sumitomo Bank (J)	498.0	61.2
Sakura Bank (J)	496.0	40.8
Sanwa Bank (J)	494.0	55.8
Mitsubishi Bank (J)	459.3	63.4
Norinchukin Bank (J)	429.0	N.T.
IBJ (J)	387.0	73.2
Credit Lyonnais (F)	339.0	2.5
Ind and Commercial Bank of China (C)	337.0	N.T.
Deutsche Bank (G)	317.2	23.0
Tokai Bank (J)	311.8	26.3
HSBC (UK)	305.0	29.4
LTCB (J)	302.0	27.0
Credit Agricole (F)	283.0	N.T.
Bank of China (C)	263.0	N.T.
Asahi Bank (J)	262.0	25.7
Société Générale (F)	260.0	8.1
ABN-AMRO (N)	253.8	8.1
Banque Nationale de Paris (F)	250.6	8.4

N.T. = Nontraded.
NOTE: Country codes are: J = Japan; F = France; C = China; G = Germany; U.K. = United Kingdom; N = Netherlands.
SOURCE: *Financial Times* (1995); Salomon Bros. (1995); Mitsubishi Bank and Bank of Tokyo will merge in 1996 (total assets = billions of $U.S. 719).

modest. Table 3–9 documents the market share of foreign institutions in the markets of various countries. One does observe wide variation between the "open" markets in the United Kingdom and the United States and the fairly "closed" markets in Germany and Japan. The case of Japan is discussed in more detail, as it casts some doubt on whether national treatment is sufficient to deliver effective market access.

The Case of Japan. The lack of foreign penetration in traditional commercial banking activities (lending and deposit taking) in Japan has raised a concern, especially in view of the Japanese penetration in foreign markets. For instance, the U.S. Treasury National Treatment Study (1994) reports that Japanese institutions control 9.4 percent of

TABLE 3–7
NATIONALITY DISTRIBUTION OF OPEN POSITIONS IN THE EURODOLLAR FUTURES AND OPTIONS CONTRACTS TRADED ON THE CHICAGO CME-IMM EXCHANGE, 1991
(billions of $U.S.)

| | Eurodollar Futures | | Options on Eurodollar Futures | | | |
| | | | Call | | Put | |
Nationality of Banks	Purchase	Sales	Purchase	Sale	Purchase	Sale
United States	153.3	104.3	40.0	24.4	57.7	39.9
Japan	93.1	97.3	37.3	28.2	13.7	82.5
France	21.3	23.4	6.1	2.4	4.4	4.8
United Kingdom	18.7	30.5	6.9	14.0	8.9	19.6
Canada	6.5	3.4	2.1	2.2	1.4	0.8
Switzerland	—		17.3	15.7	19.1	14.2
Other banks	73.6	84.1	8.6	9.5	17.0	25.3
Total no. of identified banks	366.5	343.0	118.3	96.4	122.2	187.1
Others[a]	656.7	680.2	139.7	161.6	238.7	173.8
Grand total	1023.2		258.0		360.9	

a. Positions of nonbanks or banks below the reporting cutoff point.
SOURCE: BIS (1992).

TABLE 3–8: OPEN POSITIONS IN FUTURES AND OPTIONS CONTRACTS
TRADED ON THE MATIF, 1991
(billions of $U.S.)

Contract Type	Total Face Value of Open Positions	Distributions of Open Positions (average of long plus short) Banks		Other
		French	Non-French	
Futures				
CAC-40	1.8	0.2	0.7	0.9
National French government bond	11.2	3.7	3.4	4.1
PIBOR	47.0	14.2	16.1	16.8
Options				
National French government bond (call plus put)	24.7	10.8	3.1	10.8
PIBOR (call plus put)	96.3	46.8	16.1	33.4

SOURCE: BIS (1992).

TABLE 3–9: MARKET SHARE OF FOREIGN INSTITUTIONS IN SELECTED OECD
COUNTRIES, 1986 AND 1989
(% of total assets)

Country	1986	1989
Germany	4.0	4.4
Belgium	46.0	47.0
France	10.9	13.0
Italy	2.45	2.9
United Kingdom	62.2	59.1
Japan	2.7	2.0
United States	17.9	21.4

SOURCE: Federal Reserve Bank of New York (1991), Goldberg (1992), Swary-Topf (1992).

U.S. banking assets. In California, this market share reaches 25 percent (Zimmerman 1989). This asymmetric penetration of foreign banking markets is puzzling because Japan has adopted the national treatment principle, meaning that foreign institutions operating in Japan face de jure the same regulations as domestic firms. This state of affairs has led trade negotiators of other countries to call for effective market access (de facto national treatment). A tentative explanation of the lack of foreign penetration in Japan follows.

According to Benston (1990), the determinants of bank competitiveness in foreign markets arise from four factors: comparative operating cost or innovation rate advantage, public subsidy, lower cost of capital, and services to home customers. Evidence about the total operating cost efficiency of Japanese banks is reported in Benston (1990) and Hawawini and Schill (1992), but it is unclear whether this productivity is attributable to the particular structure of Japan (very high population density, which allows for fewer branches and for the systematic use of ATMs), and whether this cost advantage can be exported abroad. The second source of competitive strength, public subsidy, could come from a privileged access at subsidized rates to the discount window of the Bank of Japan. As Benston (1990) points out, however, discount window funding by Japanese banks represents only a small fraction of deposit funding. In my opinion, it is doubtful whether the first two factors of international competitiveness—operating efficiency and discount window funding—could be the main determinants of Japanese banks' expansion.

The next factor of international competitiveness is the low-cost funding base of Japanese banks. It has been attributed to four separate sources: regulated home-based retail deposits, lower cost of subordinated debt, lower cost of equity capital, and lower equity to risk-assets ratio. The benefits arising from regulated home-based retail deposits, from de facto publicly insured subordinated debt, and from a relatively low equity to asset ratio have been well documented.[4] But these sources of lower funding costs are not specific to Japan. In most countries around the world, domestic banks have enjoyed a similar lower cost advantage that did not create the asymmetry of market penetration. For instance, public bailout has been systematic in the recent cases of Scandinavia, Spain, France, or Venezuela. The fourth source of low funding cost seems to be very specific to Japan: the cost of equity capital. Studies by Zimmer-McAuley (1991) and Abuaf-Carmody (1990) point to a lower cost of equity that allows Japanese banks to bid aggressively for loans.

---

4. Evidence on the lower cost of subordinated debt is reported in Zimmer and McAuley (1991). Scott and Iwahara (1994) argue that systematic public bailing out allows Japanese banks to operate with a lower equity requirement than their American counterparts. Packer (1994) documents the public support in facilitating the sale of bad loans to special vehicles.

Empirical evidence on various sources of lower funding cost has been demonstrated, but this factor alone is unlikely to be the main determinant of the competitiveness of Japanese banks. Indeed, since many European banks have enjoyed similar benefits, it would have to be shown that Japanese banks are using this lower funding cost to subsidize foreign activities or to fend off foreign competition at a higher degree than European firms. Moreover, this argument cannot explain the empirical evidence of the relative performance of Japanese and American firms in third countries, such as the United Kingdom. As is reported by the Federal Reserve Bank of New York (1991), American banks had an 8.1 percent market share of all commercial loans in the United Kingdom in 1989, while Japanese banks had a market share of 7.8 percent. These data being inconsistent with the low funding–cost argument, it would appear that other factors must explain the asymmetry of market penetration observed in some countries.

The last source of competitive advantage—servicing home-based customers—is a main determinant. Two studies by Zimmerman (1989) and Hultman-McGee (1989) point to the importance of trade and foreign direct investment to explain the growth of Japanese lending in the United States. Japanese banks do accompany national companies abroad. The low market share of foreign banks that is observed in Japan (as in Germany) can be explained by the close relationship between Japanese banks and their customers in the financial group structures (*keiretsu*). The same argument is advanced to explain the low market share achieved by foreign trust banks operating in Japan in the management of pension funds—lower than 0.3 percent of private funds under management.

As to the future strength of Japanese banking, one wonders whether most of these sources of competitive advantage are not fading away. The retail deposit market has been essentially deregulated since 1994; the collapse of the stock market has created an equity shortage; and perhaps most important, large Japanese firms seem to rely increasingly on bond financing in place of bank loans,[5] possibly facilitating the entry of foreign underwriters. As Semkow (1993) documents, foreign penetration has succeeded in some niches, such as the swaps and the EuroYen futures markets, where foreign banks have achieved market shares of more than 25 percent.

The wide range of success in foreign market penetration has raised the question of whether national treatment must be complemented by reciprocity clauses, an issue that will be addressed subsequently. The importance of the financial services sector in national

---

5. Hoshi, Kayshap, and Scharfstein (1993).

economies and the rapid growth of international trade in banking services raise the need for a satisfactory international regulatory and supervisory framework. In the next section, I develop an economic analysis of international banking regulations.

The Economics of Banking Regulations

Banking is a highly regulated industry. The regulatory framework includes regulations on entry (the "fit and proper" criterion), on the scope of permissible activities (banks' powers), and on rules of conduct of business (regulation on capital, on large exposure, and so forth). Regulations are applied to national and foreign suppliers of banking services. To assess the economic logic of national banking regulations and the specific issues raised by a fast-growing trade in banking services, one must first review the economics of the potential market failures that explain the need for banking regulations: imperfect (asymmetric) information, which could prevent the proper functioning of unregulated private markets; the potential for bank runs and the related fear of systemic crises; and implicit subsidies, which create distortions in international trade.

Imperfect (Asymmetric) Information and Investor Protection. The following analysis is rooted in imperfect information in banking markets and the potential need to protect consumers of financial services.[6]

The first and most important case of asymmetric information concerns the imperfect knowledge about the solvency of a banking firm. Depositors find it costly to evaluate the solvency of their bank. Additional sources of asymmetric information concern the potentially fraudulent character of management, the nature of the legal contract (for instance, the exact nature of a loan covenant), and problems related to conflicts of interest between different departments in a bank. For instance, a merger-and-acquisition advisor should not inform a fund manager about the likelihood of a transaction, lest the fund manager purchase securities of the target firm, causing the price of shares to increase, and making the acquisition more expensive.

The economics literature recognizes that the inability of consumers to evaluate the quality of a product properly can create a market failure.[7] This literature distinguishes three types of goods: search goods, whose quality is apparent before purchase; experience goods,

---

6. See chapter 2, by Lawrence White.
7. See Kay-Vickers (1986).

whose quality is apparent after consumption; and trust goods, whose quality is not always apparent even after consumption. An inefficiency may arise because the quality of a service is not valued properly by the market and reflected into higher prices, giving insufficient incentive for firms to produce quality goods. Regulation (such as minimal qualifications in the legal or medical professions) is a way to ensure a minimal level of quality. In the context of banking, quality refers in part to the degree of solvency of an institution. When depositors are uninformed, there are fewer incentives to limit the riskiness of the assets of a financial institution or its degree of financial leverage (deposit-to-equity ratio). Indeed, finance theory has shown that whenever depositors are not properly informed, shareholders of banks do benefit from an increase in risk.[8] With perfect information, depositors would react by requesting an interest rate increase to offset the transfer going to shareholders. With imperfect information this would be difficult, raising a well-identified and documented moral hazard problem.[9] The potential existence of imperfect information per se, however, does not yet justify public intervention. It has to be shown that private mechanisms cannot succeed.

There are three solutions to the imperfect information problem: information disclosure; protection of reputation for the long-term value of the franchise; and supplying risk-free deposits.

Regulation of information disclosure will reduce the degree of information asymmetry. It has been argued, however, that the evaluation of bank risks is a costly activity that could create a free rider problem. Individually, each customer may prefer not to engage in information search and analysis, on the assumption that other investors will do it. In such a situation, the provision of private information could be too low. I do not share this view. Indeed, since information once produced is available to investors at a very low transfer cost, the evaluation of banks should not be undertaken by each depositor but could be delegated to a public agency or a private rating firm. The cost of information gathering by the individual investor would be small.

A second solution to the asymmetric information problem is that firms have commercial incentives to protect their reputation. Firms who care for the value of their franchise and long-run profits have strong incentives to build internal control systems to reduce risks and

---

8. Merton (1977). The underlying intuition is that an increase in risk (variance of asset return) allows the shareholders of a firm to reap potentially large gains, while limiting the downside-risk to zero because of the limited liability characteristic of shares.

9. See the application of moral hazard to the American S&L crisis by L. White (1992).

fraud. A trade-off will always exist, however, between potentially high short-term fraudulent profit and the benefits of long-term reputation.

A third solution to information asymmetry is to create risk-free deposits. Since small account holders may find the cost of interpreting the rating high, or since they care about risk-free deposits only, two alternatives could be developed. The first is to have deposit insurance. This could be organized publicly or by the industry that guarantees the quality of the services offered. Peer monitoring and industry self-regulation prevent deviant behavior. The second mechanism is to create risk-free institutions—that is, having intermediaries invest all deposits in risk-free securities, the so-called narrow-bank proposal. Depositors would have the choice between institutions offering a higher but risky return and those providing quasi-risk–free deposits.

It would appear that the evaluation of risks is not inherently more difficult in banking than in other industries. It is quite likely that a large fraction of depositors prefer risk-free deposits, but these could be provided by the markets. One has to be extremely careful to avoid permanent regulatory interference that can create the raison d'être of public intervention. For instance, the creation of a safe and publicly insured deposit market reduces the incentives for information gathering and the creation of risk-free funds. A laissez-faire policy should not imply that there is no ground for public intervention to compensate the unlucky or imprudent investors. The argument is that transitory transfer policies should be used in these cases rather than direct and permanent interference with the functioning of private markets.

This analysis has shown that the information problem can be solved privately in the market through information disclosure, reputation, and insurance. Whenever there is evidence that the market cannot discriminate among firms, however, there is a case for the government to regulate entry and ensure minimal quality, as is done in the medical and legal professions.[10] The argument is that regulation is necessary to maintain a desired, minimal level of quality. The question arises whether this should be done privately or quasi-privately, as in Great Britain with the self-regulatory organizations (SROs), as opposed to publicly. The benefits of flexibility and industry expertise provided by private self-regulation have to be balanced against the risk of capture by the SROs, whose members have an obvious incentive to limit entry and competition. As there is currently

---

10. Evidence is a strong word. In most cases, there is a socio-political belief in the need to protect investors.

no empirical evidence demonstrating the superiority of one system or another, I suggest letting the national regulatory structures compete.[11]

The possibility of competitive deregulation raises immediately the question of the need to harmonize regulations *at the international level*. The answer is again related to imperfect information. Competition among national regulators or private clubs is desirable whenever the parties can evaluate the quality of regulatory systems. For instance, competition among regulators in Tokyo, Paris, Frankfurt, London, and New York will shape the developments of local stock exchanges, and the outcomes will be optimal if participants can discriminate among different regulatory systems. Harmonization of rules to ensure minimal quality would be necessary only if the market fails to discriminate. The degree of international harmonization could vary for different activities and classes of investors, the informed and the uninformed. An alternative to the harmonization of prudential regulations is to grant some supervisory powers to the host state, whenever it is felt that investors are inadequately protected by foreign regulation or supervision.[12]

The economics literature has identified a first potential market failure rooted in imperfect information. It is legitimate to let countries design prudential regulations to protect the uninformed investors. The implication for international trade in banking is as follows. Either prudential rules are harmonized to protect the uninformed or, as the General Agreement on Trade in Services (GATS) recommends, each host country locally supervises the rules on all banking services offered.

Bank Runs and Systemic Risks. The second market failure is the potential for bank runs and systemic crises. Banks are special because the financial contract that emerges—illiquid loans funded by short-term deposits—creates a potential market failure and a need for public intervention. The financial contract creates the risk that depositors run to withdraw their funds. A run can be triggered by bad news about the value of bank assets or by any unexplained fear.[13] In either

---

11. An additional argument to let the national regulatory structures compete is that the general-equilibrium costs of regulation are not fully understood. With the exception of a paper by Santomero-Watson (1977), most scholars have used partial-equilibrium models to analyze the effects of regulations.

12. For instance, European countries can regulate foreign firms for reason of public interest.

13. Calomiris and Gorton (1991) argue that most of the bank runs are created by a decrease in value of bank assets.

TABLE 3–10

DEPOSIT INSURANCE SYSTEMS IN SELECTED COUNTRIES

Country	Coverage, in Domestic Currency	Coverage, in $US
Belgium	BEF 500,000	14,650
Denmark	DKR 250,000	39,320
France	FF 400,000	72,660
Germany	30% of equity per deposit	
Ireland	£IRL 10,000	14,960
Italy	Lit 1 billion (100% for first 200 mil. and 75% for next 800)	650,000 (100% for first 130,000 and 75% for next 520,000)
Luxembourg	FLUX 500,000	14,650
Netherlands	DG 40,000	22,800
Spain	Pta 1,500,000	11,800
United Kingdom	75% of deposits (ceiling of £15,000)	75% of deposits (ceiling of 23,400)
Japan	Yen 10,000,000	96,900
United States	$100,000	100,000

SOURCE: National central banks.

case, a loss can ensue because illiquid assets will be sold at a discount. Moreover, a bank failure could eventually trigger a signal on the solvency of other banks, leading to a systemic crisis. Here a distinction should be drawn between the domino effect and systemic crisis.

A domino effect exists if the failure of one bank directly endangers the solvency of other banks. This risk is substantially reduced today, however, since banks are systematically measuring and controlling their counterparty exposure, for instance, through netting arrangements. A systemic run could occur if, lacking information, depositors create a run on a significant number of banks.

This market failure explains banking regulations and the establishment of safety nets to guarantee the stability of banking markets. They have taken the form of deposit insurance, lender-of-last-resort interventions, and public bailouts. As is shown in table 3–10, deposit insurance funds are unlikely to contribute much to the reduction of systemic risk because they cover only small deposits. Runs are likely to be initiated by large firms or financial institutions. Therefore, lender-of-last-resort interventions by central banks or public bailout remain the most likely tools to avoid bank runs and systemic crises.

Safety nets with deposit insurance or lender-of-last-resort intervention raise three issues at the international level: the international level playing field, when deposits are subject to different insurance coverage; the potential liability of the insurer; and the well-identified moral hazard problem.

First, since national deposit insurance coverage differs from country to country, it can be destabilizing for investors to chase the best coverage.

Second, since most deposit insurance systems currently in place cover the deposits of domestic and foreign banks operating locally, and since lender-of-last-resort intervention will be concerned primarily with domestic markets and banks operating domestically,[14] it is legitimate for insurers to keep some supervisory power over all institutions (branches and subsidiaries) operating domestically. That is, host-country regulation could apply to limit the risks taken by financial institutions and the exposure of the domestic central bank in cases of bailout.[15] The problem is well illustrated by the January 1992 winding-up order made for the Bank of Credit and Commerce International, a bank chartered in Luxembourg with significant activities in Great Britain. It automatically created a liability for the British Deposit Protection Board.

A first alternative to host-country control is to harmonize completely the solvency standards of different countries, but experience has shown that it would be very difficult to reach an agreement on harmonization of regulations and supervisory practices. Moreover, I do not believe that centralized regulation is necessary, or even desirable. Competition between national regulators should produce efficient standards and prevent regulatory capture by the regulatees, as has happened so often in banking in the past sixty years. It thus seems reasonable to let domestic supervisors keep some host supervisory powers on international banks (subsidiaries and branches) with substantial funding at risk in their own country. In the context of international trade in banking services, this view is consistent with the General Agreement on Trade in Services[16]—that is, the right for local authorities to enforce prudential solvency standards on both local and foreign firms offering services. This view is fully in line with the American Foreign Bank Supervision Enhancement Act of 1991

---

14. It is well known that the Bank of Italy did not intervene to prevent the collapse of the Luxembourg-based Banco Ambrosiano Holding because it created little disturbance on the Italian financial markets.

15. Bailout would occur if the failure of a branch of a foreign bank leads to a run on domestic banks.

16. General Agreement on Trade in Services (1994).

(Misback 1993) and the ruling of the Basel Committee on Banking Supervision accepting host-country control for international solvency rules.[17]

The third problem is that deposit insurance contributes to reducing private incentives for monitoring the solvency of banks. As was discussed earlier, the creation of risk-free deposits could be organized by the market (the narrow-bank proposal) or, alternatively, insured deposits could be made first-order claims. The uninsured deposits bearing larger losses in cases of bank failure would have additional incentives to monitor the solvency of financial institutions.

The analysis of the second type of market failure, bank runs and systemic crises, leads to the following conclusion. Since domestic central banks will be primarily concerned with the stability of their domestic markets, they should have the right to control the solvency of banks (subsidiaries and branches) operating in their domestic market. Since in many cases the solvency would depend on the solvency of an entire group, I recommend joint supervision by the home and host-country authorities.

Fair Trade. The third policy issue is the level playing field. Two issues will be distinguished. The first relates to the implicit guarantee given by central banks. The second refers to the possibility of cross-border subsidization.

Public safety nets or deposit insurance systems can provide an implicit subsidy that can alter competition. Deposit financing, for instance, can reduce the cost of funding loans, both because of the tax-deductibility of interest payments and because of the implicit guarantee given by the lender of last resort.[18] To foster stability and create a level playing field, the Basel Committee on Banking Supervision has enforced minimal capital requirements.[19] From the point of view of competition, the harmonization of prudential regulations is warranted when the objective is to create a level playing field. But harmonization should be limited only to that objective. For instance, the current efforts to harmonize the regulation on interest-rate risk and foreign exchange exposures do not appear desirable because they do not provide a clear competitive advantage to banks.[20] The exis-

17. *Financial Times of London* (1992).

18. Technically, deposit insurance creates a subsidy only in the case where the insurance premium is below its fair price.

19. According to Scott and Iwahara (1994), differences in bailout and accounting policies (such as provisioning of bad debt) substantially reduce the efficiency of these agreements.

20. Dermine (1993).

tence of large and liquid derivative markets allows the hedging of these risks at relatively low cost in most countries. Quite often the identification of a regulatory subsidy will be difficult. For instance, do links between banks and industrial groups provide a competitive advantage that is subsidized by the central bank, which takes a greater risk? There is no case for harmonization as long as the existence of a subsidy yielding a competitive advantage cannot be demonstrated. Such a case was clear in the context of loan funding and capital adequacy. It is debatable in the context of the links between banks and industrial groups.

The second issue, discussed earlier, is the possibility that oligopolistic home markets could generate rents used to subsidize foreign activities. The issue arises because of the fear that some countries do allow concentration on their domestic banking markets. This is fairly evident in the European Union, in which the competition policies in the Netherlands and the United Kingdom differ substantially. The Monopolies and Mergers Commission prevents excessive concentration on the domestic market, while the Dutch authorities have allowed the creation of a few national champions. For instance, in 1993, the British bank Lloyds withdrew its bid on Midland Bank for fear that the bid would be stopped by the merger authorities. In the Netherlands, domestic mergers have reduced the number of market players to three: ABN-AMRO, ING-Bank, and Rabobank.

Three potential sources of market failure calling for public intervention and harmonization have been discussed: imperfect information, bank runs, and fair trade. As Key and Scott (1992) have emphasized, these are quite different sources of market failure, each demanding a specific regulatory response. As concerns *imperfect information*, a market for private information would be developed allowing regulations, if necessary, to apply to specific activities and classes of investors. At the international level, banks can freely deliver services if prudential rules are harmonized. If this is not the case, countries could retain host-country power on all services offered domestically. As sovereign countries would wish to protect the *stability of their domestic markets*, it seems reasonable that they keep some supervisory power over financial institutions operating domestically. Concerning *fair trade*, public or private subsidies must not be used to subsidize international banking services.

One conclusion of this economic analysis is that individual countries should retain the right to organize their own regulations and supervision. This is consistent with the principle of national treatment, according to which domestic and foreign banks in one country would obey the same rules. In the next section, however, I evaluate more closely whether the national treatment principle underlying most trade negotiations can deal with banking, and whether it needs to be complemented by reciprocity clauses.

Reciprocity and Nondiscriminatory Barriers

The international negotiation on trade liberalization is focused on the national treatment principle, according to which there will be no discrimination between domestic and foreign firms in the application of regulatory and supervisory rules in a particular country. The United States and some European countries are not satisfied with the principle and have asked for reciprocity, according to which powers given to foreign banks operating in their own countries should also be given to banks operating in foreign countries. The economic issue with respect to reciprocity is to see whether nondiscriminatory regulations fully compatible with national treatment could raise de facto barriers to trade in banking services.[21]

In this section I will present some large differences in regulatory regimes and then analyze whether these nondiscriminatory barriers could affect trade in banking. First I will examine the scope of permissible activities, followed by restrictions on corporate control.

Scope of Permissible Activities. Table 3–11 provides information on the regulatory regimes governing the involvement of banks in the insurance sector.[22] Regulatory differences are great between a liberal Great Britain on one side and the United States and Japan on the other, separating banking from insurance. This issue is not trivial, since European banks have rapidly acquired more than 50 percent of the life insurance market in just a few years.

In a similar manner, the regulations of banks' activities in the securities markets are known to vary considerably, with European banks on the one hand enjoying great freedom with the universal banking model and Japanese and American banks on the other hand being strictly regulated by the Glass-Steagall Act and Article 65. These regulations, however, are increasingly being challenged.

Following the 1929 crisis, the 1933 Glass-Steagall Act separated commercial banks from securities activities. Since 1975, however, the Federal Reserve has progressively widened the range of securities-related activities open to some bank holding companies.[23] As con-

---

21. See Key (1993).
22. See chapter 5, by Harold Skipper.
23. See chapter 4, by Ingo Walter.

TABLE 3–11

Permissible Activities in Insurance in Selected OECD Countries, 1993

Member Countries	Direct Production by a Bank of an Insurance Product	Direct Distribution by a Bank of an Insurance Product	Creation of an Insurance Subsidiary by a Bank	Shareholding of a Bank in an Insurance Company	Financial Group in which a Bank or an Insurance Firm Is a Company of the Group
Australia	F	A	SL	L	A
Belgium	F	A	SL	SL	A
Canada	F	L	F	SL	A
Denmark	F	A	A	A	L
France	F	A	L	L	A
Germany	F	A	A	A	A
Ireland	E	A	A	A	A
Italy	F	A	A	A	A
Japan	F	F	F	SL	SL
Netherlands	F	A	L	L	A
New Zealand	N.A.	N.A.	N.A.	N.A.	N.A.
Portugal	F	L	A	A	A
Spain	F	L	A	A	A
Sweden	F	A	L	L	L
Switzerland	F	A	A	A	L
United Kingdom	F	A	A	A	A
United States	E	L	SL	SL	SL

N.A. = Not available.
Notes: A = Allowed; E = Exceptional; F = Forbidden; L = Limited; SL = Strictly limited.
Source: OECD (1993).

TABLE 3–12

PERMISSIBLE ACTIVITIES OF BANKS IN SECURITIES IN JAPAN, 1993

Activity	Primary Market	Secondary Market
Government bonds	Yes	Yes
Straight bonds	Yes	Yes
Mutual funds	Yes	Yes
Convertibles and warrants	Yes	No
Stocks and stock derivatives	No	No

SOURCE: Semkow (1993).

cerns restrictions on foreign activities of American banks, the policy has been not to undermine the competitiveness of U.S. subsidiaries that have been allowed to operate in foreign securities markets (Dale 1992).

After World War II, the United States imposed on Japan the main features of Glass-Steagall. Article 65 of Japan's Securities and Exchange Law of 1948 states that banks may not engage in securities activities. The Financial System Reform Act of 1993, however, a major reform act, will progressively allow banks and securities firms to operate in each other's territory with capitalized subsidiaries.[24] Table 3–12 documents the permissible activities of Japanese banks in securities.

The economic issue raised by the range of differences in the regulatory environment is whether the more liberal countries should be demanding reciprocity. It would appear that countries should be free to choose their regulatory regimes, and that competition between financial centers would lead to an optimal state (Walter 1992). If economies of scale and scope do exist, then European banks benefit from a liberal environment, and American and Japanese banks should pressure their home regulators to free the system. Moreover, if the European system allows banks to subsidize their insurance activities because of the implicit guarantee given by their central banks, American and Japanese firms should complain about unfairness in trade.

It would therefore appear that the demand for reciprocity is not well founded. But the arguments just proposed are incomplete; there could be specific situations in which reciprocity and the need for further harmonization of regulations are warranted. These situations

---

24. Semkow (1993).

arise when entry in a market is restricted de facto by differences in regulations. The example of *bancassurance* is such a case. If European banks adopt the *bancassurance* model to be competitive, their competitiveness in Japan and the United States would be restricted because they would have to choose between banking and insurance activities. This situation is illustrated by Internationale Nederlanden Groep (ING), the Dutch financial services group, which was given a grace period to choose between banking and insurance in the United States.[25] As in the financial services industry, restriction on entry and direct investment cannot be substituted by trade in services (physical presence is necessary in most financial services); a barrier on entry becomes de facto a barrier on trade. The case of bancassurance can be deemed special, but there are also other, more restrictive regulations on entry, all linked to corporate control, which prevents the purchase of local institutions.

Corporate Control. Some countries effectively limit the entry of foreign shareholders in limiting their percentage of ownership. Table 3–2, discussed earlier, indicates the difficulty of foreign control. Recently, the Italian authorities imposed a 3 percent voting power limit on the privatization of a large public institution. It would appear that, since entry and direct presence in a country are vital to deliver financial services, it would be reasonable to harmonize those regulations that limit ownership control and de facto entry.

The next section presents an advanced case of financial market integration, that of the single European market. It is a special case, of course, because countries willingly abandon part of their sovereignty.

The European Union Approach to International Integration

While most international agreements have used the national treatment principle, which ensures the equal treatment of all firms operating in one country, the European Commission has used a different method of integration: a single banking license, home-country control with mutual recognition, and minimal harmonization of national regulations.[26] All credit institutions authorized in an EU country will be

----

25. In 1994, the ING group decided to return its banking license to U.S. authorities.

26. These principles are incorporated in the Second Banking Directive (Directive 89/646/EEC). The principles of home-country regulation and mutual recognition have been inspired by the famous 1987 case Cassis de Dijon (EC Commission vs Germany, 205/84, ECR 3755). In this case, the European court of justice found that Germany could not prohibit the import of liqueur that was lawfully produced and sold in France solely because the alcoholic label was too low for it to be deemed liqueur under German law.

able to establish branches or supply cross-border financial services in the other countries without further authorization, provided the bank is authorized to provide such services in the home state. These services include:

- acceptance of deposits and other repayable funds from the public
- lending, including consumer credit; mortgage credit; factoring, with or without recourse; financing of commercial transactions, including forfeiting
- financial leasing
- money transmission services
- issuing and administering means of payments, such as credit cards, travelers' checks, and bankers' drafts
- guarantees and commitments
- trading for own account or for account of customers in money market instruments (checks, bills, CDs, etc.); foreign exchange; financial futures and options; foreign exchange and interest rate derivative instruments; transferable securities
- participation in securities issues and the provision of services related to such issues
- advice to undertakings on capital structure, industrial strategy and related questions, and advice and services relating to mergers and the purchase of undertakings
- money broking
- portfolio management and advice
- safekeeping and administration of securities
- credit reference services
- safe custody services

The banking model adopted by the EU is the universal banking model. It permits banks to undertake investment activities and leaves it to national regulators to control financial conglomerates, the ownership structure of banks, and their relationship with industry. The Bank of England, for instance, does not favor the ownership of banks by industrial groups, although this is allowed in France and Belgium. The Second Banking Directive calls for home-country control on solvency. This extends to the bank itself, to its foreign and national subsidiaries, which have to be consolidated for supervisory purposes, and to its foreign branches. As concerns the latter, the host state retains the right to regulate a foreign bank's activities in the host state only to the extent that such regulation is necessary for the protection of the public interest. Thus the manner in which a bank markets its services and deals with customers can be regulated by the host state.

The host state may also intervene in those matters expressly reserved to it, notably liquidity, monetary policy, and advertising.

To address a need for a minimal harmonization of regulations, the Second Banking Directive calls for an initial capital of at least ECU 5 million, harmonized capital adequacy standards and large exposure rules, and supervisory control of banks' permanent participation in the nonfinancial sector.

A supportive piece of legislation is the 1988 Directive on Liberalization of Capital Flows. That directive, however, contains a safeguard clause authorizing member states to take necessary measures in the event of balance-of-payments problems.[27]

The December 1991 Maastricht Treaty on Economic and Monetary Union has confirmed the single market program. Although the primary objective of the European System of Central Banks shall be to maintain price stability, there are explicit references to regulation and supervision.

> The European System of Central Banks (ESCB) shall contribute to the smooth conduct of policies pursued by the competent authorities relating to the prudential supervision of credit institutions and the stability of the financial system. . . . The national Central Banks are an integral part of the ESCB and shall act in accordance with the guidelines and instructions of the European Central Bank. . . . The ECB may offer advice to and be consulted by the Council, the Commission and the competent authorities of the Member States in the scope and implementation of Community legislation relating to the prudential supervision of credit institutions and to the stability of the financial system. . . . The ECB may fulfill specific tasks concerning policies relating to the prudential supervision of credit institutions and other financial institutions with the exception of insurance undertakings.

Although the exact rules governing the functioning of the new system have yet to be worked out, the treaty is explicit on the principle of decentralization and allocation of regulatory and supervisory powers to national central banks. Only in special circumstances and with

---

27. The June 1988 capital directive (Article Three) provides for the temporary implementation of capital controls. In the case of large speculative movements, after consultation with the Committee of Central Banks' governors the commission can authorize capital controls. In urgent cases a country can implement them, but must notify the commission. After consultation with the Committee of Central Banks' governors, authorization to pursue capital controls can be given for a period not exceeding six months.

unanimity in the European Council is the European Central Bank allowed to regulate or supervise financial institutions. On October 12, 1993, the last obstacle to ratification was lifted with a ruling by the German Constitutional Court, and the Maastricht Treaty has officially been in effect since November 1, 1993.

Finally, it should be recognized that the single banking market goes beyond the twelve members of the European Union. On May 13, 1992, the countries of the European Free Trade Association (EFTA),[28] with the exception of Switzerland, joined the European Economic Area (EEA). This move implies that the EEA countries accept the European banking legislation regarding single banking licenses, home-country control, mutual recognition, and acceptance of the common regulations. Moreover, Austria, Finland, and Sweden joined the European Union in January 1995, increasing the number of EU countries to fifteen.

The integration of European banking markets has raised three sets of issues: an efficient deposit insurance system, reciprocity with non-EU countries, and taxation of capital income.

Deposit Insurance in an Integrated Market. Following the collapse of Bank of Credit and Commerce International, the European Commission has worked to revise the deposit insurance systems to ensure an adequate degree of accountability for the supervisor. As discussed earlier, a solution to deposit insurance in international banking is to allocate supervisory powers to the institution in charge of insuring the deposits. A draft directive on deposit guarantee schemes was accepted by the Council of Ministers in September 1993. It provides for mandatory insurance for all EU financial institutions. The coverage per depositor is a minimum of ECU 20,000 (15,000 until 1999), with a franchise of 10 percent maximum. To ensure accountability, the principle of the home country adopted for banking supervision would apply—that is, the insurance system of the parent bank would cover the deposits collected by domestic and foreign branches. This is the principle against which two very important exceptions stand. In the case where home coverage is too large vis-à-vis the host coverage (such as for a French bank operating in Belgium), the coverage of foreign branches cannot exceed that of the host country to prevent unfair competition. In the case where the home coverage is lower than that of the host country, the foreign branch will have the right to obtain supplementary insurance from the host state. Finally, for

---

28. EFTA includes Austria, Finland, Iceland, Liechtenstein, Norway, Sweden, and Switzerland.

the branches of non-EU banks, the host country will decide whether they must or must not join an insurance system, with the provision that depositors will be informed about the magnitude of the coverage.

Reciprocity Clause. The issue of reciprocity has received considerable attention in nonmember countries. Two concerns have to be distinguished: the denial of national treatment, and effective market access, comparable to that which the community grants to third countries. Article 9(4) of the Second Banking Directive deals with the situation where there is discrimination against community financial institutions, compared with their domestic counterparts in a third country. In this case, the directive provides for the initiation of discussion with the option to suspend new banking licenses for institutions from the third country. In the second case—comparable access—Article 9(3) provides for negotiation with the country without the suspension of the right of establishment. A recent report on the Treatment of European Financial Institutions in Third Countries has been published by the commission.[29] Although it recognizes the existence of discriminatory treatment in some countries, the commission recommends negotiating in the framework of the new World Trade Organization. Moreover, the report makes no reference to a temporary suspension of authorization.

Taxation of Capital Income. To enhance the attractiveness of their home markets, various countries have reduced the taxation of income on capital, at least relative to the taxation of labor income. From a fiscal policy perspective, it would seem that the creation of an integrated financial market should not affect the relative taxation of labor and capital income. Obviously, this will not be the case as long as there is no harmonization of taxation or sharing of information by tax authorities. Table 3–13 reports the amount of liabilities of national banks vis-à-vis nonbank nonresidents.

Even acknowledging the expertise of some banking centers, it would appear that the volume of deposits housed in a few small countries is abnormally large. Proposals for a common withholding tax on interest revenue have been rejected so far by Luxembourg and the United Kingdom, with the argument that the Euromarket would be transferred to a non-EU country. An alternative proposal that would suffer a similar concern would be to lift bank secrecy. That is, the fiscal authority of one member state would have the right to obtain information about bank deposits in another EU country. An alter-

---

29. European Commission (1992).

TABLE 3–13

LIABILITIES OF NATIONAL BANKS VIS-À-VIS THE NONBANK SECTOR,

1989 AND 1994

(billions of $U.S.)

Country	1989	1994
Austria	10.9	11.2
Belgium	27.1	55.3
Luxembourg	77.2	143.5
Denmark	4.1	7.1
Finland	3.5	0.5
France	32.1	54.4
Germany	39.2	112.9
Ireland	4.4	6.5
Italy	9.1	10.3
Netherlands	31.9	52.1
Norway	1.4	1.7
Spain	20.4	33.8
Sweden	9.5	6.6
Switzerland	178.4	216.0
United Kingdom	266.4	300.1
Bahamas & Cayman	N.A.	223.0
Singapore	N.A.	65.0
Hong Kong	N.A.	47.0
Japan	13.5	22.0
United States	90.6	90.6

N.A. = not available.
SOURCE: BIS (1993). These statistics could underestimate the external position of banks to the extent that fiduciary deposits are not included.

native is to substantially modify the tax structure, focusing tax revenue on labor and corporate income while substantially reducing taxes raised on capital income.

The case of the European Union is fairly illustrative of the problems raised by integration of banking markets. The first observation is that decentralized deposit insurance systems create issues of fair trade and supervision. The second is that international banking integration can conflict with fiscal policy.

Conclusion

The banking literature has identified three main sources of potential market failure calling for public intervention: imperfect information and the protection of investors, stability of financial markets, and fair trade.

The first source of market failure is the traditional need to protect investors. I have argued that domestic regulation of solvency is warranted only in those cases where investors cannot evaluate the quality of a product. Similarly, international harmonization of regulations is necessary if the market participants cannot discriminate among different regulatory structures. Information disclosure, competition between public or private regulators, and the creation of risk-free funds will be satisfactory in most situations. In any case, different products and classes of consumers will require different regulatory treatment. To foster incentives for bank monitoring, I suggest that insured deposits be made a first-order claim. Uninsured deposits, being second-order claims, would have additional incentives for monitoring, since they would have more to lose in the event of bank failure.

A second reason for public intervention is the need to foster the stability of financial markets. As long as national authorities are responsible for the stability of their own markets, they should keep supervisory responsibilities on all firms affecting their markets, and collaborative host- and home-country supervision seems warranted.

The third potential market failure concerns fair trade. As domestic regulators will be responsible for controlling the ownership of banks (public or private), the degree of market power in their domestic market, and public bailouts, countries must ensure that banks do not exploit domestic rents to subsidize their international activities. Moreover, in this context of fair trade, harmonization of banking regulations is necessary only in the case of an identified public subsidy that confers a competitive advantage.

As concerns national treatment and reciprocity, I argue that, although the national treatment principle governing international trade seems adequate in many respects, there can be cases where differences between domestic and foreign regulations limit de facto entry in banking markets. Since entry (direct investment) is essential to the delivery of many financial services, it would seem that negotiations on reciprocity are warranted in those cases where entry is restricted by differences among national regulations.

Finally, European banking integration presents a useful case of advanced integration from which standing issues can be identified. Taxation of income on capital increasingly becomes an issue. The benefits expected from integration of banking markets should not be reversed by tax inefficiencies. Substantial work remains to be done to prevent inefficient competitive moves to reduce taxation of income on capital.

References

Abuaf, Niso, and Kathleen Carmody. "The Cost of Capital in Japan and the United States: A Tale of Two Markets." Salomon Brothers, July 1990.

Benston, George. "U.S. Banking in an Increasingly Integrated and Competitive World Economy." *Journal of Financial Services Research*, 1990.

Bank for International Settlements. "The Revised Basel Concordat, Principles for the Supervision of Banks' Foreign Establishments." Basel, Switzerland, 1983.

———. "Recent Developments in International Interbank Relations." Basel, Switerland, 1992.

———. "International Banking and Financial Market Developments." February 1995.

Calomiris, Charles, and Gary Gorton. "The Origins of Banking Panics, Models, Facts, and Bank Regulations." Wharton School, 1990, mimeo.

Dale, Richard. *Regulation of International Banking.* Cambridge, England: Woodhead-Faulkner, 1984.

———. *International Banking Deregulation.* Oxford, England: Basil Blackwell, 1992.

Dermine, Jean. "The BIS Proposals for the Measurement of Interest Rate Risk: Some Pitfalls." *Journal of International Securities Markets,* Spring 1991.

Dermine, Jean, ed. *European Banking in the 1990s.* Oxford, England: Basil Blackwell, 1993.

Diamond, Douglas. "Financial Intermediaries and Delegated Monitoring." *Review of Financial Studies,* 1984.

European Commission. *Traitement Réservé dans les Pays Tiers aux Etablissements de Crédit et aux Enterprises d'Assurance de la Communauté.* Brussels, 1992.

Federal Reserve Bank of New York. *International Competitiveness of U.S. Financial Firms.* Staff Study, 1991.

Financial Times of London. "Basel Pact on Policing the Banks Sector." July 7, 1992.

———. "FT 500." January 20, 1995.

GATT. "Revised Text on the Services Agreement." Geneva, Switzerland, 1994.

Goldberg, Larry. "The Competitive Impact of Foreign Commercial

Banks in the USA." In R. A. Gilbert, ed., *The Changing Market in Financial Services*. Boston: Kluwer Academics, 1992.

Hawawini, Gabriel, and Michael Schill. "The Japanese Presence in the European Financial Services Sector: Historic Perspective and Future Prospects." INSEAD Euro-Asia Centre, mimeo, 1992.

Herring, Richard. " '92 and After: The International Supervisory Challenge." In H. Genberg and A. K. Swoboda, eds., *World Financial Markets After 1992*. London and New York: Kegan Paul International, 1993.

Herring, Richard, and Richard Litan. "Financial Regulation in a Global Economy." Mimeo, 1993.

Hoshi, Takeo, Anil Kayshap, and David Scharfstein. "The Choice between Public and Private Debt: An Analysis of Post-Deregulation Corporate Financing in Japan." Mimeo, 1993.

Hultman, Charles W. "Regulation of International Banking: A Review of the Issues." *Journal of World Trade*, vol. 26, 1992.

Hultman, Charles W., and Randolph McGee. "Factors Affecting the Foreign Banking Presence in the U.S." *Journal of Banking and Finance*, 1989.

Kay, John, and John Vickers. "Regulatory Reform in Britain." *Economic Policy*, 1988.

Key, Sydney J. "Is National Treatment Still Viable? U.S. Policy in Theory and Practice." In H. Genberg and A. K. Swoboda, eds. *World Financial Markets after 1992*. London and New York: Kegan Paul International, 1993.

Key, Sydney J., and Hal S. Scott. "International Trade in Banking Services." In A. Steinherr, ed. *The New European Financial Market Place*. London and New York: Longman, 1992.

Luehrman, Timothy. "A Contrary View of Japan's Cost of Capital Advantage." In Ingo Walter and Taketo Hiraki, eds., *Restructuring Japan's Financial Markets*. New York: Business One Irwin, 1993.

Misback, Ann E. "The Foreign Bank Supervision Enhancement Act of 1991." *Federal Reserve Bulletin*, January 1993.

Merton, Robert. "An Analytic Derivation of the Cost of Deposit Insurance and Loan Guarantees." *Journal of Banking and Finance*, 1977.

OECD. *International Trade in Services-Banking*. Paris, 1984.

———. *Insurance and Other Financial Services*. Paris, 1992.

———. "Trade in Financial Services." *Financial Market Trends*, 1993.

———. *Labor Force Statistics*. Paris, 1991.

Packer, Frank. "The Disposal of Bad Loans in Japan: A Review of Recent Policy Initiatives." Mimeo, 1994.

Pecchioli, Rinaldo. *Prudential Supervision in Banking*. Paris: OECD, 1987.

Salomon Bros. *International Bank Weekly*, March 22, 1995.

Santomero, Anthony, and Ronald Watson. "Determining an Optimal Capital Standard for the Banking Industry." *Journal of Finance*, 1977.

Scott, Hal and Shinsaku Iwahara. *In Search of a Level Playing Field.* Group of Thirty, Occasional Paper 46. Washington, D.C., 1994.

Semkow, Brian. "Foreign Financial Institutions in Japan: Legal and Financial Barriers and Opportunities." *Butterworths Journal of International Banking and Financial Law*, February 1993.

———. "Japan's Financial System Reform Act." *Butterworths Journal of International Banking and Financial Law*, October 1993.

Skipper, Harold. "International Trade in Insurance." Chapter 5 in this volume.

Swary, Itzhak, and Barry Topf. *Global Financial Deregulation.* London: Basil Blackwell, 1992.

Treasury Department. *National Treatment Study.* Washington, D.C., 1994.

Walter, Ingo. *Barriers to Trade in Banking and Financial Services.* London: Trade Policy Research Center, 1985.

———. *Global Competition in Financial Services.* Cambridge: ASI Press/ Ballinger, 1988.

———. "The Battle of the Systems: Control of Enterprises and the Global Economy." *Journal of International Securities Markets*, Winter 1992.

———. "Global Competition and Market Access in the Securities Industry." Chapter 4 in this volume.

White, Larry. *The S&L Debacle: Public Lessons for Bank and Thrift Regulation.* Oxford: Oxford University Press, 1991.

———. "Competition versus Harmonization: An Overview of International Regulation of Financial Services." Chapter 2 in this volume.

Zimmer, Steven, and Robert McAuley. "Bank Cost of Capital and International Competition." *FRBNY Quarterly Review*, 1991.

Zimmerman, Gary. "The Growing Presence of Japanese Banks in California." *Federal Reserve Bank of San Francisco*, 1989.

4

Global Competition and Market Access in the Securities Industry

Ingo Walter

The international activities of securities firms grew far more rapidly than did global economic activity during most of the 1980s, and this differential performance has continued well into the 1990s. The reasons have to do with the competitive dynamics of the financial intermediation process itself, together with the changing financial behavior of corporate and institutional users of financial services, all set against the backdrop of shifting regulatory, technological, and macroeconomic environments.

As volatility associated with interest rates and exchange rates has increased in many parts of the world, much greater latitude has developed for profiting from cross-border speculative and arbitrage activities in financial markets—along with a greater need for risk-management services and instruments designed to help deal with the volatility. Many of these opportunities have been well suited to the capabilities of the securities industry, especially in harnessing its skills in trading and financial innovation. The continued lack of international macroeconomic policy alignments, even within tightly knit economic groups such as the European Union, suggests there will be much expansion in transaction volumes in the years ahead.

Equally important are divergent patterns of economic growth, capital investment, and savings around the world, offering financial intermediaries the opportunity to link investors with issuers globally.

The greater are such divergences, the greater is the potential for continued growth in international securities transactions. Moreover, periods of declining interest rates in a number of major currencies, along with favorable equity market conditions, have contributed to significant spurts of securities new-issues in most of the important financial markets. At the same time, industrial reconfiguration in response to changing global economics, competition policies, and trade policies has likewise been favorable to the development of the securities industry. Recapitalization of firms, as well as corporate restructuring via mergers and acquisitions, was highly supportive of the industry's development in North America and the United Kingdom in the second half of the 1980s. The action shifted in part to continental Europe and emerging-market countries in the early 1990s, including the important role of privatization transactions. Even the problem in emerging-market debt and equity securities placed with international investors, triggered by the 1994–1995 Mexican financial crisis, is likely to be only a temporary setback for the global securities industry and to give rise to yet another set of new opportunities.[1]

Not least important have been economic and financial reforms in the OECD countries that follow a decade-long pattern of economic liberalization aimed at increasing the efficiency of all kinds of markets and reducing involvement in them by governments. The principal motivation appears to have been the cumulative positive experience of the business and financial community, government officials, and the population at large with greater reliance on free-market solutions to problems of economic growth and international economic performance during the 1980s—particularly with regard to capital formation and productivity enhancement—as against traditional, socialist-oriented reliance on direct and indirect government involvement. This theme has been taken up with a vengeance in the overwhelming majority of emerging markets, as well as in countries in transition from central planning and government domination, sometimes indeed leapfrogging the reforms seen in the traditional market-economy nations beset by entrenched interests and high degrees of political inertia when faced with the need for structural change.

---

1. Earlier financial setbacks, such as the global debt crisis of the 1980s (also triggered by events in Mexico in 1982), led to a range of securities industry opportunities, such as debt-equity swaps, debt-for-bonds conversions (notably the Brady debt, restructuring initiatives in various debtor countries), and an array of privatization and financial-market liberalization programs with broad-gauge advisory, origination, and trading opportunities for international securities firms. For those who are fast on their feet and not averse to bottom-fishing, every cloud has a silver lining—sometimes several.

In reaction to these developments the securities industry, once mainly focused on national markets, has itself become highly international. Securities firms and investment banking units of universal banks based in the United States, Europe, and Japan have established or acquired significant activities in each others' markets in an effort to capture a share of cross-border business and, occasionally, domestic business in host countries as well. In the process, problems of market access have inevitably arisen, as a result either of explicit exclusionary practices, prudential regulations bearing disproportionately on foreign-based securities firms, or "structural" conduct-of-business patterns that make it difficult for foreign-based firms to penetrate local markets.

The objective of this chapter is to identify problems of market access in the securities industry, to consider the adequacy of the approaches taken under regional and global financial services liberalization negotiations, and to suggest market access issues that remain to be addressed.

Financial services are (and always will be) subject to substantial regulation, the reasons for which center on the essentially fiduciary nature of the business—handling other people's money—as well as the quasi-utility of a significant part of the industry and the unacceptable consequences of systemic damage resulting from institutional failure. White (1996) has argued that globalization of the industry and national approaches to regulation are fundamentally in conflict. Something has to give, if financial institutions subject to regulation are not to slip through the fault lines that separate national regulatory domains. Either national regulation must prevail or there must be a significant move toward global harmonization of national regulatory standards. There are pros and cons to each of these routes. National regulatory dominance may calcify inefficient financial systems and serve as a significant barrier to market access for foreign-based vendors. Harmonization may force liberalization and convergence to some sort of globally acceptable standards that are likely to embody substantial free-market attributes, including liberal market access. But harmonization is inevitably the product of negotiation and consensus building, and it may leave financial services markets less well served than if national markets were forced to compete in a "market for markets" on the basis, among other things, of net regulatory burdens imposed on financial intermediaries. This chapter examines this issue with specific reference to the global securities industry.

The first part of the chapter places the securities industry in the context of the financial intermediation process, explaining the dynamics of that process and its effect on the securities industry. The second part enumerates the scope of activities normally encompassed by the securities industry and their international dimensions, including the volume and location of transaction flows, and it reviews available evidence on the apparent performance of firms that are home-based in various countries. The third part surveys the role of financial regulation and the evidence regarding explicit and implicit barriers to market access faced by securities firms, and the extent to which these have been addressed in both regional and global trade liberalization efforts. The final section of the chapter presents some conclusions regarding outstanding market access issues.

Stylized Process of Financial Intermediation

The central component of any model of the modern financial system is the nature of the conduits through which the financial assets of the ultimate savers flow through to the liabilities of the ultimate users of finance, both within and between national economies. This involves alternative and competing modes of financial intermediation, or contracting between counterparties in financial transactions. A convenient model of financial contracting and the roles of financial institutions and markets is summarized in figure 4–1—a generic flow-of-funds diagram that can be applied at the domestic and global levels.

The diagram depicts the financial process among the different sectors of the national and international economy in terms of

- the underlying environmental and regulatory determinants, or drivers
- the financial infrastructure services that have to be provided, including market information, financial research and its dissemination, and financial rating services and portfolio diagnostics on the one hand, and trading, payments, transaction clearance and settlement, and custody services on the other hand
- the generic information, interpretation, and transaction cost advantages, or "competencies," necessary to add value and profit from the three primary intersectoral linkages, namely:
  —savings and commercial banking and other traditional forms of intermediated finance
  —investment banking and securitized intermediation
  —various financial direct-connect mechanisms between borrowers and lenders

Ultimate sources of surplus funds tapped by financial intermediaries arise in the household sector (deferred consumption or savings),

FIGURE 4–1
INTERMEDIATION DYNAMICS FOR FINANCIAL CONTRACTING

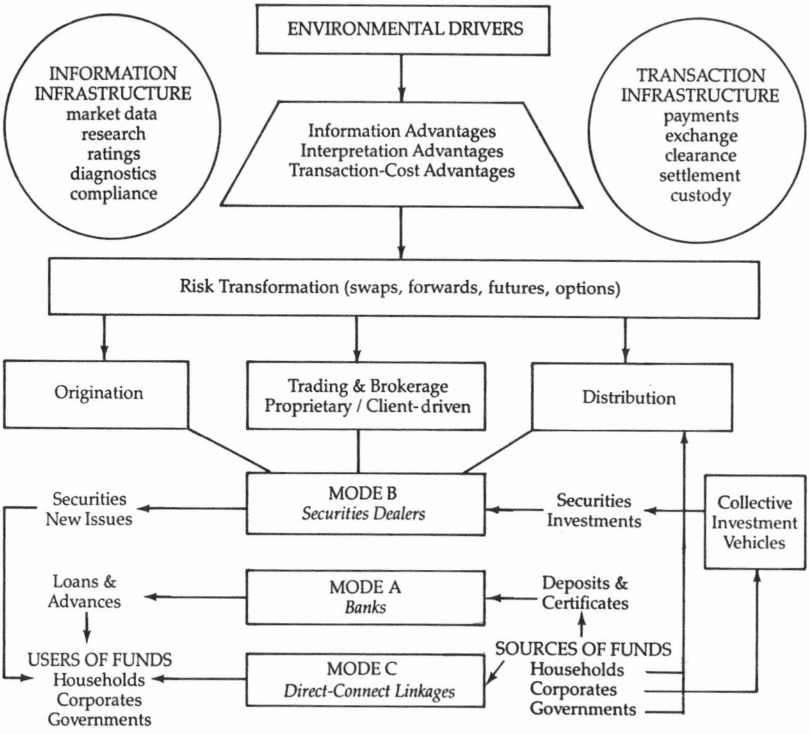

ENVIRONMENTAL DRIVERS

INFORMATION INFRASTRUCTURE
market data
research
ratings
diagnostics
compliance

Information Advantages
Interpretation Advantages
Transaction-Cost Advantages

TRANSACTION INFRASTRUCTURE
payments
exchange
clearance
settlement
custody

Risk Transformation (swaps, forwards, futures, options)

Origination

Trading & Brokerage
Proprietary / Client-driven

Distribution

Securities
New Issues

MODE B
Securities Dealers

Securities
Investments

Collective Investment Vehicles

Loans &
Advances

MODE A
Banks

Deposits &
Certificates

USERS OF FUNDS
Households
Corporates
Governments

MODE C
Direct-Connect Linkages

SOURCES OF FUNDS
Households
Corporates
Governments

SOURCE: Author.

the corporate sector (retained earnings or business savings), and the government sector (budgetary surpluses and external reserve buildups).

• Under the first, or classic, mode of financial intermediation, savings (or fund sources) are held in the form of deposits or alternative types of claims issued by commercial banks, savings organizations, insurance companies, or other forms of financial institutions entitled to finance themselves by placing their liabilities directly with the general public. Financial institutions then use these fund flows (liabilities) to purchase domestic and international assets issued by nonfinancial institution agents, such as firms and governments.

- Under the second mode of fund flows, savings may be allocated directly (or indirectly via so-called collective investment vehicles) to the purchase of securities publicly issued and sold by various governmental and private-sector organizations in the domestic and international financial markets.
- Under the third alternative, savings held in collective investment vehicles may be allocated directly to borrowers through various forms of private placement and other (possibly automated) direct-sale mechanisms to distribute their obligations, or they may be internally deployed within the saving entity (for example, retained earnings of nonfinancial corporations).

Ultimate users of funds comprise the same three segments of the economy—the household or consumer sector, the business sector, and the government sector.

- Consumers may finance purchases by means of personal loans from banks or of loans secured by purchased assets (hire-purchase, or installment loans). These may appear on the asset side of the balance sheets of credit institutions on a revolving basis for the duration of the respective loan contracts, or they may be sold off into the financial market in the form of structured securities backed by various types of receivables.
- Corporations may borrow from banks in the form of unsecured or asset-backed straight or revolving credit facilities, or they may sell debt obligations (such as commercial paper, receivables financing, or fixed-income securities of various types) or equities directly into the financial market.
- Governments can likewise borrow from credit institutions (sovereign borrowing) or issue full faith and credit or revenue-backed securities directly into the market.

With the exception of consumers, borrowers such as corporations and governments also have the possibility of privately issuing and placing their obligations with institutional investors, thereby circumventing both credit institutions and the public debt and equity markets. Even consumer debt can be repackaged as structured, asset-backed securities and sold privately to investors. And as noted, internal financial flows within economic entities comprising the end users of the financial system are an ever-present alternative to external finance.

Alternative Modes of Financial Contracting. As shown in figure 4–1, depositors buy the "secondary" financial claims or liabilities issued by credit institutions and benefit from liquidity, convenience, and safety through the ability of financial institutions to diversify risk and improve credit quality. Financial institutions can do this through professional management and monitoring of their holdings of primary financial claims—debt and equity. Savers can choose among a set of standardized contracts and receive payments, transaction services, and interest that may or may not be subject to varying degrees of government regulation. This is denoted as *mode A* in figure 4–1.

Alternatively, investors may select their own portfolios of financial assets directly from among the publicly issued debt and equity instruments on offer. This may provide a broader range of options than do standardized bank contracts and permit the larger investors to tailor portfolios more closely to their objectives while still achieving acceptable liquidity through rapid execution of trades—aided by linkages with banks and other financial institutions that are part of the domestic payments mechanism. Investors may also choose to have their portfolios professionally managed, through various types of collective investment vehicles (mutual funds, pension funds, life insurance companies). This is denoted as *mode B* in figure 4–1.

Finally, institutional investors buy large blocks of privately issued securities. In doing so, they may face a liquidity penalty—attributable to the absence or limited availability of a liquid secondary market. Normally they are compensated for this penalty via a higher yield. Conversely, directly placed securities usually involve lower issuing costs and can be specifically tailored to more closely match issuer and investor requirements than can publicly issued securities. Institutional and regulatory developments, especially in the United States, have added to the liquidity and depth of some direct-placement markets in recent years. This channel is denoted *mode C* in figure 4–1.

Value to ultimate savers and investors, inherent in the financial processes described here, accrues in the form of a three-way combination of yield, safety, and liquidity. Value to ultimate users of funds likewise accrues in the form of a combination of financing cost, transaction cost, flexibility, and liquidity. This value can be enhanced through credit backstops, guarantees, and derivative instruments, such as forward rate agreements, caps, collars, futures, and options provided by financial institutions acting either as banks or as securities firms.

Finally, the three intermediation channels identified in figure 4–1 can be linked functionally and geographically, both domestically and internationally.

Functional linkages permit bank receivables, for example, to be repackaged and sold to nonbank securities investors. Or bank credit facilities or insurance company guarantees can support the issuance of securities. Or privately placed securities may eventually be eligible for sale in public markets.

Geographic linkages make it possible for savers and issuers to have access to foreign and offshore markets, thereby improving risk, liquidity, and yield, or reducing transaction costs.

If permitted by financial regulation, various kinds of financial firms emerge to perform one or more of the roles suggested in figure 4–1—commercial banks, savings banks, postal savings institutions, savings cooperatives, credit unions, securities firms (full-service firms and various kinds of specialists), mutual funds, insurance companies, finance companies, finance subsidiaries of industrial companies, and others. Members of each strategic group compete with one another, as well as with members of other strategic groups. Assuming it is allowed to do so by the regulators, each firm elects to operate in one or more of the three financial-process modes identified in figure 4–1, according to its own competitive advantages—that is, its comparative efficiency in the relevant financial production mode compared with that of other firms. Tables 4–1 and 4–2 provide a dramatic example of how strategic groups have evolved from 1950 to 1990 in providing financial services in the United States.

Structural Shifts in the Intermediation Process. As noted, the three alternative channels of financial fund flows identified in figure 4–1 often compete vigorously with each other for transaction volume in the financial intermediation process. The winners and losers among institutions competing in this process tend to be relatively consistent across national and international financial markets. In the case of the most highly developed financial systems, the securities industry (mode B in figure 4–1) has gained at the expense of the banking industry (mode A)—see table 4–3 for the United States as an example. The reason for this migration of financial flows from one process to another arguably has much to do with changes in the relative static and dynamic efficiency characteristics and costs (or spreads) of inter-mediation via traditional financial institutions. The migration of flows does not so much stem from more direct securities market processes that result from superior static and dynamic efficiency properties, and less oppressive regulation.

On the borrower side of figure 4–1, this migration of flows has

TABLE 4-1

FUNCTIONS AND PRODUCTS OF THE FINANCIAL SERVICES INDUSTRY, CIRCA 1950

Function or Institution	Payment Services	Savings Products	Fiduciary Services	Lending		Underwriting Issuance of		Insurance and Risk Management Products
				Business	Consumer	Equity	Debt	
Insured depository institutions	●	●	●					
Insurance companies		●		○	●			●
Finance companies			●	○	●			
Securities firms		●				●	●	
Pension funds		●						
Mutual funds		●						

○ = minor involvement.

SOURCE: General Accounting Office.

TABLE 4–2
FUNCTIONS AND PRODUCTS OF THE FINANCIAL SERVICES INDUSTRY, CIRCA 1995

Function or Institution	Payment Services	Savings Products	Fiduciary Services	Lending		Underwriting Issuance of		Insurance and Risk Management Products
				Business	Consumer	Equity	Debt	
Insured depository institutions	●	●	●	●	●	○	○	●
Insurance companies	●	●	●	●	●	○	○	●
Finance companies	●	●	●	●	●	○	○	●
Securities firms	●	●	●	●	●	●	●	●
Pension funds			●	●				●
Mutual funds	●	●	●					●
Diversified financial firms	●	●	●	●	●	●	●	●
Specialist firms	●	●	●	●	●	●	●	●

○ = selective involvement via affiliates.
SOURCE: General Accounting Office.

TABLE 4–3

PERCENTAGE SHARES OF ASSETS OF FINANCIAL INSTITUTIONS IN THE UNITED STATES, 1860–1993

	1860	1880	1900	1912	1922	1929	1939	1948	1960	1970	1980	1993
Commercial banks	71.4	60.6	62.9	64.5	63.3	53.7	51.2	55.9	38.2	37.9	34.8	25.4
Thrift institutions	17.8	22.8	18.2	14.8	13.9	14.0	13.6	12.3	19.7	20.4	21.4	9.4
Insurance companies	10.7	13.9	13.8	16.6	16.7	18.6	27.2	24.3	23.8	18.9	16.1	17.4
Investment companies	N.A.	N.A.	N.A.	N.A.	0.0	2.4	1.9	1.3	2.9	3.5	3.6	14.9
Pension funds	N.A.	N.A.	0.0	0.0	0.0	0.7	2.1	3.1	9.7	13.0	17.4	24.4
Finance companies	N.A.	0.0	0.0	0.0	0.0	2.0	2.2	2.0	4.6	4.8	5.1	4.7
Securities brokers and dealers	0.0	0.0	3.8	3.0	5.3	8.1	1.5	1.0	1.1	1.2	1.1	3.3
Mortgage companies	0.0	2.7	1.3	1.2	0.8	0.6	0.3	0.1	N.A.	N.A.	0.4	0.2
Real estate investment trusts	N.A.	N.A.	N.A.	N.A.	N.A.	N.A.	N.A.	N.A.	0.0	0.3	0.1	0.1
Total	100.0	100.0	100.0	100.0	100.0	100.0	100.0	100.0	100.0	100.0	100.0	100.0
Total, in $ millions	.001	.005	.016	.034	.075	.123	.129	.281	.596	1.328	4.025	13.952

N.A. = not available.
SOURCE: Randall Krozner, "The Evolution of Universal Banking and Its Regulation," in Anthony Saunders and Ingo Walter, eds., *Financial System Design: Universal Banking Considered* (Homewood, Ill.: Richard D. Irwin, 1996).

been manifested in the increasing use of the commercial paper markets as a substitute for bank credit lines, medium-term note programs, and domestic and international bond issues for long-term debt financing. Nonbank lending to business by finance companies and insurance companies, as well as private placements of securities with such institutions, have further eroded the market share of banks in a number of national financial environments. Whereas corporate and institutional access to the securities markets is obvious, even households have greatly increased their access to financing—through securities issues in a number of countries, and through securitized liabilities such as mortgage loans and credit card debt. For example, traded financial instruments are issued against anticipated cash flows of interest and principal from various kinds of receivables. Securitization allows increased asset portfolio liquidity and better ability to manage interest-rate risk exposures. Most types of bank loans have become potentially securitizable—a trend that has not necessarily abated, as governments in various countries change bank and securities regulations to allow the process to spread, and as pressure mounts from financial services as well as nonfinancial firms to attain access to this technology. Thus, a major integrating factor in world financial markets is likely to come from the direct recycling of bank loans through one of the many available securitization vehicles.

On the investor side of figure 4–1, the same migration from banks to the securities industry is evident in the growing share of investments as a form of savings, particularly through fiduciaries such as pension funds, insurance companies, and mutual funds.

The next set of developments in some of the most innovative financial markets is likely to involve replacement of traditional banking and securities forms of financial intermediation by direct financial links between sources and users of funds that have the potential of further cutting out traditional financial intermediaries—the direct-connect mechanisms identified as mode C in figure 4–1. This includes direct intercompany–payment clearing, such as electronic data interchange (EDI) and automated private placements of securities, as is already done in some European financial markets using electronic Dutch auction distribution of government securities. Although they are often closely interrelated, the three intermediation modes in figure 4–1 thus compete with one another in a modern financial system on the basis of static and dynamic efficiency, as well as differential regulatory burdens to which they are exposed.

As a consequence of these developments, borrowers in many national financial systems today face a range of alternatives for obtaining financing. Even households and small or medium-sized companies that are basically limited to bank credit can have their loans securitized and can benefit from access to a broader pool of funding sources, as well as from conversion of illiquid bank loans into liquid securities forms. The gains from both activities will be partially passed backward to the borrower. Similarly, today's modern financial systems provide a wide range of opportunities and services to investors, allowing them to optimize their asset portfolios by taking advantage of the domestic and international portfolio diversification across the range of financial instruments being offered, as well as improvements in the securities market infrastructure services. Again, even the retail investor can access these investment alternatives and process-technology improvements by taking advantage of the broad array of mutual funds, unit trusts, and other collective investment vehicles being aggressively marketed to households. In many cases these vehicles are imaginative, high-technology, nonstationary distribution techniques backed by extensive macroeconomic, financial market, and securities research.

In short, the economic dynamics of financial intermediation appears to have systematically favored the securities industry at the expense of the banking industry because of the process of disintermediation and securitization based on superior static and dynamic efficiency attributes. Financial intermediation may yet be challenged, however, by various direct-connect and private placement linkages between issuers and investors. The pace of change has hardly been uniform around the world, however, as seen in the differences in household asset composition in the United States, Europe, and developing countries. Still, more efficient modes of financial contracting will progressively encroach on less efficient ones. To the extent that the securities industry is in the vanguard of this development, a growing demand for its services seems ensured—as does the international competitive positioning of securities firms based in countries with financial systems that lead this development.

Even as intense competition across financial intermediation channels has developed, similar competition has emerged among national financial systems, as well as between them and offshore financial markets. Again, the borrower not only has the choice between bank credits and securities issues in the domestic market, but also has the alternative of borrowing or issuing abroad if foreign or offshore financing alternatives are more attractive. Similarly, savers and their fiduciaries have the option of going abroad to place funds if the returns and portfolio alternatives on offer are superior to those available at home. Securities firms active in the most competitive markets thus have a dual advantage in this bidirectional financial intermediation competition. They can export to others the product and process technologies they have honed in the most advanced markets, and they can attract lending, underwriting, trading, and distribution activities to these markets from less efficient markets. Policies that prevent either of these developments largely define the realm of protectionism in the global securities industry.

Character of the International Securities Industry

The previous section of this chapter has positioned the international securities industry in terms of mode B of the domestic and international financial intermediation process depicted in figure 4–1. In broad outline, the industry encompasses the activities listed in figure 4–2. These activities can be elaborated as follows below.

Capital Markets. At the center of table 4–4 are the capital market activities of securities firms, comprising underwriting securities new-issues, dealing in these securities for the firm's own account and on behalf of clients, providing brokerage services, conducting and disseminating research on issuers, markets, and macroeconomic developments, and supplying risk-management services to issuers and investors. These can be detailed as follows:

- First is the underwriting of new issues of debt and equity securities—both seasoned and initial public offerings—for a range of clients, including private-sector corporations, government-owned or government-controlled entities, sovereign governments, and multilateral agencies. The underwriting function involves purchasing the securities from the issuer and selling them either in public markets or to large institutional investors in the form of private placements. Earnings, and exposure of the firm to underwriting risk, typically come from the spread between the buying and selling prices.

    —Bond (fixed-income) underwriting is usually carried out through domestic and international underwriting syndicates of securities firms with access to local investors, investors in various foreign markets, such as Switzerland, and investors in offshore markets using one of several alternative distribution techniques. Placements may also be restricted to selected institutional investors (private placements) rather than the general public. Access to various foreign markets is facilitated by means of interest-rate and currency swaps, and some widely distributed multimarket issues have become known as global issues. In some markets, intense competition and deregulation have nar-

FIGURE 4–2

DIAGRAM OF A FULL-SERVICE SECURITIES FIRM

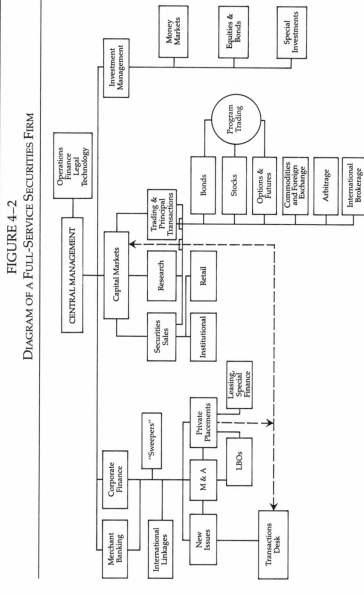

SOURCE: Roy C. Smith and Ingo Walter, *Global Banking* (New York: Oxford University Press, 1996).

TABLE 4–4
PRODUCTS AND SERVICES OF SECURITIES FIRMS

Corporate Finance	Capital Markets	Investment Management
Mergers and Acquisitions	New Issues in Global Markets	Investment Participations
National markets	Short-term debt	Principal Equity Investments
Cross-border transactions	Long-term debt	Leveraged buyouts
Foreign markets	Private placements	Venture capital
Strategic advice	Asset securitization	Recapitalizations
General Client Service	Equities	Real estate
Market access	Global Market-Making	Oil and Gas
Ratings	Securities	Arbitrage
Recapitalizations	Fixed income	Merger
Corporate restructuring	Equities	Equity
Divestitures	Collateralized mortgage	Fixed income
Bankruptcy workouts	obligations	Equities
Real Estate Finance	Asset-backed securities	Derivatives
Mortgages	Foreign exchange	Global Asset Management
Equities	Commodities	Fixed income
	Swaps and Derivatives	Equity
	Investment Research and Ideas	Indexed funds
	Loan Syndications and Bridge	Private Banking and Custody
	Lending	Services
	Hedging and Risk Management	Domestic
	Pension Fund Services	Global

SOURCE: Author.

rowed spreads to the point that the number of firms in underwriting syndicates has declined over time, and in some cases a single firm handles an entire issue—the so-called bought deal.

—Stock underwriting is usually heavily concentrated in the home country of the issuing firm, which is normally where the secondary-market trading and liquidity is to be found. New issues of stock may be offered to investors for the first time (initial public offerings, or IPOs), to the general public on a repeat basis (seasoned issues), to existing holders of the stock (rights issues), or only to selected institutional investors (private placements).

• Second is the secondary market trading of cash instruments such as stocks, bonds, asset-backed securities, foreign exchange, and sometimes commodities such as cereal grains, pork bellies, and gold—as well as derivatives on individual securities or commodities (mainly futures and options) or on indexes. Activities include customer trading (executing client orders), proprietary trading (for the firm's own account), and market-making and arbitrage—buying and selling simultaneously in at least two markets to capitalize on price discrepancies between different markets for underlying financial instruments or derivatives, or between cash and derivatives markets. Some firms also engage in risk arbitrage, usually involving speculative purchases of stock on the basis of public information relating to mergers and acquisitions.

• Brokerage involves executing buy or sell orders for customers without actually taking possession of the security or derivative concerned, sometimes including complex instructions based on various contingencies in the market.

• Research is conducted into factors affecting the various markets as well as individual securities and derivatives. Securities research is made available to investor clients by presumably independent analysts within the firm whose opinion can be taken seriously, as opposed to validating vested interests of the firm by analysts whose careers depend on the quality and objectivity of their work. The value of research provided to clients depends critically on its quality and timeliness and is often compensated by business channeled through the firm, such as brokerage commissions and underwriting mandates. Closely allied are research activities—often highly technical modeling exercises—involving innovative financial instruments that link market developments and sources of value-added to issuer-clients or investor-clients.

• Hedging and risk management mainly involve the use of derivative instruments to reduce exposure to risk associated with individual transactions or markets affecting corporate, institutional, or individual clients. These include interest-rate caps, floors and collars, various kinds of contingent contracts, and futures and options on various types of instruments. It may be quicker, easier, and cheaper, for example, for an investor to alter the risk profile on an investment portfolio by using derivatives rather than by buying and selling the underlying instruments.

Corporate Finance. At the left side of table 4–4 are the corporate finance activities of the typical securities firm, predominantly involving advisory work relating to mergers, acquisitions, divestitures, recapitalizations, leveraged buyouts, and a variety of other generic and specialized corporate transactions.

• Mergers and acquisitions involve fee-based advisory assignments to firms wishing to acquire others (buy-side assignments) or firms wishing to be sold or to sell certain business units to prospective acquirers (sell-side assignments). The mergers and acquisitions (M&A) business is closely associated with the market for corporate control, and it may involve advisories and fund-raising efforts for hostile acquirers, or plotting defensive strategies and recapitalizations for firms subject to unwanted takeover bids. It may also involve providing independent valuations and fairness opinions to buyers or sellers of companies, to protect against lawsuits from disgruntled investors alleging that the price paid for a company was either too high or too low. Such activities may be domestic, within a single national economy, or cross-border, between a buyer in one country and a seller in another.

• Recapitalizations involve advice to corporations concerning optimum capital structure, increasing or decreasing the proportion of debt to equity in the balance sheet, types and maturity structure of liabilities, stock repurchases programs, and the like. The securities firm may supply financial advice on these matters, as well as providing the required execution services through its capital markets activities.

• Real estate and other special transactions include advisory services for energy, transportation, or project financings requiring specialized industry expertise.

• Merchant banking involves securities firms putting their clients' and their own capital on the line in M&A transactions and other equity participations. This could involve buying control of entire firms to restructure and eventually sell them, in whole or in part, to other

101

companies or to the investing public. It may also involve large, essentially permanent stakeholdings in business enterprises, including board-level representation and supervision of management. Or it may involve short-term subordinated lending (bridge loans or mezzanine financing) to ensure the success of an M&A transaction, intended to be quickly repaid out of the assets of the surviving entity. Other areas of significant direct investments may include real estate and leveraged lease transactions.

Investment Management and Investor Services. On the right hand of table 4–4 are investment services provided to institutional and individual asset-holders and sometimes involving a good deal of the firm's own capital in debt or equity investments.

- Investment management for institutions and individuals is one such service. With respect to institutions, major investors such as pension funds and insurance companies may allocate blocks of assets to securities firms to manage against specific performance targets (usually stock or bond indexes), or bogeys. Individuals may also assign discretionary management to securities firms. Those with significant assets (high net worth clients) may couple asset management with tax planning, estates and trusts, and similar services in a private banking relationship with the securities firm, either directly or with the help of independent financial advisers. Closed-end or open-end mutual funds or unit trusts may also be operated by a securities firm and either marketed to selected institutions and high net worth individuals or mass-marketed to the general investor community as tax-advantaged pension holdings or to capture general household savings.
- Investor services are a second type. There is an array of services that lie between buyers and sellers of securities, domestically as well as internationally, which are critical for the effective operation of securities markets. Such operation centers on domestic and international systems for clearing and settling securities transactions via efficient central securities depositories, which in turn are prerequisites for a value chain of services, often supplied on the basis of quality and price by competing private-sector vendors of information services, analytical services, trading services and information processing, credit services, custody and safekeeping, and portfolio diagnostic services. Many such infrastructure services, including trading information, securities clearance, settlement, and global custody, are supplied internationally by specialized firms or commercial banks and a number of securities firms as well.

Figure 4–2 may be taken as a typical organizational structure of an American or British securities firm. It shows how the activities listed in table 4–4 tend to be structured. Examples among U.S. investment banks include Morgan Stanley, Goldman Sachs, and Merrill Lynch. A British merchant bank such as Shroders or Robert Fleming would be similarly structured, with the added element of limited commercial lending to clients. A French *banque d'affaires* such as Banque Indosuez or Paribas would have a greater emphasis on quasi-permanent holdings of securities in nonfinancial corporations. Japanese securities companies such as Nomura, Nikko, Daiwa, and Yamaichi would be similarly structured, traditionally with a relatively greater emphasis on retail brokerage and no commercial lending. All such firms select in various ways from the above menu of services and organize themselves in various strategic configurations. Some securities firms encompass the entire range of activities as full-service vendors, supplying such services to institutional and retail clients, with other full-service firms providing more or less the same range only to institutional (wholesale) clients. Others specialize in a narrower range of services, including financial "boutiques" that may limit themselves to a few or only one area, such as M&A advisory services or leveraged buyout transactions.

Still other securities firms are units of universal banks. Securities activities can be linked to banking activities in various ways (Saunders & Walter 1994). In the pure universal bank and in the German variant of universal banking, securities and corporate finance activities are carried out by the bank itself. In the British version of universal banking, they are carried out by a separately capitalized securities subsidiary of the bank, competing with similarly structured firms and with free-standing merchant banks. Most major British merchant banks have been acquired by continental European universal banks: Morgan Grenfell by Deutsche Bank AG, Kleinwort Benson by Dresdner Bank AG, Barings by Internationale Nederlanden Groep, and S. G. Warburg by Swiss Bank Corporation. In the U.S. version of universal banking, such as it is, they will be organized as separately capitalized subsidiaries of bank holding companies—so-called Section 20 subsidiaries that are engaged in underwriting and dealing in corporate bond stocks, municipal revenue bonds, and their derivatives, all prohibited under Section 20 of the Glass-Steagall Act of 1933, up to a statutory 10 percent revenue limit. These subsidiaries exist alongside separately capitalized commercial banking subsidiaries of the same holding companies and are competing with free-standing investment banks of various configurations.

A final and related dimension of investment banking organization is its relationship to the ownership and control of nonfinancial corporations (Walter 1993). In the typical Anglo-American approach, individuals hold shares in both banks and nonfinancial companies, either directly or through collective investment vehicles such as mutual funds and pension funds. In the German or continental European approach, this pattern of shareholding is complemented—and to some extent supplemented—by permanent large-scale bank shareholdings of nonfinancial companies (and bank voting of fiduciary shareholdings), as well as by nonfinancial corporate shareholdings in banks. In the Japanese *keiretsu* approach, this is further complemented by reciprocal shareholdings among companies in often elaborate industrial crossholding structures. How investment banking services are supplied and the extent to which foreign-based firms are able to achieve effective market access may be affected in important ways by the structure of bank-industry linkages and the "inside" versus "public" flow of information between corporations and the financial markets.

Investment Banking Market Dimensions and Transaction Flows. Given the activities mix described in the preceding section, it is logical that securities firms must be positioned to have access to the principal arenas in which those activities are conducted—securities new issues, trading, sales, and corporate finance advisory work. This section provides a brief overview of market volumes and locations in each of these activities. Although size of deal-flow is hardly a foolproof guide to market attractiveness for firms in the securities industry—depending heavily on the market's competitive structure—it does have considerable importance from the perspective of market access and regulatory policies.

Table 4–5 provides an overview of international capital-raising activity during the period 1990–1994—cross-border bank lending, European bond and foreign bond new issues, international tranches of equity issues, medium-term notes, syndicated loans, and committed European note programs. Note that international bond and stock issues have captured the lion's share of capital-raising activity, certainly relative to bank-related facilities, including asset-backed securities placed with international investors. This illustrates the growing importance of the securities linkage as against the banking linkage depicted in figure 4–1 with respect to the international markets.

Table 4–6 gives an indication of corporate finance–deal flow in the form of global merger and acquisitions and related transactions during the period 1985–1994. Note that the bulk of M&A activity during the late 1980s (61 percent) was centered in the United States

TABLE 4-5: U.S. AND INTERNATIONAL CAPITAL MARKET ACTIVITY, 1990–1994
($U.S. billions)

Activity	1990	1991	1992	1993	1994
U.S. domestic new issues					
U.S. medium-term notes	100.0	142.3	169.4	260.3	282.8
Investment grade debt	106.7	193.7	281.1	389.2	342.5
Collaterialized securities	180.6	292.6	428.2	478.9	252.5
Junk and convertibles	6.6	20.9	53.7	69.5	36.4
Municipal debt	124.8	162.8	231.7	287.8	161.3
Total debt	518.7	812.3	1,164.1	1,485.7	1,075.5
Preferred stock	4.6	20.1	20.9	22.4	15.5
Common stock	19.2	54.8	72.4	101.7	61.6
Total equity	23.7	75.0	93.3	124.1	77.1
Total U.S. debt and equity	542.4	887.3	1,257.4	1,609.8	1,152.5
International issues					
Euro medium-term notes	21.9	38.5	96.9	149.8	257.2
Euro and foreign bonds	184.3	260.8	335.9	482.7	485.2
International equity	7.4	12.0	17.8	27.7	32.4
Total international debt and equity	213.6	311.4	450.6	660.2	774.8
Worldwide total debt and equity	756.0	1,198.7	1,708.0	2,270.0	1,927.3
Global syndicated bank loans and backstop facilities	467.9	727.0	403.0	555.4	785.6

Source: Securities Data Corporation, *Investment Dealers' Digest*.

TABLE 4–6
U.S. AND INTERNATIONAL VOLUME OF TRANSACTIONS IN GLOBAL MERGER AND ACQUISITIONS DEVELOPMENTS, 1985–1994
($U.S. billions)

Transactions	1985	1986	1987	1988	1989	1990	1991	1992	1993	1994
U.S. domestic	192.3	200.9	203.9	293.2	250.1	124.9	108.5	119.3	101.1	199.8
U.S. cross-border	15.9	39.3	50.2	77.9	85.6	73.0	40.5	33.5	34.9	58.4
Intra-European	11.5	20.7	54.9	86.4	130.1	127.2	117.2	91.0	59.9	85.6
European cross-border	8.8	35.4	41.4	54.6	74.3	97.7	53.8	43.0	33.0	57.1
U.S.-European cross-border	(5.9)	(17.4)	(28.3)	(38.2)	(46.3)	(36.6)	(22.8)	(13.3)	(27.4)	(39.0)
All other	10.5	15.9	28.2	37.5	69.7	47.8	54.2	43.0	60.2	34.3
Global total	233.1	294.8	350.3	511.4	563.5	434.0	351.4	316.5	261.7	406.9
Percentage of U.S. total	89.3	81.5	72.5	72.6	59.6	45.6	42.4	48.3	52.0	63.5
Percentage of European total	8.7	19.0	27.5	27.6	36.3	51.8	48.7	42.3	35.5	35.1
Percentage of U.S. domestic total	82.5	68.1	58.2	57.3	44.4	28.8	30.9	37.7	38.6	49.1

SOURCE: Securities Data Company.

(both domestic and cross-border transactions). By 1992 the largest share of such activity occurred outside the United States, mainly in Western Europe, as economic restructuring triggered by events such as the EU single-market initiative began to take hold. By 1994, however, U.S. M&A volume had once again reached preeminence.

Each of these major activity areas of the securities and investment banking industry has become dramatically more international over the years, and so have the firms engaged in them. No major securities firm has failed to establish (or is in the process of establishing) a viable presence in the three principal securities hubs—London, New York, and Tokyo, or in important regional centers such as Frankfurt, Paris, Singapore, Hong Kong, or other specific centers of interest in industrial countries and emerging markets. Consequently, policy measures that inhibit access to such markets can seriously impede their development on the basis of competitive advantage, as well as impeding the linkage of sources and users of finance worldwide, arguably at significant efficiency and growth costs to borrowers, investors, and national economic and financial systems.

Regulatory Determinants of Financial Structures

The financial flows that are the basis of the preceding discussion of financial intermediation in general and investment banking in particular are dramatically affected by regulatory factors—including regulation related to market access. Financial services make up an industry that has usually been, and will continue to be, subject to significant public-authority regulation and supervision because of its fiduciary nature and the possibility of social costs associated with institutional failure. Indeed, small changes in financial regulation can bring about truly massive changes in financial activity. In the process, they can affect the competitive viability and performance of different types of financial institutions spreading their activities across the financial spectrum depicted in figure 4–1.

Regulatory Trade-offs. The right-hand side of figure 4–3 depicts the policy trade-offs that invariably confront those charged with designing and implementing a properly structured financial system. On the one hand, they must strive to achieve static and dynamic efficiency, with respect to the financial system as a whole, as well as the competitive viability of financial institutions that are subject to regulation.

On the other hand, policy makers must safeguard the stability of institutions and the financial markets as a whole, in addition to encouraging what is considered acceptable market conduct, including

FIGURE 4–3
Policy Trade-offs and Techniques of the Regulatory Overlay

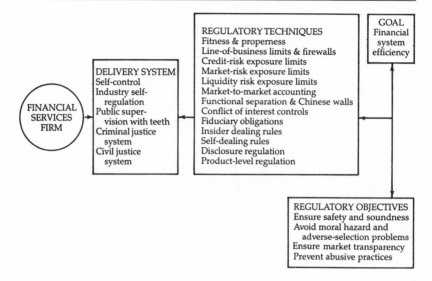

SOURCE: Author.

the politically sensitive implied social contract between financial institutions and small, unsophisticated customers.

The problem of financial "safety-net" design is beset with difficulties such as moral hazard and adverse selection, and it becomes especially problematic when products and activities shade into one another, when on- and off-balance sheet activities are involved, and when domestic and offshore business is conducted. Regulators constantly face problems of inadequate regulation, resulting in costly failures, versus overregulation, resulting in opportunity costs in the form of efficiencies not achieved.

Some of the principal options that regulators have at their disposal—specified in figure 4–3—include fitness-and-properness criteria, under which a financial institution may be established, continue to operate, or be shut down; line-of-business regulation, as to what specific types of institutions may do; as well as regulations as to liquidity, exposures, and capital adequacy. Regulatory initiatives, however, can have their own distortive effect on financial markets, and regulation becomes especially difficult when financial markets evolve rapidly.

The final element of figure 4–3 involves the regulatory vehicles that may be used, ranging from reliance on self-control on the part of boards and senior managements of financial firms concerned with protecting their franchises, through industry self-regulation, to public oversight by regulators with teeth—including criminal prosecution.

Just as there are trade-offs implicit in figure 4–3 between financial system performance and stability, so also there are trade-offs between regulation and supervision, with some regulatory options fairly easy to supervise but full of distortive potential, because of their broad-gauge nature. Other options are possibly cost-effective but devilishly difficult to supervise. Finally, there are trade-offs between supervision and performance, with some supervisory techniques far more costly than others. Regulators must optimize across this set of trade-offs under conditions of rapid market and industry change, blurred institutional and activity demarcations, and international regulatory fault lines.

Net Regulatory Burden and Transactional Mobility. It is useful to think of financial regulation and supervision as imposing a set of taxes and subsidies on the operations of financial firms, whether banks or securities firms, exposed to them. On the one hand, the imposition of reserve requirements, capital adequacy rules, interest-usury ceilings, and certain forms of financial disclosure requirements can be viewed as imposing additional implicit taxes on a financial firm's activities in that they increase the costs of financial intermediation. On the other hand, regulator-supplied deposit insurance, lender-of-last-resort facilities, and institutional bailouts serve to stabilize financial markets and reduce the risk of systemic failure, thereby lowering the costs of financial intermediation. They can therefore be viewed as implicit subsidies by taxpayers.[2]

The difference between these tax and subsidy elements of regulation can be viewed as the net regulatory burden (NRB) faced by financial firms in any given jurisdiction. Private, profit-maximizing financial firms migrate toward those financial centers where the NRB is lowest—assuming all other economic factors are the same. Thus, at any point NRB differences will induce firms to relocate as long as NRB savings exceed the transaction, communication, information, and other economic costs of doing so. Since one can argue that, in today's global financial marketplace, transaction and other economic costs of relocating are likely to be small, one can expect financial market participants to be extremely sensitive to changes in current and perceived NRBs among competing regulatory environments. To

---

2. See Kane (1987).

some extent, the regulators responsible for particular jurisdictions appear to recognize this sensitivity, and in their competition for employment and value-added creation, taxes, and other revenues have engaged in a form of competition over their levels of NRB.[3]

In an individual economy with a single regulatory body, competition will spark a dynamic interplay between demanders and suppliers of financial services. Banks and securities firms will seek to reduce their NRB and increase their profitability. If they can do so at low cost, they will actively seek product innovations and new avenues that avoid cumbersome and costly regulations. This may be facilitated both in the case of multiple and sometimes overlapping domestic regulatory bodies, as well as in the global case of multiple and often competing regulatory bodies.

A single economy may have multiple national regulatory authorities, complemented by a host of other regulatory groups at the state and local levels—especially in countries organized politically along federal lines. In the case of the United States, for example, at the federal level financial activities could fall into the regulatory domain of the Federal Reserve Board, the comptroller of the currency, the Securities and Exchange Commission, and the Commodity Futures Trading Commission. Each of the fifty states has its own regulatory bodies to deal with banking and insurance. Every city and municipality has an agency responsible for local income taxes, real estate taxes, transfer taxes, stamp duties, and so on, all of which affect the NRB falling on financial institutions. The situation is complicated still further by ambiguity regarding the definition of a bank, a security, an exchange, and so forth—blurring the lines of demarcation between both products and institutions, and raising questions about which regulatory agency holds jurisdiction.[4]

In the international financial system, with many governments and many regulatory authorities, there is fertile ground for banks and securities firms to reduce NRB. National regulatory authorities may compete among each other on the basis of NRB to preserve or reclaim financial activities within their respective regulatory domains, and

---

3. See Levich and Walter (1990).

4. Edward Kane (1987) has argued that regulation itself may be thought of in a market context, with regulatory bodies established along geographic, product, or functional lines competing to extend their regulatory domains. Financial firms understand this regulatory competition and try to exploit it to enhance their market share or profitability, even as domestic regulators try to respond with reregulation in an effort to recover part of their regulatory domain.

firms benefit from such international competition, especially if financial innovation and technological change allow them to operate successfully at a distance from their home bases. Users of financial services also benefit to the extent that competition forces financial firms to pass through to them the lower NRB.

NRB associated with regulations in onshore financial markets creates opportunities to develop a parallel, offshore market for the delivery of similar services. Barriers such as political risk, minimum transaction size, firm size, and credit quality help temper the migration of financial activity offshore, although offshore markets can be used to replicate a variety of financial instruments, such as long-term forward contracts, short-term commercial paper, long-term bonds, European currency interest rate futures, and the like. Many of these are exposed to significant NRB by onshore financial authorities, and they pose a general competitive threat to onshore securities or banking activities.

The rise of regulatory competition and the existence of offshore markets thus underscores the fact that market participants face a range of alternatives for executing transactions in any of several financial centers. The development of offshore currency and bond markets in the 1960s represents a case in which borrowers and lenders alike found that they could carry out the requisite market transactions more efficiently and with sufficient safety by operating offshore—in a parallel market. If domestic regulators wish, they can attempt to have the transactions conducted within their respective financial centers; such a preference may be driven by a desire to maintain an adequate level of prudential regulation, to sustain their revenues from the taxation of financial services, to support employment and output in the financial services industry, or simply to maximize their regulatory domain. Regulatory requirements cannot be set arbitrarily. Consequently, national financial regulations are determined competitively after taking account of regulations (both present and prospective) in other financial centers. The essence of this analysis is that the market for suppliers of financial regulation is highly competitive. As such, the movement to liberalize regulations is a consequence of national regulators' vying for market share. The market for financial regulation is contestable in that other national regulatory bodies offer (or threaten to offer) rules that may be more favorable than those of the domestic regulator. This actual or threatened competition may serve to constrain the actions of financial regulators and tax authorities from increasing levels of NRB.

This view results in a regulatory dialectic—a dynamic interaction between the regulator and the regulated in which there is continuous action and reaction by all parties, the players may behave aggressively or defensively, and they may adapt with varying speed and degrees of freedom in line with their average adaptive efficiencies as follows (Kane 1987):

- less regulated players move faster and more freely than more tightly regulated players
- private players move faster and more freely than governmental players
- regulated players move faster and more freely than their regulators
- international regulatory bodies move more slowly and less freely than all the other players

Given this ordering of adaptive efficiencies, we expect that the lag between a regulation and its avoidance is on average shorter than the lag between avoidance and reregulation. The lag in reregulation may be shorter for industry-based self-regulatory groups than for governments. It may be longer when international regulatory efforts are involved.

Financial firms constantly monitor their NRB and transfer activities into other regulatory regimes when their NRB can be reduced. Various imperfections exist that permit some variance in NRB across countries. For example, when transaction costs and information costs are significant, firms will have to be located in those regulatory domains where they intend to sell their services. Nevertheless, this dispersion among NRBs cannot be too great, otherwise private firms will have an incentive to relocate their activities. Entry and exit costs, currency conversion costs, distance-related delivery costs, and uncertainties surrounding these costs and other control measures act as effective barriers to complete NRB equalization across countries. But technological change that has markedly lowered communications and information processing costs, combined with the rapid growth of international financial transactions, has cut the gap in NRB needed to induce regulatory arbitrage.

The point is simply that, as any factor of production or economic activity gains mobility, it becomes increasingly difficult to subject it to regulation. In today's world, communications costs are low and capital mobility is high, so that it is becoming less feasible for a state or a nation to impose an NRB that stands too far apart from world norms. Still, it is likely that a long-run equilibrium can be maintained with a positive NRB. Financial transactions involve uncertainty— about the monetary unit of account, about the creditworthiness of the financial institutions and other counterparties, and about the political stability of the financial center. Financial institutions ought to value their access to lender-of-last-resort facilities, to deposit-liability insurance, to the opportunity to be headquartered in a stable political climate, and the like. Indeed, we observe that those markets that are almost totally unregulated, such as the European currency market (with an NRB approaching zero), have not completely dominated financial transactions subject to location-shifting. If financial institutions find it in their interest to pay some regulatory tax, the economic question then concerns the sustainable magnitude of this net regulatory burden.

NRB in most countries creates a variety of constraints on financial firms, ranging from capital adequacy standards, exposure limits, and liquidity requirements to fitness-and-properness criteria and periodic compliance reviews—usually set in place to mitigate concerns related to fiduciary responsibilities, market conduct, and systemic safety and soundness. Each concern imposes economic costs and may therefore erode the static or dynamic efficiency properties of the financial intermediation process depicted in figure 4–1. Improved stability is rarely costless, and the question of whether the social gains in terms of improved firm and industry stability and fiduciary performance exceed these costs is a complex and difficult matter for debate. Since any such improvements can be measured only in terms of damage that did not occur and costs that were successfully avoided, the argument is invariably based on "what if" hypotheticals. There are no definitive answers with respect to optimum regulatory structures— only better and worse solutions, as perceived by those ultimately responsible for the regulators, and their collective risk aversion and reaction to past regulatory failures.

The regulatory environments and NRBs associated with national bond and stock markets have certainly changed dramatically over the years. Starting in 1975 with the U.S. introduction of negotiated securities commission rates on "Mayday" and working through assorted deregulation in the 1986 "Big Bang" reforms in London, as well as significant reforms in Tokyo, Toronto, and Paris, restrictive pricing conventions have been eliminated and business practices liberalized. Regulatory convergence has thus come some distance. Despite this, especially international equity markets have remained relatively fragmented. Each country maintains its own (often multiple) securities exchanges. Each exchange operates according to its own regulations, which have been subject in recent years to widespread reforms, and many countries have implemented over-the-counter markets that form a second-level trading structure that is in the process of being institutionalized and integrated. Offshore, the

European markets form an integrated self-regulated, over-the-counter market trading in deposits and debt securities—listed, unlisted, and derivative.

It seems likely that progressive convergence in regulation of securities firms will continue, with players based in the more heavily regulated countries successfully lobbying for liberalization and the emergence among regulators of a consensus on minimum acceptable standards. The objective, once again, is to optimize the balance between market efficiency and regulatory soundness, so that market forces are the main determinants of what investments are carried out, where, and by whom in the global capital market.

Trade Policy Aspects of Investment Banking Regulation

The foregoing discussion of the regulatory context of international financial services, securities services in particular, suggests that there exists broad scope for barriers to market access that may have little or nothing to do with protectionism. In attempting to apply a rational regulatory framework consistent with a country's history, traditions, and attitudes toward risk, foreign-based firms may find themselves inadvertently discriminated against or market access impaired in one or more aspects of investment banking activity. Nonetheless, regulatory arbitrage and activity in response to NRB differentials limit the extent to which discrimination can be applied. It is in the interest of both the vendor of securities services and the client to shift to a location offering lower NRB levels, and this in itself is the source of continuing pressure for regulators and supervisors to align their practices with international norms. It may be useful, however, to identify a number of market-access barriers to foreign-based securities firms, whether or not they originate in the regulatory context, in terms of the basic activity range discussed earlier.

In addition to conventional forms of fiduciary and stability-oriented regulation, the financial services industry in some countries—most notably in the United States and Japan—has been subject to activity limitations that constrain access to geographic markets, services, or clients. These can be considered aspects of NRB, and can be discussed in terms of market-entry barriers, operating restrictions that affect access to specific client groups, and operating restrictions affecting the ability to supply the market with specific types of investment banking products.

Capital Markets Activities. Capital raising (fixed-income and equity underwriting and distribution) by foreign-based financial firms in national markets is usually constrained by limited access to local corporate clients, and especially by limited access to local institutional and individual investors. It is well known, for example, that foreign-based securities firms have made few inroads in raising capital for corporates in the U.S. debt and equity markets, despite the fact that no explicit barriers exist. They simply have had little value-added to offer in comparison with their U.S. competitors.[5] This does not constrain them, however, from leading foreign issuers (usually from their home countries) into the U.S. public or private placement markets, normally jointly with U.S. investment banks, or from leading U.S. issuers into foreign markets—again, usually their domestic markets or the European bond market. Similar conditions exist abroad, although the problem of issuer and investor access may be made more difficult by closer relationships between securities firms or universal banks and their clients (equity shareholdings, for example) in certain countries than exist in the United States. But these are structural impediments rather than protectionist measures, and they are alleviated by increasingly aggressive searches on the part of clients for lower-cost financings.

More serious market-access problems are posed by underwriting cartel arrangements and "fidelity" requirements, such as existed in Switzerland until the mid-1980s, for example, which freeze out foreign-based participants from significant underwriting roles. Similarly, queuing procedures used by regulators to limit the flow of securities new issues may be biased against issuers brought to market by foreign-based firms. Or regulators may mandate that only banks under the local definition may underwrite new issues of securities, freezing out firms that are not organized as banks or making things more expensive or difficult by requiring a bank charter. Foreign universal banks have long complained about the U.S. Glass-Steagall restrictions as an effective market-access barrier, forcing them to abandon the grandfathering of their securities powers under the 1978 International Banking Act to set up holding companies with Section 20 subsidiaries. In this way they can conduct the kinds of expanded securities activities (including equity derivatives) necessary to be seri-

---

5. According to IDD Information Services, during the 1980s, ninety-four foreign acquisitions of domestic securities firms took place, or about 17 percent of the total. Using a definition that a foreign-controlled securities firm is one in which foreign citizens own at least a 25 percent share of the firm, the proportion of all public offerings underwritten by foreign firms peaked at 19 percent in 1987, and their share had declined to 15 percent as of the end of 1989.

ous players in the American market. The range of permissible securities activities available to foreign-based universal banks in the United States under national treatment following the International Banking Act of 1978 is discussed below and in table 4–7.

Structural impediments include traditional *Hausbank* relationships in Germany, which have limited the volume of capital market new issues of debt and equity securities and encourage reliance on traditional bank-debt financing. Only 425 German companies listed shares in mid-1993, compared with 1,950 in the much smaller United Kingdom economy. A progressive search for lower-cost capital, however—including foreign debt issues and stock listings—as well as a growing role for non-German investors is likely to transform German corporate financing patterns and improve access to foreign-based investment banking firms. Moreover, in the absence of such progress, Germany has few real prospects to develop into a significant global financial center.

Corporate Finance. It is difficult to prevent international flow of ideas. Consequently, the corporate-finance business stream of investment banks enjoys relatively unimpeded market access. Usually delivered by a combination of corporate finance generalists supported by specialists in areas such as mergers, acquisitions, and corporate recapitalizations, advisory functions are not easy to impede. Consequently, firms such as Lazard Frères and Goldman Sachs have won far more than their proportionate share of advisory assignments covering domestic and cross-border acquisitions, divestitures, and privatizations away from their home markets. While domestic transactions in markets such as the German, dominated by close bank-industry relationships, continue to be dominated by local universal banks, a gradual transition to a more market-driven approach seems to be taking hold.

A more serious impediment is the continued lack of development, or complete absence, of an active market for corporate control in many countries because of shareholder rights restrictions, antitakeover measures, limited "free" registered shares trading in open markets, and similar factors.[6] Such measures can be expected to ease gradually in many countries, because of their adverse impact on the cost of capital and because developing legal infrastructures incorporate viable takeover codes and dispute-settlement processes.

---

6. This has limited industrial restructuring through mergers and acquisitions—specifically, unsolicited takeovers (Walter and Smith 1991).

TABLE 4–7
RANGE OF PERMISSIBLE SECURITIES ACTIVITIES FOR U.S. AND FOREIGN-BASED
COMMERCIAL BANKS, 1968–1987

Activity	When Permissible
Underwriting and dealing	
U.S. Treasury securities	Always
U.S. agency securities	Always
Commercial paper	1987
Mortgage and other asset-backed securities	1987
Municipal securities	
General obligation	Always
Some revenue bonds	1968
All revenue bonds	1987
Corporate bonds	1989
Corporate equity	1990
Private placements of bonds and equity securities	Always
Sponsoring closed-end funds	1974
Deposits with returns tied to stock market performance	1987
Underwriting and dealing in securities offshore	Always
Mergers and acquisitions	Always
Trust investments	
Individual accounts	Always
IRA commingled accounts	1982
Automatic investment service	1974
Dividend investment service	Always
Financial advising and managing	
Closed-end funds	1974
Mutual funds	1974
Brokerage	Always
Securities swaps	Always
Research advice to investors	
Separate from brokerage	Always
Combined with brokerage	
Institutional	1986
Retail	1987

SOURCE: J. P. Morgan & Co., *Glass-Steagall: Long Overdue for Repeal* (New York: J. P. Morgan, 1995), drawing upon George G. Kaufman, *The U.S. Financial System* (Englewood Cliffs: Prentice-Hall, 1995). Foreign-based firms with securities activities were grandfathered under the 1978 International Banking Act but stopped from expanding unless approved via a Section 20 subsidiary.

Investment Management and Investor Services. Market access in investment management usually requires obtaining approvals from domestic securities regulators with respect to fitness and properness to advise investors, to manage investment portfolios for individual and institutional clients such as pension funds, and to assemble market collective investment vehicles, such as mutual funds. Blockage of foreign-based fund managers from a given national market can sometimes be overcome through offshore vehicles located in such jurisdictions as Luxembourg, the isle of Jersey, or Nassau.

One example of market-access problems in this sector of the securities industry involves management of Central Provident Fund (CPF) assets in Singapore—a compulsory saving scheme that was significantly liberalized in 1993 to allow participants a broad range of investment options. Liberalization did not include, however, foreign equity or debt investments (despite the demonstrable benefits of international portfolio diversification) or the use of most foreign-based managers of mutual funds, such as the Fidelity Group of the United States. Another example is Germany, where foreigners remain barred from joining the national association of mutual funds and have had to patch together their own group (Vereinigung Ausländischer Investmentgesellschaften) to promote their interests in a decidedly hostile environment.[7] Countries like Singapore and Germany are extremely attractive in the investment management business because of their high saving rates (42 percent and 15 percent, respectively). Moreover, foreign-based funds usually have superior track records to local funds—of the one hundred top-performing (in DM) bond and stock funds available to German investors in 1993, only eighteen were German-run and a mere three of the ten top performers were German-run.[8]

Other market-access barriers of concern to the investment management business of securities firms involve limits on foreign shareholdings in local companies, proxy voting, shareholder rights, and related corporate control issues, as well as the important role of in-

---

7. The Germanic investment environment is nicely captured in the following anecdote: "An elderly Austrian lady ordered her local bank to put $5,014 worth of shares in a blue-chip U.S.-run umbrella fund readily available in Europe. It was a standing order, the same amount of the mutual fund to be bought every month. Two months later she complained she hadn't received a statement. The bank's director summoned the client to his office, imperiously informing her that he hadn't executed her order because the U.S. fund was bad. He was 'protecting' her money. The American fund, he said darkly, could be a front for Scientology." *Forbes*, August 16, 1993.

8. Ibid.

sider transactions in many markets, placing foreigners at a decided disadvantage. As in the case of Germany, countries hoping to play a significant role as financial centers are under pressure to clean up financial market practices such as insider dealing and to increase transparency and fairness, so that the problem may be self-limiting in nature.

Finally, some market access barriers may affect providers of financial infrastructure services—financial information, trading systems, clearance and settlement, and custody services. Countries usually run highly centralized clearance and settlement utilities, such as the U.S. Depository Trust Company (DTC) or the German *Kassenverein*, which limit competitive utilities originating abroad. Economies of scale, security, and payments linkages may favor the economics of centralized systems, however. Lack of direct access to such clearance and settlement systems by end-users such as large institutional investors, forcing them to deal through securities firms, could also be viewed as a trade barrier—one that protects the securities industry.

Data on market shares and league tables of firms engaged in the international securities industry is necessarily partial in coverage. Available information suggests, however, that much of the market is highly competitive and contestable, even though in some areas market structure is quite concentrated. Figures 4–4 and 4–5 show market-share evolution in the international equities and fixed-income securities new-issue businesses, respectively, for different types of firms. Note the progressive market share gains of the U.S. investment banks at the expense of the European universal banks in the equities area, and the continuing major role of the latter in the fixed-income area—as well as the dramatic rise and fall of the Japanese securities firms in this sector.[9]

Table 4–8 provides an assessment of investment banking activities (plus syndicated bank loans) conducted on international markets in 1995, as a rough guide to firms' prominence or visibility in the market. Note that, of the top ten firms, all are American except for one, CS First Boston, which is partially American. The top twenty

---

9. This was triggered by a boom phase in the Japanese stock market, making it possible for corporations to issue warrant bonds (bonds linked to warrants to buy stock at a fixed price) at very low interest rates. The warrants could be stripped and sold separately, as could the underlying bond at a discount. To a significant extent, both were heavily sold to Japanese investors. The Big Four Japanese securities houses dominated this business, centered in London to take advantage of NRB differentials, which declined precipitously with the collapse of the Japanese stock market after 1990.

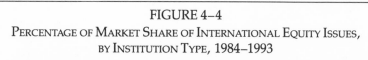

FIGURE 4-4

PERCENTAGE OF MARKET SHARE OF INTERNATIONAL EQUITY ISSUES,
BY INSTITUTION TYPE, 1984–1993

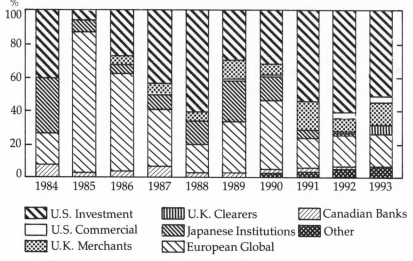

SOURCE: Salomon Brothers, based on International Financing Review and Securities Data Corporation data.

listing contains a good mixture of U.S., European, and Japanese firms—but again, with three-fourths wholly or partially American—suggesting access broadly compatible with contestable markets. This is corroborated by table 4–9—a weighted composite score of underwriting, trading, research, and advisory activities of investment banks compiled in 1995 by *Euromoney*, a trade publication.

While U.S. securities firms may (often justifiably) complain about barriers to access to individual markets abroad for specific financial services, they have certainly achieved a disproportionately large share of international business in this industry. How this will develop in the years ahead as the industry consolidates globally—including such major cross-border acquisitions as Morgan Grenfell by Deutsche Bank of Germany, Barings by ING Groep of the Netherlands, and S. G. Warburg by Swiss Bank Corporation—remains to be seen.

Rules of the Game. Market access in the securities industry is determined largely by national rules, which in turn are heavily driven by fitness and properness, prudential, and market-conduct concerns, as well as occasional protectionism. Not being credit institutions, and therefore more easily able to lead transactions for local issuer or inves-

FIGURE 4–5
Percentage of Market Share of European and International Bond Issues, by Institution Type, 1984–1993

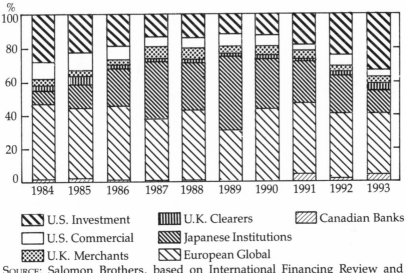

U.S. Investment   U.K. Clearers   Canadian Banks
U.S. Commercial   Japanese Institutions
U.K. Merchants   European Global

Source: Salomon Brothers, based on International Financing Review and Securities Data Corporation data.

tor clients into offshore and foreign environments, market access for securities firms has arguably been less problematic than for banks and other types of credit institutions. Since markets compete and vested interests are often substantial, efforts to harmonize such securities rules between countries have often failed—the role of industry organizations such as IOSCO notwithstanding. This failure has perhaps led to lower NRB levels by the industry than otherwise, and it has allowed for substantial regulatory arbitrage as well as for occasional "accidents." There are, however, a number of both global and regional changes in this picture that may have important market access implications in the future.

The United States. The U.S. securities industry environment, despite the strong commitment and occasional strong-arm tactics shown by the government with respect to opening foreign markets, remains one of the most difficult in the world for foreign-based investment banks. This is in part attributable to the high level of concentration of many securities activities, which makes it difficult for foreign firms to contest the market. In part as well, it is attributable to the remnants of the Glass-Steagall barriers between commercial and investment

121

TABLE 4–8
Global Wholesale Banking and Investment Banking, Full Credit to Book Running Manager Only, 1995
(billions of $U.S.)

Firm	Global Debt and Equity Securities Underwriting and Placement[a]	Global M&A Advisory[b]	International Loans Arranged[c]	Medium-Term Notes Lead Managed[a]	Total	Percentage of Industry Total
Merrill Lynch	173.43	34.76	2.00	208.80	418.99	10.8
CS/First Boston	109.58	66.22	45.90	69.00	290.70	7.5
Chemical/Chase	11.30	—	272.40	—	283.70	7.3
JP Morgan	76.32	53.72	128.60	—	258.64	6.7
Morgan Stanley	104.52	113.77	—	18.00	236.29	6.1
Goldman Sachs	96.44	83.64	2.00	39.06	221.14	5.7
Lehman Brothers	91.15	46.17	—	55.00	192.32	5.0
Salomon Brothers	82.28	39.34	—	21.40	143.91	3.7

Citicorp	10.70	—	116.50	10.30	137.50	3.6
Bear Stearns	38.31	47.81	—	31.50	117.62	3.0
SBC Warburg	36.75	31.50	11.30	—	79.55	2.1
Deutsche MG	23.87	21.35	20.40	12.50	78.12	2.0
UBS	30.06	15.81	31.10	—	76.97	2.0
Lazard Houses	—	75.45	—	—	75.45	2.0
NationsBank	18.40	—	38.90	13.00	70.30	1.8
Smith Barney	29.33	25.75	—	5.96	61.04	1.6
ABN/Amro	20.94	—	23.10	7.50	51.54	1.3
Bank of America	7.00	—	42.20	—	49.20	1.3
Nomura	48.32	—	—	—	48.32	1.2
DLJ	32.26	14.83	—	—	47.09	1.2
Total industry	1535.10	575.80	1098.40	656.70	3866.00	100.0
Top 10% as % of total	51.72	84.31	51.66	68.99	59.49	59.49
Top 20 as % of total	67.81	116.38	66.86	74.92	75.98	75.98

Empty cells = no involvement.
SOURCES: For a, global rankings, top 25, completed deals only, including all U.S. private placements; Securities Data Corp. For b, by market value of completed global transactions, full credit to both advisors, top 25 advisors; Securities Data Corp. For c, full credit to book manager, top 25 managers as reported, *IFR International Financing Review*; Jan. 20, 1996. For d, global MTNs, top 25 managers; Securities Data Corp.

TABLE 4-9

WEIGHTED COMPOSITE SCORE OF UNDERWRITING, TRADING, RESEARCH, AND
ADVISORY ACTIVITIES OF INVESTMENT BANKS, 1993 AND 1994

Rank 1993	Rank 1994	Bank	Country	Total, out of 1,000	Underwriting, out of 400	Trading, out of 400	Advisory, out of 200
1	1	Goldman Sachs	U.S.	520.14	247.09	171.70	101.35
2	2	Merrill Lynch	U.S.	457.06	252.82	136.51	67.73
5	3	Morgan Stanley	U.S.	355.62	139.49	116.12	100.01
12	4	Lehman Brothers	U.S.	321.10	120.84	144.34	55.92
3	5	JP Morgan	U.S.	276.64	56.33	160.49	59.82
4	6	CS First Boston/Credit Suisse	Switzerland	244.55	130.14	70.21	44.20
8	7	Swiss Bank Corporation	Switzerland	222.59	61.86	147.59	13.13
6	8	Deutsche Bank	Germany	213.21	109.70	97.01	6.50
9	9	Union Bank of Switzerland	Switzerland	201.59	58.55	128.94	14.11
10	10	Citibank	U.S.	185.03	21.01	131.06	32.96
7	11	SG Warburg	U.K.	179.49	75.44	29.47	74.58
11	12	Barclays de Zoete Wedd	U.K.	175.95	35.81	107.65	32.50
13	13	Salomon Brothers	U.S.	147.24	31.74	62.27	53.22
17	14	Chase Manhattan	U.S.	146.50	1.90	94.60	50.00
15	15	HSBC Group	U.K.	139.20	18.16	100.14	20.90
19	16	NatWest	U.K.	120.36	30.26	77.16	12.94
14	17	Chemical	U.S.	104.69	11.83	84.27	8.59
16	18	Paribas	France	92.81	42.56	48.71	1.54
20	19	Bankers Trust	U.S.	88.70	11.51	75.90	1.29
23	20	Nomura	Japan	88.26	55.23	28.86	4.17

SOURCE: *Euromoney*, April 1995.

banking, which clash with the universal banking structures that exist in essentially all other significant financial markets in the world.

The principal ways a foreign universal bank can enter the U.S. banking market are through

- a commercial bank subsidiary chartered under state or federal law
- a branch office licensed under state or federal law
- an agency licensed under state or federal law
- an edge corporation subsidiary chartered under federal law to engage in international or foreign banking operations

Also possible are "agreement corporations," organized under state law and subject to Federal Reserve Board Regulation K; investment corporations organized under New York state law; and representative offices. Under the International Banking Act of 1978 (IBA), in states that allow branch or agency operations, a foreign bank has the same option of choosing a state or federal license for branch or agency operations. The parent of a federal branch of a foreign bank must establish a capital adequacy deposit with a Federal Reserve member bank. Limits on lending and investment by the branch are based on consolidated worldwide parent capital. The Federal Reserve Board (FRB) has authority to impose reserve requirements on U.S. branches and agencies of foreign banks if the parent bank's worldwide assets are greater than $1 billion. Branches are able to apply for federal deposit insurance, required to hold reserves, and able to have access to Federal Reserve facilities, including the discount window.

Unlike domestic banks, before the passage of the 1978 International Banking Act, foreign banks were able to establish branches and agencies in more than one state. The IBA restricted the establishment of new deposit-taking offices to a home state selected by the bank. Existing interstate operations were grandfathered.

National or state chartered commercial banks, including subsidiaries, and bank holding companies or their subsidiaries can underwrite and deal in obligations of the U.S. government, general obligations of state and local governments, obligations of the government of Canada, and some municipal bonds. They also may engage directly in brokerage and may own discount brokerages. The Glass-Steagall provisions of the 1933 Banking Act and Federal Reserve regulation, however, prohibit a bank or an affiliate of a member bank of the Federal Reserve System from being "principally engaged" in underwriting or dealing in nongovernment securities. Before the IBA, this provision applied only to the U.S. subsidiaries of foreign banks, not to their branches or agencies. Consequently, foreign universal banks effectively had universal banking powers in the United States. The IBA applied the Glass-Steagall restrictions to federal branches of foreign banks and to state licensed branches of foreign banks. All nonbanking activities dating from before 1978 were grandfathered— the bank can continue the operations and can expand the number of locations, but it is not permitted to expand through merger or acquisition of existing operations. The IBA also grandfathered any investments foreign banks had before 1978 in securities companies—but it prevented acquisition of additional securities companies or entering new securities activities, although the securities affiliate could expand through internal growth.

The Federal Reserve Board determined that "principally engaged" meant that 10 percent or more of revenues are derived from underwriting or dealing in nongovernment securities. In January 1989 under Section 20 of the Glass-Steagall Act, the FRB approved applications by five U.S. bank holding companies to underwrite and deal in all types of debt and equity securities, subject to the revenue limitations and other prudential restrictions—so-called firewalls. The additional restrictions include prohibiting affiliated banks from providing credit to or for the benefit of the securities affiliate; preventing the sharing of directors, officers, employees, or customer information; and requiring deduction of the securities affiliate's capital from the bank holding company's capital in calculated capital requirements. Furthermore, preauthorization reviews on applicants' operating and managerial infrastructure are required. All foreign banks are subject to the same requirements, and in 1990 five foreign banks received similar authorizations. As of April 1995 there were approximately thirty Section 20 securities affiliates of U.S. commercial banks or foreign banks in operation.[10] Banks may also act as agents for private placements or as primary dealers in U.S. government securities new issues, and they may engage in some futures, options, and commodities activities.

U.S. securities activities and transactions involving securities are regulated under federal securities laws administered and enforced by the SEC. The laws provide for the national treatment of persons engaged in the securities business within the United States. The Securities Acts Amendments of 1975 limit the ability of registered broker-dealers to be excluded from membership, ensuring that foreign ownership does not constitute grounds for denial. Registered broker-dealers are not required to report the extent of foreign ownership,

---

10. J. P. Morgan & Co., *Glass-Steagall: Overdue for Repeal* (New York: J. P. Morgan, 1995).

although if ownership is greater than 10 percent it must be reported to the Commerce Department's Bureau of Economic Analysis. The Primary Dealers Act of 1988 requires the Federal Reserve to determine whether U.S. firms operating in the government debt markets of foreign countries have "the same competitive opportunities" as domestic companies in those markets. If this is not deemed to be the case, an individual or company from that country may not control a primary dealer in the United States.

As it is the principal regulator of securities firms, rule changes by the SEC have a major effect on both the growth of the securities industry in the United States and market access on the part of foreign-based firms. Certain SEC rules (and rule changes) have had favorable effects on the industry's NRB, while others have had negative effects. Foreign-based securities firms, however, have generally felt that SEC regulations are overly intrusive and involve considerable compliance and information costs. One example is the requirement that foreign investment advisers (under the Investment Advisers Act of 1940) must register with the SEC, although a foreign broker-dealer does not have to register if it is associated with a broker-dealer already registered with the SEC. This barrier to foreign-based investment advisers might be reduced by treating foreign advisers on a similar basis to foreign broker-dealers. One approach is part of the Canada–U.S. Free Trade Area, whereby advisers registered with one jurisdiction are automatically accepted by the other. Although implementational issues are difficult, an extension of this concept to cover investment advisers licensed in other major financial markets would do much to alleviate this problem.

An important and often hidden cost or regulatory burden facing foreign firms considering U.S. public offerings is the SEC's requirements on financial statement or accounting disclosure. Many countries (such as Germany) operate under accounting standards that are quite different from U.S. Generally Accepted Accounting Practices (GAAP) standards. Currently, in registration and other SEC disclosure documents, a foreign issuer has to present a quantitative reconciliation between its financial statements (based on its home-country accounting standards) and U.S. GAAP standards. The production of such information is both costly and difficult, and it acts as a significant barrier to foreign firms considering whether to issue securities in U.S. markets rather than in their domestic markets or in the European markets. This requirement may be one reason why so few foreign-based firms (only 95 out of the 1,800 largest foreign companies) are listed on the New York Stock Exchange and why no world-class German firm was listed until Daimler-Benz's listing in 1993. It is not

127

unreasonable to believe that for first-class foreign issuers such as Deutsche Bank, Dresdner Bank, Imperial Chemical Industries, Honda, and the like, U.S. investors already know a sufficient amount through their financial statements, due diligence, and Standard & Poor's and Moody's ratings as to render such required accounting reconciliations excessively costly relative to their supposed benefits to investors. Because of recent EU directives, for example, German authorities have removed most of the non-GAAP information-disclosure problems affecting German companies. Given this, the SEC might be encouraged to allow large, first-class foreign firms publicly to offer securities in the United States based on full SEC-mandated disclosure, but excluding the mandated quantitative reconciliation requirement. For example, such a requirement could be optional for the largest foreign issuers. In October 1990, the SEC issued a revised proposal for a multijurisdictional disclosure system between the United States and Canada. Such a system might usefully be extended among the United States, the European Union, and Japan.

Unlike commercial banks, securities firms in the United States have not been limited in setting up nationwide networks of outlets, even though commercial banks were limited in doing so under the McFadden Act and the Bank Holding Company Act. Consequently, foreign universal banks seeking to establish nationwide branch networks to be used as well for securities activities were doubly impaired, although they could keep preexisting branches under the IBA's grandfathering provisions. The Interstate Banking Act of 1994, however, authorized interstate acquisitions by both domestic and foreign banks one year after the date of enactment and full interstate branching by acquisition and consolidation on June 1, 1997.

There have been two major SEC rule changes providing positive benefits for foreign-based firms. In November 1983, the SEC approved Rule 415, which allowed large firms to preregister new issues of debt (and eventually equity). Thus, firms had up to two years after SEC registration to offer securities to the market (by taking them "off the shelf"), thereby better synchronizing an issue to a time when market conditions are right and benefiting from greater competition among underwriters based on price.

The second potentially positive development was the approval by the SEC of changes in the rules governing the private placement market in the United States (Rule 144A). Before this rule change, market liquidity had been inhibited by SEC restrictions on the secondary market resale of privately placed issues, and it was reflected in an interest-rate penalty that issuers had to pay to compensate investors for the reduced liquidity. The rule change allows privately placed securities to trade in a secondary market between qualified institutional buyers—defined as those with owned or managed assets exceeding $100 billion—without the type of disclosure required for public issues. As a consequence of Rule 144A, a safe haven thus is provided to any issuer, domestic or foreign, offering securities to qualified institutional buyers on an unregistered basis.

Whereas SEC Rule 415 earlier permitted qualified issuers to sell securities under a shelf-registration procedure, Rule 144A omitted registration requirements altogether, thereby greatly simplifying new-issue procedures for international borrowers unwilling to submit to the trouble and cost of preparing a registration statement. This was viewed as having the potential of attracting foreign and domestic issuers utilizing U.S. markets, as opposed to the European markets, in a so-called capital market "flow back" or "reintegration" effect. Rule 144A thus had the potential of transforming the U.S. institutional market for debt (and to a lesser extent equity) securities into an equivalent of the self-regulated and highly innovative European bond market.

Several proposals surfaced in 1994 and 1995 for the repeal of the Glass-Steagall Act, which continued to represent arguably the most important single barrier to international market access in the securities industry. At this writing, the fate of this legislation remains uncertain. Nevertheless, U.S. banking and securities regulation is in conformity with national treatment, although proposed legislation (the Fair Trade in Financial Services Act) suggested a change from unconditional national treatment to a policy of reciprocal national treatment. This bill was passed by the Senate as part of the Community Act in 1994, but Congress could not decide who should have jurisdiction regarding determination of reciprocal treatment.

The European Union. In Europe, where universal banking predominates and there is often an unclear institutional distinction between investment and commercial banking, liberalization of intra-EU financial services activities can be traced to the 1977 First Banking Directive, which allowed banks based anywhere in the EU to establish branches or subsidiaries in any other member country (freedom of establishment) on the condition that banking regulations in the host country were fully observed. It also required member states to establish a licensing system for credit institutions, including minimum "fitness and properness" criteria for authorization to do business.

Under the 1988 Second Banking Directive, a single EU banking license allowed credit institutions (authorized to do business in any single member state) to have full access to other national markets for all credit services without separate authorization. This includes deposit-taking, wholesale and retail lending, leasing, portfolio advice and management, as well as trading in securities. In line with the broader dictates of the Basel Accord of 1986, prudential control over all banks authorized to do business in the EU is exercised by home countries, including subsidiaries (which come under a separate 1983 EU directive on consolidated supervision).[11]

Nonbanking securities firms are covered by the Investment Services Directive, originally proposed in 1985 but still not in force a decade later, intended to apply to all securities firms but not to insurance companies, to firms that provide investment services exclusively for their parent companies or for other subsidiaries, to investment services provided in an incidental manner, or to firms that provide investment services for employee-participation schemes and the central banks of EU member states or other public entities managing public debt. The supervision of an EU securities firm is the responsibility of its home state. Notification is required before the acquisition of (or increase in shareholdings in) an EU securities firm when voting rights or capital reaches levels of 20 percent, 33 percent, and 50 percent. Authorities have three months to oppose such a proposal.

An EU securities firm with approval from the regulatory bodies of its home state is authorized to operate on an EU-wide basis. The firm must be authorized by the state where it has its registered office, but it is not permitted to be authorized in one state to avoid the stricter standards in force in a second state, where it carries out the greater part of its activities. Authorization will not be granted unless the firm has sufficient capital (see below) and unless the individuals who direct the business are of "sufficiently good repute and are sufficiently experienced." Authorization is also dependent on the suitability of the shareholders or members with qualifying holdings exceeding 10 percent.

Foreign-based financial institutions are treated in accordance with the principle of reciprocal national treatment and, once certified by a member country, notionally fall under the same single-passport rules as EU financial institutions as long as their home countries are not found to discriminate against EU-based institutions. Reciprocal national treatment, however, must be understood in the context of the procedural requirements of the banking and investment services directives, which limit the possible misuse of reciprocity. The benefit of the single passport is available only to EU subsidiaries of foreign financial institutions. Branches are not eligible and cannot be certi-

---

11. See chapter 3 of this volume.

fied. This is a major point, because of the capital cost of putting significant operations into subsidiaries. The same issue comes up in U.S. banking law—certain agencies, such as the SEC, have aggressively favored forcing the use of Section 20 subsidiaries, thus raising a reciprocity threat against U.S. branches in Europe. Requirements to use subsidiaries rather than branches arguably constitute significant barriers to competition.

Whenever authorization is granted to a direct or indirect subsidiary of a parent firm governed by a non-EU country, or when a parent securities firm acquires a majority interest in an EU firm, the commission must be notified. It must also be notified when firms of member states have difficulty establishing themselves in third countries, and when the concept of reciprocity or national treatment is not adhered to. In such cases the commission may initiate negotiations or EU member states may limit or suspend their decisions on authorizations for securities firms from the third country in question. This suspension may last three months, during which time a decision on possible further action will be made.

Member states may not make establishment subject to any authorization requirement, and securities firms must be directly or indirectly able to become members of or have access to the regulated markets and clearing and settlement systems of the host member state. Limitation of access to regulated markets because of national rules or laws is prohibited. Host member states may require all securities firms operating within their borders to report on their activities—reporting that may be the same as for domestic firms, but not more stringent.[12] All firms have until December 31, 1996, to comply with the Investment Services Directive (ISD).

The ISD is paralleled by the EU's Capital Adequacy Directive (CAD), and it applies to all firms that provide (1) reception and transmission of investors' orders for financial orders for financial instruments, (2) execution of investors' orders for financial instruments, or (3) management of individual portfolios of investments in financial instruments, without trading for its own account or underwriting issues of financial instruments on a firm commitment basis. When a firm is not authorized to hold clients' money or securities, to deal for its own account, or to underwrite on a firm commitment basis, the capital must be ECU 50,000. Firms in category 3 above must have registered capital of ECU 125,000, while all others must have ECU

---

12. Securities firms already authorized by a home member state before December 31, 1995, will be able to continue operations as long as they meet the capital requirements and have suitable supervision.

730,000 in capital. Specific provisions relate capital adequacy to the relative size of the trading book.

Like the ISD, the CAD has a grandfather clause, and firms in existence before the directive is in force will be continued even if the capital levels are not met. Registered capital may not fall below a reference level calculated from the average daily levels for the six months before the calculation date, and it must be recalculated every six months. If the ownership of the firm changes hands, capital levels must meet the CAD requirements unless the change of hands is caused by an inheritance or unless one partner involved before the CAD remains at the firm. In the case of a merger, under the consent of the authorities, the combined capital may be exempt from the requirements but may not fall below the level set at the time of the merger.

The CAD requirements are applied on a consolidated basis when a securities firm is part of a credit institution (a universal bank), when it is a subsidiary of another financial institution, or when the institution has a financial holding company as a parent. The regulatory authorities may supervise institutions at an individual level, rather than a consolidated level, when the requirements are met on a solo basis and systems are in place to monitor the capital of all other financial institutions in the group. Alternatively, the authorities may waive the requirements on a solo basis if the parent undertaking is subject to supervision on a consolidated basis.

The CAD requires securities firms to provide "own funds," which are always more than or equal to the sum of the requirements for (1) position risk;[13] (2) settlement and counterparty risk[14] and large exposures for their trading book business;[15] (3) the capital required for foreign exchange risk for all their business;[16] and (4) the minimum

---

13. Position risk as defined includes specific risk associated with a change in price in an instrument attributable to factors related to its issuer (or the issuer of the underlying) and general risk related to interest rates or a broad equity-market move. All positions are netted and classified according to maturity and duration. These positions are weighted and own-funds requirements are calculated.

14. Settlement and counterparty risk is calculated according to the length of time the payment or exchange is overdue and according to the risk weighting of the counterparty.

15. The large-exposure requirement is that institutions must monitor and control their exposures to individual clients and groups.

16. Foreign exchange risk exposure is defined as the net foreign exchange position in excess of 2 percent of the firm's own funds; the excess is multiplied by 8 percent to determine the requirement to hold capital against foreign exchange exposures.

registered capital requirement specified under the directive; and (4) any risks outside the scope of the CAD and the own-funds directive. A fund must be established that holds a minimum of one-quarter of the preceding year's fixed overheads.

Treatment of foreign-based firms differs significantly in the various EU member states. For example, the Banking Law of 1984 allows any institution holding a banking license to participate in all securities activities in France. Similarly, nonbank financial institutions licensed as Maisons de Titres are also authorized to undertake securities activities. In general, over the past decade, U.S. and foreign securities firms have been invited to operate in France for their capital and expertise in an effort to make Paris a financial center in Europe. In order to operate in France, a foreign-based securities firm must obtain a license from the Bank of France. The application process is identical to that required of French applicants, which allows them to accept deposits and to engage in commercial banking, securities activities, money market and forex operations, underwriting, portfolio management, and investment advice. The foreign bank or securities firm has the option of establishing as a branch or as a subsidiary, both of which require capital separate from their parent. The French banking laws do not contain reciprocity provisions, but the treatment of French institutions in another country can be considered when reviewing a license for an institution from that country. Purchases of an existing French financial institution by a foreign firm are subject to a one-month review, and they may be denied for reasons of national interest. As of 1990, U.S. banks were prohibited from underwriting public and corporate bonds, although they were permitted to participate in syndicates, since under Glass-Steagall French banks cannot perform this role in the United States if they are operating as a commercial bank, unless a Section 20 application is approved.

Both France and Italy have favored concentration of the European securities industry in a relatively small number of firms that can be easily monitored under ISD and CAD, although this position has been criticized as protectionist in nature, fundamentally favoring established domestic firms.[17]

Under the German universal banking system, both banks and securities firms must secure a German banking license. The procedure is the same for both domestic and foreign applicants. A more

---

17. Jonathan Story and Ingo Walter, *The Battle of the Systems* (Manchester, England: Manchester University Press, forthcoming). The author suggests that the EU governments have come forward with "a raft of new proposals designed to halt, or at least slow, the integration process."

limited license is available for firms trading solely for their own accounts. Entry to the German market may be through branching, through establishment of a subsidiary, or through acquisition. Lack of reciprocity as a reason for refusal is allowed, although it has not been used. Legal treatment is the same for both domestic and foreign firms.

Before 1993, a German branch's operations were limited by its own capital, not that of its parent. Therefore branching was effectively a less viable means of entry. With the implementation of the EU's second banking directive, branches of other EU member states were no longer required to maintain additional capital. The minister of finance has authorized the extension of this treatment of branches to banks from non-EU states and they have been extended to U.S. banks.

Authorization and regulation of securities firms in the United Kingdom is controlled by the Department of Trade and Industry, but it is largely delegated to the Securities & Investments Board (SIB) and its Self Regulatory Organizations (SROs). Applicants must have sufficient capital, must demonstrate adequate controls, and must be considered "fit and proper" by the Bank of England. Foreign firms are treated the same as domestic firms and can enter the United Kingdom by forming a subsidiary, by branching, or through an acquisition. U.K. law does not mandate national treatment, although it is practiced. It does permit reciprocity—never used but considered a good bargaining chip, for example, to help force open the Japanese market for British firms.

Also of interest in the EU context is that it is not necessary to block establishment of securities firms in order to distort competitive conditions. The Dutch government, for example, has insisted that the ISD does not apply to screen-based trading systems emanating from other EU states, and therefore it does not have to accept them automatically. This position may be increasingly important if secondary-market trading increasingly occurs in order-driven electronic markets, where location and distance essentially have no meaning—as exemplified by the growing share of trading in continental European stocks on the London Stock Exchange.

In the European Union, then, public authorities or professional self-regulatory organizations appointed by public authorities retain the power of licensing, supervising, and regulating investment firms. Institutions duly registered and supervised by EU home countries are essentially free to establish a commercial presence and to supply securities services in any member country without separate authorization. Investment firms holding membership in stock exchanges in their home countries are likewise free to apply for full trading privileges on all EU stock, options, and futures exchanges. Close collaboration is envisaged between the EU Commission, the authorities responsible for securities markets and institutions, and banking and insurance authorities.

Foreign financial institutions are treated in accordance with the principle of reciprocal national treatment and, once certified by a member country, notionally fall under the same single passport rules as EU financial institutions as long as their home countries are not found to discriminate against EU-based institutions. But reciprocal national treatment has to be understood in the context of the procedural requirements of the banking and investment services directives, which limit the possible misuse of reciprocity. The benefit of the single passport is available only to EU subsidiaries of foreign financial institutions. Branches are not eligible and cannot be certified. This is significant because of the capital cost of putting significant operations into subsidiaries. The same issue comes up in U.S. banking law—certain agencies, such as the SEC, have been aggressively in favor of forcing use of Section 20 subsidiaries, thus raising a reciprocity threat against U.S. branches in Europe. Requirements to use subsidiaries rather than branches arguably constitute significant barriers to competition.

The EU's ISD is closely linked to its Capital Adequacy Directive (CAD), with respect both to securities firms and the securities activities of banks. The issues include matching capital against market risks, establishing minimum levels of firm capital covering all eventualities, and EU-wide enforcement of maximum exposure limits. Given the EU tradition of universal banking, whatever capitalization requirements emerge will also have to be aligned, such as between banks and nonbanks doing securities business, to achieve regulatory parity. Indeed, implementation of the ISD in the absence of an EU capital-adequacy directive bearing on nonbank securities firms could lead to significant competitive dislocations among such firms and between independent securities firms and banks. The question of whether the CAD should be enacted in the absence of the ISD or both must be enacted simultaneously has created a major debate.

The EU single passport for banks and securities firms will be under the control of home-country authorities, but conduct-of-business rules regarding EU financial markets themselves are the exclusive responsibility of host-country authorities. As it stands, under existing EU agreements, financial institutions must deal with thirteen different sets of rules, including the European bond market, plus those of nonmember countries. This increases regulatory confusion and leaves open the possibility of rule-based protectionism against nondomestic firms. It seems likely, however, that EU rules will gradually converge toward a consensus on minimum acceptable conduct-of-business standards, which will seek to optimize the balance between market efficiency and regulatory soundness. Areas of particular interest with respect to conduct-of-business rules include insider trading and information disclosure. With regard to information disclosure in securities new issues, there has been consistent opposition to efforts at standardizing the content and distribution of prospectuses covering equity, bond, and European bond issues for sale to individuals and institutions in the member countries. An EU disclosure directive put forward in 1988 for application in 1992, involving a common prospectus but exempting European securities not sold to the general public, was initially defeated. Two prospectus directives have since been adopted, however.

Trading conduct has not so far been addressed at the EU level, and it continues to evolve in the member countries. Basic principles include the independence of the investment adviser, the adequacy of client information (including risk preference) suitable to a fiduciary relationship, and warnings against tied sales, exploitation of conflicts of interest, self-dealing, material interest in customer transactions, front-running, overcharging, churning of portfolios, and insider trading. Also included among the principles are the effective dissemination of research and the prompt and timely execution at best price. There are also issues related to client responsibility, including periodic statements and clarity of agreements, deceptive advertising, and disclosure of material interest of the firm in client transactions. Also included are rules governing management of discretionary accounts, pressure tactics, staff supervision, compliance and complaint procedures, custody procedures, and segregation of client securities. The omission of investment advice and secondary market trading (including short-selling and margin rules) from the EU investment services directive was controversial, as were the complaint procedures specified in the directive in the event of infractions of host-country rules. For some critics, inclusion of nongovernmental self-regulatory organizations such as the SIB as competent authorities was also objectionable.

The European investment management environment has been altered by an EU directive governing the operation and sale of mutual funds—Undertakings for the Collective Investment of Transferable Securities (UCITS)—which came into force on October 1, 1989, after fifteen years of negotiation. It specifies general rules for the kinds of investments appropriate for mutual funds and how they should be sold. The regulatory requirements for fund management and certification are left to the home country of the firm, while specific rules for adequacy of disclosure and selling practices are left to the respective host countries. Funds duly established, monitored, and in compliance with UCITS in any EU member country can be sold without restriction to investors in local markets communitywide and promoted and advertised through local selling networks and direct mail, as long as selling requirements applicable in each country are met. Permissible investment vehicles include high-performance synthetic funds, based on futures and options, not previously permitted in some financial centers. Under UCITS, 90 percent of assets must be invested in publicly traded companies; no more than 5 percent of the outstanding stock of any company may be owned by a fund, and there are limits on investment funds' borrowing rights. Real estate funds, commodity funds, and money market funds are excluded.

The EU approach to liberalization of the playing field for securities services seems both rational and fair, with a basic principle of national treatment combined with hints of reciprocity. Europe's universal banking tradition has not burdened the system with U.S.-type line-of-business restrictions, which have made it easier both to create a single market for securities firms and to provide consistent market access for firms from third countries. Of course, universal banking may involve market-access barriers of its own—for example, through close *Hausbank* relationships between bank and client, major bank or government shareholdings, and the like. These, however, fall under the heading of structural impediments rather than explicit barriers to trade in securities services. At the same time, the EU initiatives have been severely criticized as fundamentally distortive of market competition, threatening to wreck prospects for a single capital market and to raise the cost of capital for EU firms. "Harmonization along the lines of the ISD concentration provisions is damaging . . . in the sense that it serves neither to liberalize mallets nor to mitigate negative externalities and systemic risks, but rather simply to protect the narrow interests of favored producers of financial services."[18]

Japan. As in the United States and Europe, banks in Japan—beleaguered in the first half of the 1990s by a massive number of bad debts—will eventually have to find a new domestic business, for which many believe the greatest promise lies in securities activities. Similarly, Japanese brokers want to be able to move into lucrative

---

18. Benn Steil, *Illusions of Liberalization: Securities Regulation in Japan and the EU* (London: Royal Institute of International Affairs, 1995).

areas traditionally set aside for banks, if possible without giving up their exclusive hold on their extremely profitable securities business. The question of reforming Article 65 (the Japanese law that closely resembles the U.S. Glass-Steagall provisions) has been on the agenda for some time. Absent meaningful reform, the Japanese market will be entirely out of alignment with markets in Europe and the United States. European and American banks and securities firms will use every opportunity (as they have over matters of Tokyo Stock Exchange membership) to force roughly equivalent Japanese deregulation and substantial equality of market access.

De facto repeal of Article 65 will dramatically alter the competitive structure of financial intermediation in Japan. A dozen or so large securities firms in the United States are preparing to face competition from a handful of large, adequately capitalized banks with the demise of Glass-Steagall. In Japan four large securities firms face a dozen or so large but in many cases wounded city banks, three long-term credit banks, and a dozen trust or cooperative banks, with major aspirations in the securities field.

Fixed commission rates in Japan have been required by the Tokyo Stock Exchange—virtually the last major exchange in the world that does not mandate negotiated commissions between customer and broker—although in recent years there have been a number of authorized institutional discounts from standard rates for large orders. It is inevitable that the Japanese commission structure will collapse, after which competition for securities transactions will—as in the case of Mayday in the United States, Big Bang in Great Britain, and any comparable catastrophe virtually everywhere else negotiated rates have been introduced—become very bloody indeed, once the Japanese economy recovers. This will be true especially if the big banks are allowed into the game at the same time, as was the case in the United Kingdom.

Japanese brokers have traced virtually all their profitability to domestic brokerage commissions. They are reluctant block traders, they offer little in the way of service beyond taking orders against the latest stock ideas, and they are heavily overstaffed for what they do. Profit pressure has been exceedingly tough for these firms for some time, especially as competent, smaller-sized Japanese and foreign brokers nick off their clients with block trading and research services. Several foreign firms operating in Tokyo have been able to demonstrate their ability to do this, and a few have introduced U.S. trading techniques into Tokyo and have become very profitable in the process. It is certainly not unthinkable for foreign firms to develop a significant share of securities market business in Japan, assuming a fully level playing field and large commitments of time and resources.

Japan must also bring its domestic new-issue capital market–access conditions into line with those of the United States and Europe. This has not been the case in the past, new securities issues being subject to substantial regulations that limit market usage to a comparatively small number of blue-chip companies, queuing delays, interest-rate controls, collateralization requirements, and approval of "commission banks" (city banks acting as trustees for bondholders). Accordingly, many Japanese corporations have preferred to utilize the European bond market, where none of these obstacles exist, even when the investors in their securities are overwhelmingly Japanese. The round-trip circuitousness taken to escape the confinement of new-issue conditions in the domestic market was motivated almost entirely by financial arbitrage on the part of the issuers. The authorities finally began to act in 1989 to bring this business back to Japan. They liberalized the standards for Japanese companies seeking to use the domestic public bond markets, they introduced shelf registration procedures to provide quicker access to markets, and they proposed that securities issued abroad and purchased by Japanese investors be registered in Japan. An important result of recapturing this business for Japan, however, is the continued liberalization of market-access rules, in turn increasing the volume of corporate new issues in the Japanese market. Many of these issues, like Rule 144A issues in the United States and European market issues, could well be sold on a global basis to foreign investors.

As is the case of some European countries, tight links between Japanese securities firms and their clients have limited penetration of the securities underwriting business by U.S. and European securities firms. Nothing prevents them from taking Japanese firms to foreign markets, however, if they are able to obtain mandates. Non-Japanese firms complain that regulators prohibit or impair precisely the kinds of innovation-driven value-added products in which they have a competitive edge, and which could help pry Japanese clients away from their traditional securities firms—and from conventional bank lending. Foreign firms have argued that guidance from the Ministry of Finance has influenced the underwriting rotations of investment banks among issuers in the Japanese corporate bond market, locking them into a minuscule share.[19] Resolving this issue is all the more important in light of the ministry's efforts to repatriate transactions to the onshore market by lowering the NRB differentials.

---

19. See Walter and Hiraki, *Restructuring Japan's Securities Markets*.

Secondary market trading by foreign-based securities firms in Japan may be impaired by factors such as licensing requirements, the need to be qualified as a bank, restricted or costly memberships on exchanges, and the like. Occasionally, foreign-based firms, drawing on their trading experience in their home markets, initiate new types of trading activities or come to dominate leading-edge trading businesses—as is the case for equity derivatives, where NRB differentials drove a significant part of the market offshore (to Singapore), and it continues to be dominated by non-Japanese players.

GATS. The General Agreement on Trade in Services (GATS) provides a "legal basis on which to negotiate the multilateral elimination of barriers that discriminate against foreign services providers"—barriers embedded in the countries' domestic laws and regulations. The GATS comprises three parts. The first is a framework agreement that sets out general rules governing trade and investment in services. These services can be provided as services supplied from the territory of one party to the territory of another; or services supplied in the territory of one party to the consumers of any other; or services provided through agents or subsidiaries of one party in the territory of any other (such as banking); or services provided by the nationals of one party in the territory of any other. The second part is a set of schedules or binding agreements to market access and national treatment for individual services industries. These commitments result from iterative bilateral "request and offer" negotiations. Once a country has made a commitment to market access or national treatment, the other rules, such as those on payments and transfers or domestic regulation, go into effect for that particular sector for that country. The third part is a set of annexes outlining more specific detail on individual sectors.

GATS rules are based on most-favored-nation (MFN) obligations, which have the effect of turning a bilateral agreement into a multilateral one. A problem occurs when the bilateral measure is not applicable to third parties for regulatory or free-rider reasons. Some flexibility has been incorporated, however, by allowing a country to exclude some sectors or countries from the application of MFN. These exemptions were included as an annex to the agreement, are subject to review after five years, and have a maximum duration of ten years. There is no explicit mechanism and there are no standards for granting exemptions.

Transparency requires all relevant laws and regulations to be published. Since domestic regulations are the primary influence on trade in services, GATS requires that "parties establish the means for prompt reviews of economic decisions relating to the supply of services." The agreement acknowledges that governments will pass prudential bank regulatory standards, which raises the question of how these affect the MFN, national treatment, and market-access obligations. GATS states simply that "where such measures do not conform with the provision of the Agreement, they shall not be used as a means of avoiding the Member's commitments or obligations under the Agreement." It does, however, include obligations on recognition requirements (such as education) for licenses or authorizations in the services sector, and it encourages agreements based on international criteria and reliance on the licensing of the institution's home country. Before this recognition is achieved, however, some agreement on minimum standards of capital adequacy, management quality, and supervision is required.

For industries covered by the GATS, there are obligations not to restrict international transfers and payments for current transactions. Under balance-of-payments difficulties there may be some restrictions, but they may not be imposed in a discriminatory manner. Signatories are permitted to enter into free trade agreements with other countries, provided that internal liberalization is increased and that third parties benefit from the arrangements. Government procurement is exempted from the rules on MFN, national treatment, and market access, although there are provisions for future negotiations. The national treatment provision allows for *different* treatment of service providers of other countries as compared with the treatment of domestic suppliers, although the conditions of competition should not be modified in favor of the domestic providers. A problem with this provision is that it concentrates on regulatory measures and does not bear on restrictive business practices, although it does require parties to "enter into consultations with a view to eliminating (such) practices." The concept of continued liberalization is left on an informal basis, and there are no conditions or time guidelines for holding successive rounds of negotiations. Any further agreements are added as schedules and annexed to the GATS. The bargaining process can include different services, such as giving concessions in aviation for concessions in banking and securities services.

Market access under GATS is maintained through the inclusion of six measures a country cannot take once it has made a market access commitment:

1. There can be no limits on the number of foreign service providers.
2. Limitations on the total value of service transactions are banned.

3. Limiting the total number of service operations or the total quantity of service output by using quotas or economic needs test is prohibited.
4. A limit on the number of employees in a service sector is not permitted.
5. A member cannot restrict or require a service provider to operate through a specific type of legal entity.
6. There can be no limits or caps on the percentage of foreign shareholding or the total value of foreign investment.

Dispute settlement under GATS is an inclusive process. That is, if direct negotiation between two parties fails, then either party can consult with a third party or with the Council for Trade in Services or the Dispute Settlement Body (DSB). The DSB can investigate the problem, make recommendations or rulings, and authorize the member to suspend its GATS obligations. The Council for Trade in Services is structured to maintain the operation or objectives of the GATS. There are safeguards regarding the operation of the council: the chairman is elected by the full membership, not the council itself; the council must further the objectives of GATS; the council can perform only the functions assigned by the full membership.

GATS recognizes the importance of the development of financial institutions and the service sector more generally of developing countries. To this end it includes an article stating obligations toward developing countries, although there is no definition of a developing country and no statement as to who is obligated. Developed countries must grant access to technology and must open their markets for services to developing countries.

In the U.S. view, GATS failed to achieve the desired degree of liberalization of foreign financial services markets, and this led the United States to the MFN exemption to deal with the free-rider problem. But GATS does provide for continued negotiation toward full liberalization. Up to the implementation of the Uruguay Round agreement, the United States could use existing trade laws or could enact new ones that do not have to be applied on an MFN basis and could continue bilateral discussions for trade liberalization. Following the entry into force of the Uruguay agreement the U.S. MFN exemption was subject to suspension for six months, during which time the United States and its trading partners would continue to negotiate toward a comprehensive financial services agreement. After four months the GATS Committee on Trade in Financial Services was to report on the progress of the negotiations. If the United States is not satisfied with the progress at the end of the six-month period, the MFN exemption will remain in place.

Failure of the financial services sector to be included in the GATT Uruguay Round agreements makes the EU's and NAFTA's regulatory and market-access approaches particularly important and helpful in setting the standard for future policy initiatives affecting the international securities industry.

Progress on a multilateral level is particularly significant because of market access problems in the case of Japan and many emerging market countries, which represent some of the most attractive environments for investment banking activity. In Japan, a recent study has suggested that Japanese securities market reforms have been limited in terms of improved market access for foreign-based firms because powerful financial institutions and Ministry of Finance bureaucrats conspired to thwart liberalization. The result has been to stifle innovation, to distort the allocation of capital, to increase risks in the banking sector, and to drive profitable securities business offshore.[20] Certainly the diversity of treatment of foreign firms undertaking securities activities around the world (see table 4–10) suggests that a great deal remains to be done.

Conclusion

This chapter has assessed global competition in the securities industry and market access. I began with a framework intended to identify the positioning of the investment banking sector in the process of domestic and international financial intermediation. I then described the disintermediation and securitization process both conceptually and factually, in terms of past and prospective developments. There are significant leads and lags in this process across national and international financial markets, with correspondingly different effects on firms positioned at various points across the competing financial conduits. I then described how the securities industry is positioned across the financial intermediation process in its core activities—securities underwriting and dealing, derivative transactions, corporate finance, and investment management—and how public policy via regulatory "taxes" and "subsidies," or net regulatory burden, affects the direction and volume of these flows and hence the securities industry's activities. Certain NRB dimensions can be applied in a protectionist way to affect market-access conditions for domestic versus foreign-based securities firms. Finally, the market access issue was addressed directly via the CAP matrix, relevant market-access issues facing the main business streams of the securities industry. In

---

20. Steil, *Illusions of Liberalization.*

TABLE 4–10

ACCESS OF FOREIGN-BASED SECURITIES FIRMS TO NATIONAL MARKETS, 1994

Argentina	Permitted; certain activities must be conducted through subsidiaries
Australia	Permitted
Austria	Permitted
Bahrain	Permitted, but limited by terms of license and supervisory guidelines
Belgium	Permitted; some activities must be conducted through subsidiaries
Bolivia	Permitted through subsidiaries
Brazil	Permitted through subsidiaries
Canada	Permitted through subsidiaries
Cayman Islands	Permitted
Chile	Permitted to some extent; certain activities through subsidiaries
China	Permitted through subsidiaries
Denmark	Permitted
European Union	Not applicable; permissibility is subject to home-country authorization and limited host-country regulation
Finland	Permitted
France	Permitted
Germany	Permitted
Greece	Underwriting permitted by certain credit institutions; brokerage and dealing permitted through subsidiaries
Hong Kong	Permitted, except for limitation on shareholding in certain listed companies and subject to limits based on the capital of the bank
India	Permitted; some activities through subsidiaries
Ireland	Permitted; usually through a subsidiary
Italy	Permitted, but not permitted to operate directly on the Stock Exchange.
Japan	Permitted through subsidiaries, except for equity brokerage for the time being
Korea	Permitted through affiliates
Mexico	Permitted through affiliates
The Netherlands	Permitted
New Zealand	Permitted, but in practice through a subsidiary
Norway	Generally permitted through subsidiaries; stockbrokerage activities need no longer be conducted in separate subsidiaries

TABLE 4–10 (continued)

Pakistan	Permitted, except for some specifically disallowed securities
Panama	Permitted
Peru	Permitted through subsidiaries; banks have recently been authorized to issue mortgage-backed securities
Poland	Permitted
Portugal	Generally permitted; mutual funds only through subsidiaries
Singapore	Banks may hold equity participations in stockbrokering firms with approval of the Monetary Authority of Singapore
Spain	Permitted; banks are permitted to own up to 100% of stock exchange members
Sweden	Permitted
Switzerland	Permitted
Thailand	Permitted through subsidiaries; banks were recently given authority to underwrite debt securities
United Kingdom	Permitted; usually through subsidiaries
United States	Permitted for government securities; stockbrokerage activities are also generally permitted; however, corporate securities underwriting and dealing activities must be conducted through specially-authorized affiliates, which must limit such activities to 10% of gross revenues
Uruguay	Underwriting authority is permitted, and dealing is limited to public debt; brokerage and mutual funds not permitted

Source: Institute of International Bankers, *Global Survey 1994* (New York: Institute of International Bankers, 1994).

this context I examined continuing changes in access rules in the world's largest capital market (the United States), regional developments in Europe and North America, and global developments under GATS.

I conclude that the dynamics of finance have been highly favorable to enhancing the transaction flow of investment banking internationally and within many national markets, so that this has been one of the most rapidly growing sectors in the international economy. Nondiscrimination against foreign players prevails in most major markets, whose interests are closely aligned with global financial flows. The United States is less open than most major markets in this regard, because of the continuation of Glass-Steagall distortions, despite their considerable weakening in recent years.

Although many countries throw up barriers to market access by foreign-based securities firms, in the end countries that persist in this course cannot be part of the "club," and they consequently pay significant penalties in terms of the static and dynamic efficiency properties of their financial systems. This has been recognized in important market-opening moves by countries such as China, India, Malaysia, and Chile. Fundamentally as well, the mobility of many investment banking activities in response to explicit market-access barriers or NRB differentials arguably renders protectionism in this sector significantly less problematic than in many other industries.

In discussions of global harmonization of the rules of the game covering market-access issues in the securities industry, it is tempting to suggest that the markets will take care of themselves.

First, the European markets represent a largely self-regulated benchmark that has functioned very well for more than two decades. There have been no major disasters, and the market is highly efficient. To compete, national bond markets have to show that they can do as well or better, or transactions will simply flow to this offshore market.

Second, transactions in equities and other financial instruments where there are no offshore markets flow toward the lowest transaction costs, the highest transparency and liquidity, and ensured fairness. This may mean not the least regulated but rather the optimally regulated markets, from the perspectives of both issuers and investors. Nothing could be better for liberal market access for vendors of financial services than vigorous competition across such markets, in the process leading toward global norms that arise without the products of harmonization.

Third, end-users of financial markets have become highly performance-oriented. If they are to do well, borrowers in capital markets will seek out those with optimum efficiency, transparency, and liquidity characteristics. The same is true of institutional investors, whose fiduciary clients will desert them if they fail. Increasingly, end-users cannot afford to be left behind, and this places enormous pressures on financial intermediaries as well as market regulators. Nobody likes to be forced to pay more (or receive less) than is necessary.

Fourth, the battle for market share among financial centers (and the employment gains, income generation, and multiplier effects it

146

entails) amplifies the underlying competitive dynamics of the markets.

Finally, reciprocity pressures put laggard markets on notice that their institutions cannot expect unfettered access to major markets without meaningful concessions once they appear on the radar screen of firms seeking to exploit their competitive advantages in less efficient markets.

To be sure, plenty of problems remain for market access in securities services, especially with respect to retail transactions. But the transactional mobility of this industry has become extraordinary, and it is almost certainly sufficient to ensure liberal market access and regulatory outcomes.

References

Aliber, Robert Z. "International Banking: A Survey." *Journal of Money, Credit, and Banking* (November 1984).

Bank for International Settlements. *Recent Innovations in International Banking*. Basel: Bank for International Settlements, 1986.

Baumol, William, J. Panzar, and R. Willig. *Contestability of Markets and the Theory of Industry Structure*. New York: Harcourt Brace Jovanovich, 1982.

Cable, J. "Capital Market Information and Industrial Performance: The Role of West German Banks." *The Economic Journal* (1985), pp. 118–32.

Caves, Richard, and Michael Porter. "From Entry Barriers to Mobility Barriers: Conjectural Decisions and Contrived Deterrence to New Competition." *Quarterly Journal of Economics* (May 1977).

Dermine, Jean, ed. *European Banking after 1992*. Rev. ed. Oxford, England: Basil Blackwell, 1993.

Edwards, James, and Klaus Fischer. "An Overview of the German Financial System." Center for Economic Policy Research. Working paper: November 1992.

Federal Reserve Board of Governors. "The Separation of Banking and Commerce in American Banking History." Appendix A, P. Volcker's statement before the Subcommittee on Commerce, Consumer, and Monetary Affairs of the House Committee on Government Operations: June 1986.

Gnehm, A., and C. Thalmann. *Conflicts of Interest in Financial Operations: Problems of Regulation in the National and International Context*. Paper prepared for the Swiss Bank Corporation. Basel, Switzerland: 1989.

Goldberg, L., and G. Hanweck. "The Development and Growth of Banking Centers and the Integration of Local Banking Markets."

The Review of Research in Banking and Finance (Spring 1990), pp. 85–105.

Goldberg, M., R. W. Helseley, and M. D. Levi. "The Location of International Financial Centers." *Annals of Regional Science* (1988), pp. 81–94.

———. "The Location of International Financial Center Activity." *Regional Studies* (1989), pp. 1–7.

Hayes, Samuel III, A. M. Spence, and D.v.P. Marks. *Competition in the Investment Banking Industry.* Cambridge, Mass.: Harvard University Press, 1983.

Herring, Richard J., and A. M. Santomero. "The Corporate Structure of Financial Conglomerates." *Journal of Financial Services Research* (December 1990), pp. 471–97.

Hoshi, T., A. Kayshap, and D. Sharfstein. "The Role of Banks in Reducing the Costs of Financial Distress in Japan." *Journal of Financial Economics* (1991), pp. 151–67.

———. "Corporate Structure, Liquidity, and Investment: Evidence from Japanese Industrial Groups." *Quarterly Journal of Economics* (1991), pp. 33–60.

Institute of International Bankers. *Global Survey 1994.* New York: Institute of International Bankers, 1994.

Jensen, Michael, and Richard Ruback. "The Market for Corporate Control: The Scientific Evidence." *Journal of Financial Economics* 11 (April 1983), pp. 5–50.

Kane, Edward J. "Competitive Financial Reregulation: An International Perspective." In R. Portes and A. Swoboda, eds., *Threats to International Financial Stability.* London, England: Cambridge University Press, 1987.

Kaufman, George, ed. *Banking in Major Countries.* New York: Oxford University Press, 1992.

Kim, S. B. "Modus Operandi of Lenders-Cum-Shareholder Banks." Federal Reserve Bank of San Francisco. Mimeo (September 1990).

Krümmel, Hans-Jakob. "German Universal Banking Scrutinized." *Journal of Banking and Finance* (March 1980).

Levich, R., and I. Walter. "Tax-Driven Regulatory Drag: European Financial Centers in the 1990s." In Horst Siebert, ed., *Reforming Capital Income Taxation.* Tuebingen, Germany: J.C.B. Mohr (Paul Siebeck), 1990.

Mayer, Colin P. "Corporate Control and Transformation in Eastern Europe." Paper presented at a SUERF conference, "The New Europe: Evolving Economic and Financial Systems in East and West." Berlin, Germany (October 8–10, 1992).

Neave, Edwin. *The Economic Organization of a Financial System.* London, England: Routledge, 1992.

Newman, H. "Strategic Groups and the Structure-Performance Relationships." *Review of Economics and Statistics* (August 1978).

Panzar, John C., and Robert D. Willig. "Economies of Scope." *American Economic Review* (May 1981).

Pastré, Olivier. "International Bank-Industry Relations: An Empirical Assessment." *Journal of Banking and Finance* (March 1981).

Pozdena, Randall J. "Do Banks Need Securities Powers?" *Federal Reserve Bank of San Francisco Weekly Letter* (December 29, 1989).

Reed, H. C. *The Preeminence of International Financial Centres.* New York: Praeger, 1981.

Röller, Wolfgang. "Die Macht der Banken." *Zeitschrift für das Gesamte Kreditwesen* (January 1, 1990).

Rybczynski, T. N. "Corporate Restructuring." *National Westminster Bank Review* (August 1989).

Saunders, Anthony. "The Separation of Banking and Commerce." New York University Salomon Center. Working paper (September 1990).

Saunders, Anthony, and Ingo Walter. *Universal Banking in America.* New York: Oxford University Press, 1993.

Schott, Jeffrey J. *The Uruguay Round.* Washington, D.C.: Institute for International Economics, 1994.

Sheard, P. "The Main Bank System and Corporate Monitoring and Control in Japan." *Journal of Commercial Banking and Organization* (1989), pp. 399–422.

Smith, George D., and Richard Sylla. "Wall Street and the Capital Markets in the Twentieth Century: A Historical Essay." New York University Salomon Center. Working paper (September 1992).

Smith, Roy C. *Comeback: The Restoration of American Banking Power in the New World Economy.* Boston, Mass.: Harvard Business School Press, 1993.

Smith, Roy C., and Ingo Walter. *Global Financial Services.* New York: Harper & Row, 1990.

———. "Bank-Industry Linkages: Models for Eastern European Restructuring." Paper presented at a SUERF conference, "The New Europe: Evolving Economic and Financial Systems in East and West." Berlin, Germany (October 8–10, 1992).

Steinherr, Alfred, and Christian Huveneers. "On the Performance of Differently Regulated Financial Institutions: Some Empirical Evidence." Université Catholique de Louvain. Working paper (February 1992).

Story, Jonathan, and Ingo Walter. *The Battle of the Systems.* Manchester, England: Manchester University Press, forthcoming.

Task Force on the International Competitiveness of U.S. Financial Institutions, Subcommittee on Financial Institutions, Committee on

Banking, Finance, and Urban Affairs, U.S. House of Representatives. "Report of the Task Force" (November 1990).

United States Treasury. *Modernizing the Financial System: Recommendations for Safer, More Competitive Banks.* Washington, D.C.: Department of the Treasury, 1991.

Walter, Ingo. *Barriers to Trade in Banking and Financial Services.* London, England: Trade Policy Research Center, 1985.

———. *Global Competition in Financial Services.* Cambridge, Mass.: Ballinger-Harper & Row, 1988.

———. *The Battle of the Systems: Control of Enterprises and the Global Economy.* Kiel, Germany: Institut für Weltwirtschaft, 1993.

Walter, Ingo, ed. *Deregulating Wall Street.* New York: John Wiley & Sons, 1985.

Walter, Ingo, and Roy C. Smith. *Investment Banking in Europe: Restructuring for the 1990s.* Oxford, England: Basil Blackwell, 1989.

Walter, Ingo, and Takato Hiraki, eds. *Restructuring Japan's Financial Markets.* Homewood, Ill.: Business One Irwin, 1993.

White, L. J. *The S&L Debacle: Public Policy Lessons for Bank and Thrift Regulation.* Oxford: Oxford University Press, 1991.

———. "Competition versus Harmonization." Chapter 2 in this volume.

5

International Trade in Insurance

Harold D. Skipper, Jr.

This study of international trade in insurance services continues the sectoral examination of financial services with a view toward exploring the issue of whether regulatory harmonization is a necessary precondition for insurance market liberalization. In fundamental ways, insurance does not differ greatly from other financial services.[1] Retail banks, investment banks, and insurers all perform the financial intermediation function. Risk assessment and risk assumption lie at the heart of all operations.

Indeed, banks increasingly manufacture and sell insurancelike products, and insurers increasingly manufacture and sell banklike products. The distinctions among banking, securities firms, and insurers are expected to continue to blur, as financial service conglomerates seek economies of scope.

Given this trend, one may legitimately ask why financial services should be examined on a sectoral basis. From the insurance perspective, there is insight to be gained by such an approach.

First, even with a similarity of conceptual activities, the actual production, underwriting, and marketing of the various services can differ dramatically. Bankers have not, to date, successfully marketed—let alone underwritten and priced—complex insurance products. The successes of *bancassurance* have been largely confined to the life branch, and only with commoditylike products.

---

1. See Lewis (1990).

Second, the different evolutionary paths followed by each sector's regulatory bodies have led to varied, not-yet-equivalent supervisory approaches. Until greater cross-sector regulatory convergence is achieved, a sector-by-sector approach seems reasonable.

Third, insurance is often slighted, if not omitted altogether, in policy papers on financial services. By an explicit examination of insurance, we hope to draw broader lessons for all financial service sectors, including insurance.

Finally, in many ways, insurance issues are less critical than those in banking. Banking is directly involved with national macroeconomic policy, including monetary policy and credit allocation. Insurance is less often so involved. As such, public policy makers might logically conclude that liberalizing or other policy actions appropriate for one financial sector might be less appropriate for another. A sectoral approach will facilitate this examination.

The approach taken here includes first providing an overview of the nature and functioning of insurance. The second section examines the structure of insurance markets, including insurance supply and demand.

The third section provides an overview of governmental intervention into insurance markets. This section includes a discussion of the general purposes and types of trade barriers extant worldwide in insurance services.

Section four then focuses on this study's central question: Is regulatory harmonization necessary for insurance liberalization? Arguments both for and against harmonization are examined. Finally, section five presents study conclusions.

The Nature of Insurance

Insurance is both a risk-shifting and risk-sharing device. For a consideration (the premium), the insured is guaranteed to be made whole financially by the insuring organization (the insurer) if a covered loss occurs. The entire scheme functions because the insurer (presumably) insures a sufficient quantity of similar loss exposures such that its total claims experience is reasonably predictable. The greater the number of similarly situated, independent insureds, the more predictable the insurer's experience—thanks to the law of large numbers.

This comfortably predictable experience does not always materialize. The independence criterion is often violated because of catastrophic exposures, as when Hurricane Andrew smashed through

Florida in 1992, ultimately causing the failure of seven insurance companies and the weakening of dozens more.[2]

Even when independence is not a problem, unforeseen environmental changes can wreck insurers' pricing assumptions. Life and health insurers had not anticipated the additional AIDS claims; liability insurers still do not know how much environmental impairment losses will cost them—losses that they never intended to cover. In spite of these and a host of other possible operational glitches, the world's insurers are largely profitable, stable financial institutions.

The Benefits of Insurance. Besides that peace-of-mind feeling that insurance brings to individuals and executives, it offers more tangible benefits as well. Insurance underpins almost all major private economic undertakings and probably the great majority of lesser ones.[3] Thus, investors do not finance construction of new manufacturing facilities without property insurance; airplanes, ships, and trains do not move without liability insurance; and banks often will not make loans to small businesses without adequate life insurance on key employees. Through its transfer of risk, insurance is said to be the "lubricant of commerce." There is probably no country—irrespective of its level of economic development or political philosophy—wherein insurance fails to play such a role.

Insurance companies are also important financial intermediaries. Because they must carry sufficient assets to back their typically large liabilities, insurers are major sources of funds for national money and capital markets. For example, as contrasted with commercial banking's 21.5 percent share, insurance companies supplied 16 percent of all U.S. money and capital market funds during 1994.[4]

Finally, certain types of insurance policies include a substantial savings element, thereby providing a mechanism for consumers to accumulate funds—usually in more or less direct competition with other savings media. Thus, for example, life insurance accounted for almost 14 percent of private household financial assets in Japan in

---

2. Unexpectedly high claim payments by the Prudential Property and Casualty Insurance Company (PRUPAC) resulted in the loss of its entire $900 million surplus. PRUPAC was saved by its parent, the Prudential Insurance Company of America, making a surplus contribution to PRUPAC.

3. The use of insurance by large corporations has been the subject of debate. In theory, portfolio diversification by shareholders should largely obviate corporate demand for insurance. See Mayers and Smith (1982, 1990) and Grace and Rebello (1993).

4. American Council of Life Insurance (1995).

FIGURE 5–1

PERCENTAGE OF HOUSEHOLD SAVINGS THROUGH LIFE INSURANCE AMONG THE G-7 COUNTRIES, 1980 AND 1990

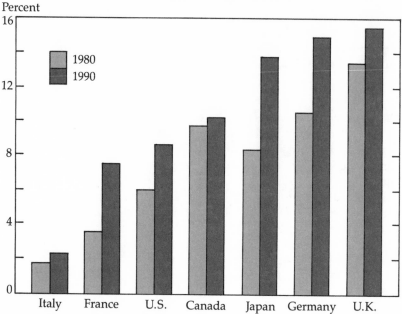

Percent

SOURCE: Swiss Reinsurance Company.

1990, up from 7.5 percent a decade earlier.[5] Figure 5–1 shows the relative importance of life insurance in household savings for the G7 countries. In each instance, life insurance's share of such savings has increased over the 10 year period shown.

Insurance Classifications. Insurance can be classified in numerous ways. For purposes of this study, four means are relevant: social versus private, life versus nonlife, commercial versus personal, and direct versus reinsurance.

Social versus private insurance. Governments have determined that they—as opposed to the private sector—must provide some types of insurance. Thus, all developed market-economy countries have extensive government-administered social security schemes that provide survivor, retirement, disability, and unemployment benefits. Health insurance and workers' compensation benefits are provided

---

5. Swiss Reinsurance Company (1993).

by either government or the private sector or some combination of the two.

Social insurance may be distinguished from private insurance through its emphasis on social equity (income redistribution), as contrasted with actuarial equity (premiums reflect the expected value of losses). Also, participation in social insurance schemes is compulsory, and financing relies on government-mandated premiums (taxes).

This study is concerned solely with private insurance. Certain lines of insurance, however, are private in some markets and public in others. Also, a few governments, including that of France, own or control nonmonopolistic insurers, although the trend is to divest such shareholdings. Such insurers typically compete with private insurers and, for purposes of this study, no distinction is made by nature of ownership.

Life versus nonlife insurance. The insurance business has historically divided itself between companies that sell insurance on the person (life insurance) and those that sell insurance to protect property (nonlife insurance). This classification is not completely satisfactory, as overlaps exist, yet will serve our purposes.

The life branch includes insurance that pays benefits on a person's death (usually termed life insurance); living a certain period of time (endowments and annuities); disability (disability insurance); and injury or incurring a disease (health insurance). In some markets, notably in Europe, health insurance is classified as nonlife insurance.

The nonlife branch—often referred to as property-casualty insurance in the United States and general insurance in the United Kingdom—includes insurance to cover property losses (damage to or destruction of homes, automobiles, businesses, aircraft); liability losses (payments attributable to professional negligence, product defects, negligent automobile operation); and, in some countries, workers' compensation (and health insurance) payments.

The life and nonlife branches of insurance perceive themselves quite differently, and with some justification. Indeed, most countries prohibit a single corporation from selling both types, although joint production via holding companies and affiliates is usually permitted. This study is concerned with both life and nonlife insurance.

Commercial versus personal insurance. Nonlife insurance purchased by individuals (such as homeowners' insurance or automobile insurance) is classified as personal insurance. Within the European Union (EU), such insurances are generally referred to as insurance for mass risks.[6]

---

6. Technically, small businesses also are considered mass risks.

Nonlife insurance purchased by businesses and other organizations (such as product liability, business interruption, and automobile insurance) is classified as commercial insurance. Within the EU, such insurances are generally referred to as insurance for large risks.

As will be made clear later, government oversight is more stringent in the personal than in the commercial lines because of greater information asymmetry problems in personal lines. This study is concerned with both personal and commercial lines.

Direct insurance versus reinsurance. Insurance sold to the general public and to noninsurance commercial and industrial enterprises is classified as direct insurance. Insurers selling such insurance—both life and nonlife, as well as both personal and commercial lines—are referred to as direct writing insurers and attendant premiums are direct written premiums.

Insurance purchased by direct writing insurers is classed as reinsurance and is sold by reinsurers, with some also being sold by the reinsurance departments of direct writing companies. Reinsurance is wholesale insurance. Direct writing companies purchase reinsurance to avoid undue potential loss concentrations, to provide the direct insurer with greater underwriting capacity, to stabilize total financial results, and to take advantage of special expertise of the reinsurer.

Almost all insurers, worldwide, purchase reinsurance.[7] Indeed, reinsurers themselves purchase reinsurance—that is, they retrocede business to other reinsurers and the reinsurance departments of direct writing companies. Thus, it is not unusual for dozens of insurers and reinsurers to "have a line" on insurance policies with high limits.

The insured may be unaware that the insurer has reinsured the policy. This fact ordinarily poses no difficulties, as the insured's legal relationship is with the direct writing company and not the reinsurer. The direct writing company remains obligated to pay legitimate claims under the reinsured policy, even if the reinsurer is unable to do so. Some reinsurer failures, however, have contributed to the failure of direct writing insurers.

Reinsurance typically involves large exposures to loss, often with a catastrophic loss potential. As such, great underwriting and pricing expertise is required. As the direct writing company is ordinarily

---

7. In fact, State Farm Insurance Company (U.S.) is one of the very few that purchases virtually no reinsurance. It did so until recently, when it concluded that its spread of risk, great size, and other operational characteristics were such that the added cost of reinsurance was not justified. State Farm's Hurricane Andrew losses, totaling almost $4 billion, resulted in a substantial direct surplus loss.

FIGURE 5–2
INSURANCE MARKET SHARES WORLDWIDE, TOTAL BUSINESS, 1985 AND 1993

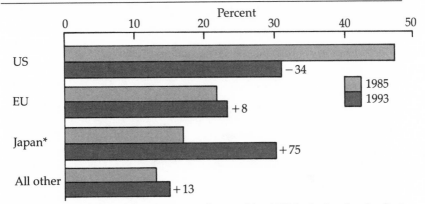

NOTE: For Japan, premium growth is influenced by 1993 inclusion for the first time of two major life insurers and by increased value of years.
SOURCE: Swiss Reinsurance Co. (1995).

a knowledgeable buyer and the reinsurer a knowledgeable seller, government intervention into the transaction has historically been nonexistent or kept to a minimum. Reinsurance tends to be highly specialized and is probably the most international insurance business. This study focuses on both direct insurance and reinsurance.

The Structure of Insurance Markets

The structure of an insurance market is determined, first, by the nature of the demand for insurance, which itself is most heavily affected by the level of economic development, and second, by the character of the insurance supply.[8] Each of these elements is discussed below.

Overview of Insurance Markets Worldwide. The most commonly accepted measure of insurance market size is gross direct premiums written.[9] Globally, direct written premiums exceeded $1.8 trillion in

---

8. Several studies investigate the structure of insurance markets, including Joskow (1973) and Cummins and Vanderhei (1979). See Grace and Barth (1993) for an overview of nonlife market structure research. See Black and Skipper (1994) for a discussion of market structure in life insurance.

9. Unless otherwise indicated, all data are from Swiss Reinsurance Company (1995).

FIGURE 5–3
PERCENTAGE CHANGE IN NONLIFE AND LIFE INSURANCE MARKET SHARES
WORLDWIDE, 1985 AND 1993

A. NONLIFE INSURANCE MARKET

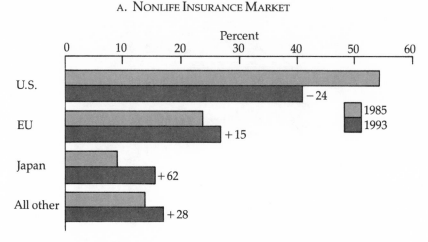

1993, having grown an average of 6 percent per year over the preceding six years.[10] Considerable regional diversity exists in growth rates. After experiencing the highest regional real growth rate at 13.2 percent in 1992, Latin American growth in 1993 was down to 5.9 percent. Premium growth in Africa was only 1.2 percent in 1993, down from 7.0 percent in 1992. Europe posted a healthy 7.5 percent growth rate in 1993, followed by Asia, at 6.0 percent. Premium growth rates in Oceania and North America were 5.5 and 4.9 percent, respectively.

The United States is the world's largest insurance market, accounting for 31.3 percent of total direct premiums written, followed closely by Japan's 30.4 percent share. As figure 5–2 shows, the European Union (EU) countries' share was 23.8 percent. The U.S. worldwide market share generally has been declining over the previous years, as other countries' shares have risen.

When analyzed between the life and nonlife sectors, results differ. The first panel of figure 5–3 shows the dominant position of the United States in the nonlife business, at a 41.5 percent world market share, with the EU at 26.8 percent, and Japan at 14.7 percent. The high U.S. nonlife market share is driven mainly by significant increases in liability insurance premiums and the large amount of health insurance financed through private insurance.

10. Worldwide premium figures omit some countries' premiums as their writings are small or because data are unavailable.

FIGURE 5–3 (continued)

B. Life Insurance Market

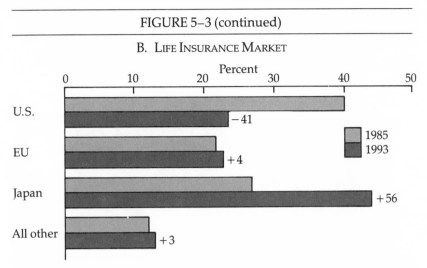

NOTE: For Panel A, for Japan, premium growth is influenced by increased value of yen. For Panel B, for Japan, premium growth is influenced by 1993 inclusion for the first time of two major life insurers and by increased value of yen. The data source classifies health insurance as nonlife insurance.
SOURCE: Swiss Reinsurance Co. (1995).

In the second panel of figure 5–3, the high propensity of Japanese to save in general and via life insurance products in particular is evident, with a 42.6 percent Japanese market share in the life insurance branch. The United States is second at 23.3 percent, followed by the EU at 21.4 percent.

The OECD countries accounted for 92 percent of worldwide life and nonlife premiums in 1993, with the G7 countries alone having an 83 percent world share. Figure 5–4 shows world insurance market shares by selected country groupings.

Two measures are used traditionally to indicate the relative importance of insurance within national economies. Insurance density indicates the per capita premium within a country. Values are usually converted to special drawing rights or to U.S. dollars. As such, comparisons are affected by currency fluctuations, and this fact may lead to distortions. Even so, the measure is a useful indicator of insurance purchases within national economies.

The other measure, insurance penetration, is the ratio of direct premiums written to GDP. It indicates roughly the relative importance of insurance within national economies and is unaffected by currency fluctuations. Even so, it does not give a complete picture, as it ignores price, product mix, and other market variations.

159

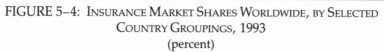

FIGURE 5–4: Insurance Market Shares Worldwide, by Selected Country Groupings, 1993
(percent)

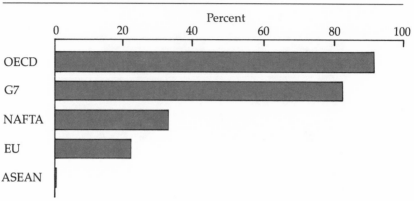

Source: Swiss Reinsurance Co. (1995).

Figure 5–5 is a reproduction from a Swiss Reinsurance Company publication giving insurance density and insurance penetration figures for seventy-eight countries for 1993. As can be seen, the Japanese per capita expenditure of $4,395 is easily the world's highest, with Switzerland ($3,096), the United States ($2,191), Great Britain ($1,913), and most other OECD countries following. The OECD average was $1,895. The EU average was $1,234. Developing countries' figures fall uniformly at the end of the list.

Insurance penetration was highest in Japan (12.6 percent), followed by South Africa (12.2 percent) and Zimbabwe (11.7 percent). Ratios greater than 8 percent were recorded in Great Britain, South Korea, Switzerland, Japan, Barbados, the United States, and the Netherlands. The OECD average penetration was 8.8 percent, while the EU average was 6.9 percent. Again, with important exceptions, developing countries anchor the bottom of the list.

Countries with high penetration tend to be those with high levels of saving through life insurance. Thus, while the life sector accounts for 56.1 percent of worldwide premiums, it accounts for approximately 80 percent of the total insurance business in Japan, South Korea, and South Africa.

The Nature and Determinants of Insurance Demand. The demand for insurance within national economies is a function of a myriad of influences. Culture and religion can exert powerful influences. For example, the high cultural propensity to save in Japan, Korea, and some other Asian countries has enhanced the demand for saving-oriented life insurance products. Conversely, the perception by many Muslims that life insurance is contrary to the Koran often depresses demand in countries with large Muslim populations.

Countries wherein the people have little private property or where property rights are not well developed exhibit correspondingly little demand for property insurance. Likewise, if people are generally poor, they have little need for liability insurance to protect themselves and have few funds with which to purchase insurance.

Extensive government-provided security schemes depress the demand for private insurance.[11] Fortunately for private insurers, the trend worldwide is for governments to diminish their role as purveyors of individual financial security. Such actions increase the demand for private insurance.

The political and economic stability of a country influences insurance demand.[12] An unstable environment depresses insurance demand. The generalization should be qualified somewhat, in that citizens in unstable environments often avoid local insurance purchases but purchase insurance from foreign companies that offer greater financial strength and policies, especially life insurance policies, denominated in strong currencies. Such purchases are often made in spite of domestic prohibitions.

Of course, price is an important determinant of insurance demand and supply. The price an insurer charges is influenced by its cost structure, by the competitiveness within the particular line of insurance, and by government tax and other policy. Unfortunately, no completely satisfactory national measures of price exist. Proxies are used, but the fact remains that the price elasticities of the various insurance lines are not well understood.[13]

As alluded to above, the magnitude of national economic activity has an important effect on insurance demand. In fact, if it is assumed that countries follow a more or less common development path, it can be concluded that the income elasticity of insurance premiums is greater than 1.0. A recent study found a total income elasticity of 1.35.[14] Thus, a 1.0 percent increase in GDP can be expected to give rise on average to a 1.35 percent increase in insurance premiums written.

---

11. See Beenstock, Dickinson, and Khajuria (1986) and Kim (1988).

12. See Beenstock, Dickinson, and Khajuria (1986) and Wasow (1986).

13. See Cummins and Weiss (1991) for a discussion of nonlife prices, and Diacon (1980) and Black and Skipper (1994) for a discussion of life prices.

14. Swiss Reinsurance Company (1993b). Other studies have found elasticities greater than 1.0. See Grace and Skipper (1991).

FIGURE 5–5
Insurance Density and Penetration, by Country, 1993

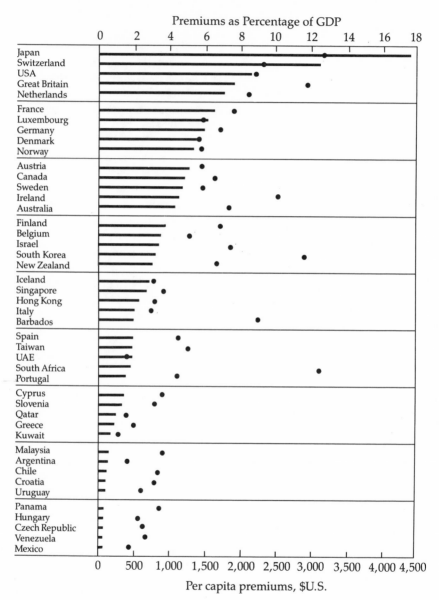

- Premiums/GDP
- Per capita premiums

FIGURE 5–5 (continued)

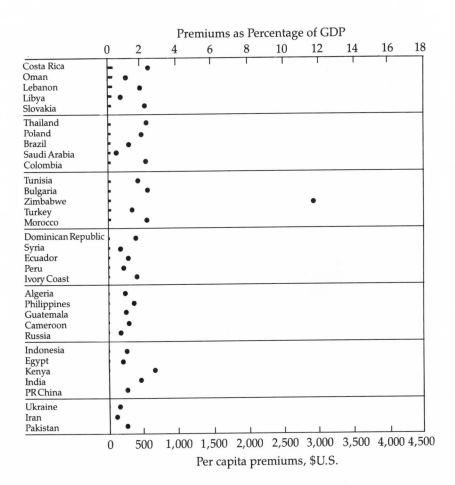

Premiums as Percentage of GDP

SOURCE: Swiss Reinsurance Co. (1995).

The demand for each line of insurance varies with the nature and character of its purchasers. All lines within the life insurance sector tend to be purchased from locally established companies, with only negligible amounts purchased on a cross-border basis. Life insurance consumers generally seem to prefer to deal with domestic companies, steering clear of foreign companies even in those markets where they can conduct an insurance business (such as the United Kingdom). This preference flows from the fact that life insurance buyers are often poorly informed and therefore prefer to deal with better known, local companies. As life insurers continue to increase their services and product offerings to commercial accounts, it is reasonable to expect demand to become less domestically oriented.

The nature and character of the nonlife insurance demand can vary substantially, as between personal and commercial lines. Personal automobile, homeowners', and other lines of insurance tend overwhelmingly to be purchased from domestic firms. As with the typical life insurance consumer, a less-informed nonlife consumer seems to reveal a preference for better known, locally regulated companies.

In large part, this revealed preference for local firms is government-driven. Personal automobile liability insurance is compulsory in all OECD countries. Domestic laws typically prohibit the purchase of compulsory insurance from any but locally established companies.[15] The logic for this requirement is that such insurance, being closely related to public policy and the protection of innocent third parties, requires the utmost in government scrutiny—which cannot be adequately achieved with foreign companies, especially when their assets are not held locally.

The typical commercial-lines consumer is better informed than the typical personal-lines consumer and can thereby better protect its own interest. As such, demand in commercial insurance lines is often less domestically oriented. Also, large commercial and industrial firms have more options than do individuals. If insurers fail to offer terms or prices that these firms believe they warrant, they may form their own captive insurer. Access is thereby gained to the wholesale insurance market (reinsurance) and greater control exercised over cash flow and policy coverage.

The Nature and Determinants of Insurance Supply. We know surprisingly little about the nature and determinants of insurance supply—either life or nonlife insurance. Theoretical analyses assume that

---

15. See OECD (1983). This study is currently being updated by the OECD.

insurance supply is a function of expected profit—a reasonable assumption, but one that neither adds much insight nor aids in examining the practical realities. In any event, the supply of insurance is not subject to direct measurement, as insurance output is not subject to precise definition or measurement.[16] Even so, we know that the insurance supply—however defined—is positively related to insurer-risk–bearing capacity. Risk-bearing capacity, in turn, is generally a function of insurer capital. For a market, insurance capacity is therefore some function of the total capital that investors are willing to put at risk and the intensity with which managers expose the capital to risk.

If investors are unwilling to supply additional capital or if managers are unwilling to expose a given capital level to additional risk, a so-called capacity crisis can develop. Such crises occur periodically within the nonlife branch, with the result that some lines of insurance become scarce or even unavailable—a so-called hard market. With such market tightening, insurers are able to raise prices and profits rise, inducing more capital to flow into the business and inducing managers to write more insurance with a given capital level. A soft market evolves, which is typically followed within five to eight years by another hard market.

Such profit cycles are not generally found in the life branch and do not exist in all countries.[17] The causes of cycles remain poorly understood, with recent research suggesting institutional differences, regulation, interest rates, and the general business cycle as contributing factors.[18] Whatever the causes, cycles affect worldwide insurance and reinsurance capacity.[19]

Number and types of firms. National insurance markets differ markedly. In some, state-owned monopolies remain the sole suppliers, although the trend is away from such monopolies. In many developing countries, foreign-controlled firms still deny effective market access. Most OECD country markets exhibit a blend of domestic and foreign companies, with domestic-controlled undertakings dominat-

---

16. See Doherty (1981) and Weiss (1991) for nonlife studies, and Hirshhorn and Geehan (1977) and Gardner (1992) for life studies. Geehan (1986) provides an overview of all important output studies published through 1985.

17. Cummins and Outreville (1987).

18. See Cummins and Outreville (1990), Tenneyson (1991), NAIC (1991), and Grace and Hotchkiss (1995).

19. Although the existence of cycles in most markets is inconsistent with the rational expectations model (see Cummins and Outreville 1987), there is no evidence of industrywide collusion.

TABLE 5–1

NUMBER AND TYPES OF INSURANCE COMPANIES IN OECD MEMBER
COUNTRIES, 1993

Country	Life	Nonlife	Composite	Reinsurance	Total
Australia	48	129	0	32	209
Austria	6	29	32	3	70
Belgium	43	169	54	—	266
Canada	142	195	9	53	399
Denmark	41	175	0	29	245
Finland	16	31	0	9	56
France	147	467	—	20	634
Germany	326	410	0	31	767
Greece	25	121	32	—	178
Iceland	5	19	0	2	26
Ireland	31	65	0	—	96
Italy	71	162	26	9	268
Japan	40	56	0	3	99
Luxembourg	34	32	2	173	241
The Netherlands	97	673	—	17	786
New Zealand	39	128	—	—	167
Norway	10	133	—	2	145
Portugal	24	54	9	1	88
Spain	68	315	84	7	474
Sweden	29	105	6	—	140
Switzerland	30	93	0	19	142
Turkey	9	22	19	4	54
United Kingdom	196	566	62	—	824
United States	1,678	2,694	0	465	4,837
Total	3,155	6,843	335	879	11,211

NOTE: Cells without data indicate either not applicable or none.
SOURCE: OECD (1994).

ing. Some markets are quite concentrated, while others are not. Table
5–1 lists the number and types of insurers within the OECD countries.

The two most prevalent forms of insurers worldwide are stocks
and mutuals. Stock insurers are owned by shareholders with profits
accruing to them. Mutual insurers have no shareholders, being
owned by policyholders, with profits flowing to them. The stock-
insurer form predominates in most lines and markets, worldwide.
Mutuals control important market shares in Japan, the United Kingdom, and the United States.

Table 5–2 lists the world's twenty-five largest insurers, based on

TABLE 5–2

TWENTY-FIVE LARGEST INSURANCE COMPANIES WORLDWIDE,
RANKED IN ASSET ORDER, 1994

(millions of $U.S.)

Company	Assets	Capital
Nippon Life (Japan)	348,597	4,164
Zenkyoren (Japan)	247,700	3,551
Dai-Ichi Mutual Life (Japan)	245,926	3,412
Sumitomo Life (Japan)	214,835	3,067
Prudential Insurance (U.S.)	211,902	11,711
Allianz Holding (Germany)	164,601	13,759
Compagnie UAP (France)	160,376	17,369
Meiji Mutual Life (Japan)	148,640	2,498
AXA (France)[a]	145,031	13,470
Metropolitan Life (U.S.)	131,177	8,258
American International (U.S.)	114,346	27,047
Asahi Mutual Life (Japan)	112,139	1,501
Prudential (U.K.)	98,063	13,041
Equitable (U.S.)	94,640	5,818
Aetna Life & Casualty (U.S.)	92,906	6,790
Mitsui Mutual Life (Japan)	92,779	1,112
CIGNA (U.S.)	83,838	7,200
Internationale Nederlanden Groep (Netherlands)[b]	82,163	12,092
Yasuda Mutual Life (Japan)	82,050	1,742
Assurances Generales de France (France)	79,681	16,735
Aegon (Netherlands)	78,992	8,865
State Farm (U.S.)	76,677	21,165
Teachers Insurance & Annuity (U.S.)	73,348	5,103
Tokyo Marine & Fire (Japan)	72,990	22,320
Commercial Union (U.K.)	72,715	9,235

NOTE: Companies are ranked by assets, as of December 31, 1994.
a. Includes consolidation of Equitable Companies.
b. Insurance operations only.
SOURCE: Worldscope.

assets, and their country of domicile. Japan is home to nine, and the United States is second-largest, with eight. Most of the insurers listed in table 5–2 write the great majority of their business within their domestic markets.

Perhaps fewer than a dozen insurers are truly international—capable of servicing their customers worldwide. Among such firms

TABLE 5-3
ESTIMATED NUMBER OF CAPTIVE INSURERS IN MAJOR CAPTIVE
DOMICILES, 1994

Domicile	Number
Bermuda	1,200
Cayman	350
Guernsey	250
Vermont (U.S.)	241
Barbados	190
Luxembourg	170
Isle of Man	120
Ireland	78
Singapore	47
Hawaii (U.S.)	33
BVI	30
Bahamas	30
Colorado (U.S.)	29
Tennessee (U.S.)	17
Other U.S.	218
Other Non-U.S.	222
Total	3,225

SOURCE: Tillinghast, Captive Insurance Company Report (1994).

are the American International Group, CIGNA, and Aetna in the United States; the Royal and General Accident in the United Kingdom; the Zurich in Switzerland; and Allianz in Germany.

Thousands of businesses worldwide are involved in captive and other sophisticated self-insurance programs. It is estimated that these nonconventional self-funding approaches may equal one-third of U.S. commercial nonlife-insurance direct written premiums, and the proportion is growing. For tax and regulatory reasons, most captive insurers are not domiciled in the parent company's jurisdiction. Table 5-3 lists the major captive domiciles, along with the number of captives in each. Insurance placed with such captives technically is cross-border insurance. Such flows, however, are clearly of a different character from arms-length cross-border insurance transactions.

The international dimensions of insurance supply. With the increasing internationalization of business comes a corresponding internationalization of financial services. Additionally, the size and concentration of many purely domestic loss exposures requires a mustering of international insurance capacity. No one country's market can provide needed cover for property- and liability-loss exposure arising from oil refineries, tankers, offshore rigs, satellites, jumbo jets, environmental impairment, and the like. An international spread is essential if such large risks are to be insured. Also, for many insurers, the only effective means of achieving additional growth is through international expansion, as their domestic markets may be saturated, as is largely the case in the United States.

Of course, national markets benefit from a greater international presence. Domestic capacity (supply) is increased, thereby enhancing competition and providing better consumer value and choice. As with other international operations, knowledge-sharing can bring innovative products, production and underwriting techniques, and claims-settling practices. With increasing competition and innovation in insurance, the international competitiveness of domestic firms that must purchase insurance is enhanced.

Insurance services can be delivered by foreign interests through either cross-border trade or establishment. Cross-border insurance trade exists when the buyer purchases (imports) insurance from an insurer or reinsurer domiciled in another country; for example, a U.S. corporation (importer) purchases insurance directly from a U.K. insurer (exporter). In EU terminology, this category of international transactions is referred to as services business.

Delivery via establishment insurance trade exists when the buyer purchases insurance from a domestic, foreign-owned entity. The foreign presence may be via a local agent with authority to underwrite business on the foreign insurer's behalf, through a branch office, or through the creation or purchase of a local insurer or reinsurer.

Data on the dimensions of international insurance supply are sparse, so assessing its magnitude and importance is difficult. Most national accounting systems fail to make appropriate allowance for insurance and reinsurance trade (the United Kingdom being an important exception). Additionally, classification problems exist with trade-related insurance, such as marine insurance—a particularly important line in many countries (less so in the United States).

Cross-border insurance trade. Cross-border trade in life insurance is believed to be minuscule. Carter (1990) estimates that cross-border trade in nonlife insurance accounts for about 4 percent of total world nonlife premiums. Bedore (1991) offers a 2 to 3 percent estimate. For the United States, cross-border exports and imports of direct insurance accounted for 0.5 percent and 0.3 percent respectively of U.S. direct premiums written in 1992.[20]

---

20. Calculated by author from U.S. Department of Commerce (1994) figures.

TABLE 5–4: U.S. Cross-Border Trade in Insurance, 1990–1992
($U.S. millions)

Item	1990	1991	1992
Net exports[a]	751	1,028	1,069
Direct premiums received	2,834	1,845	2,623
Reinsurance premiums received	2,009	2,192	2,900
Net imports[b]	1,910	2,450	1,373
Direct premiums paid	1,006	1,107	1,348
Reinsurance premiums paid	9,216	9,962	10,527
Net balance of insurance trade	(1,159)	(1,422)	(303)

a. Premium receipts of U.S.-based insurance companies from foreign-based insureds net of losses.
b. Premium payments of U.S.-based insureds to foreign-based insurance companies net of losses.
Source: U.S. Department of Commerce (1994).

TABLE 5–5
U.S. Reinsurance Market, 1987–1991
($U.S. billions)

Premiums	1987	1988	1989	1990	1991
Total reinsurance	22.5	21.2	21.6	23.0	25.3
Domestic reinsurers[a]	15.2	13.4	12.8	13.9	14.9
Professional reinsurers	12.2	11.1	10.7	11.7	12.7
Direct writers	2.9	2.3	2.1	2.2	2.2
Foreign reinsurers[b]	7.3	7.8	8.8	9.1	10.4

a. Net written premiums; detail may not add to total, because of rounding.
b. Net written premiums paid to reinsurers outside the United States. Includes life insurance ceded abroad.
Source: U.S. Department of Commerce (1993).

Table 5–4 gives figures for U.S. cross-border trade in both direct insurance and reinsurance for 1990 through 1992. Most U.S. insurance imports are from Europe (especially reinsurance imports) and from Bermuda, the major captive insurer domicile. The United States is a net importer of reinsurance. In fact, cross-border trade in reinsurance accounted for more than 40 percent of the total U.S. reinsurance market in 1991, as illustrated in table 5–5.

Establishment insurance trade. Important differences exist in establishment by agency, branch, or subsidiary.[21] Although an agency has

21. The OECD Invisibles Code and Capital Movements Code explicitly

authority to represent the insurer, it typically performs the distribution and possibly underwriting and claim settlement functions only. It is not a risk-bearing entity. No insurer assets are held or managed by the agency. Payments to claimants must come from funds held by the insurer in its home country. This form of establishment closely resembles cross-border trade with the principal regulatory responsibility resting with the home-country supervisor, except for marketing practices.

Branches represent a more substantial form of establishment, in that assets to back local reserves are usually maintained in the host country. Local deposits equal to minimum capital and surplus requirements are often mandatory. Nonetheless, branches are not separate corporations. They are a part of the home-country insurer. As such, they are subject to dual regulatory oversight, which can create problems.[22]

Establishment by purchasing or creating a subsidiary poses far fewer policy issues. The local subsidiary of a foreign insurer is a domestic corporation, fully subject to host-country laws and regulation.

Precise insurance establishment worldwide trade figures are not available. Carter (1990) estimates that about 9 percent of nonlife premiums and 4 percent of life premiums are written worldwide by foreign insurers through local establishment. Bedore (1991) uses a 10 percent estimate that includes cross-border transactions.

Foreign insurance firms' success within a market is a function of the market's structure. Foreign firms have traditionally been most successful in the more complex insurance lines, such as commercial insurance, marine insurance, and reinsurance. Their typically large size, geographic spread of risk, in-depth knowledge of complex risks, and management efficiency have enabled them to compete successfully with local firms.

With important exceptions, the less complex personal lines and life insurance segments are dominated by domestic firms. The main reasons for this situation relate to the high information and distribution costs associated with mass risks and to restrictive regulations.

The extent of foreign presence within domestic insurance markets varies greatly worldwide, from nil within closed markets such as

---

recognize these differences and permit correspondingly different regulatory responses. See OECD (1990).

22. See Key and Scott (1991) for a discussion of these and related problems in the context of banking. Their discussion also applies to insurance branching.

FIGURE 5–6

MARKET SHARE OF FOREIGN-CONTROLLED UNDERTAKINGS AMONG SELECTED
OECD COUNTRIES, AS PERCENTAGE OF LIFE AND NONLIFE BUSINESS, 1992

A. LIFE BUSINESS, 1992

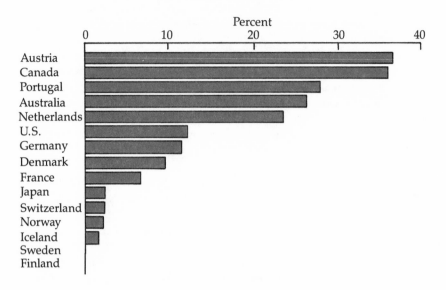

B. NONLIFE BUSINESS, 1992

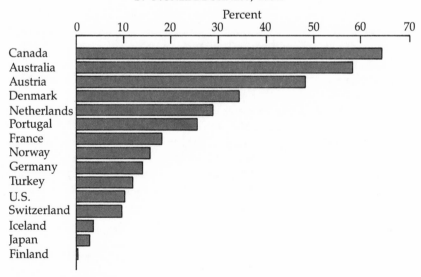

SOURCE: OECD (1994).

172

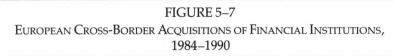

FIGURE 5–7

EUROPEAN CROSS-BORDER ACQUISITIONS OF FINANCIAL INSTITUTIONS, 1984–1990

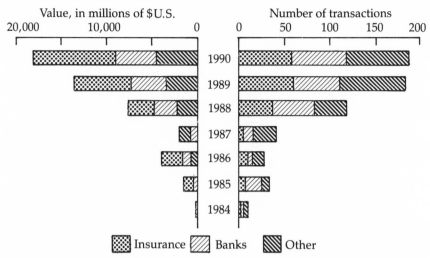

SOURCE: Wasserstein Perella & Co.

India to well over 30 percent in Canada and Austria. Figure 5–6 shows foreign presence within the life and nonlife insurance markets of OECD countries for which data are available. A foreign presence is defined as the proportion of domestic direct business written by foreign-controlled companies, branches, and agencies (for instance, through establishment). Cross-border (services) business is excluded. By this measure, Austria, Australia, and Canada are among the most international of the group, with Finland, Iceland, Japan, and Sweden among the least.

The pace of financial service firm mergers and acquisitions (M&A) has been brisk during the past ten years. The EU Single Market program has resulted in significant European M&A activity. Figure 5–7 shows the number and the aggregate value of cross-border financial service firm transactions by European acquirers for the period from 1984 to 1990. A great proportion of these transactions is intra-European. This European activity may be contrasted with the less vigorous U.S. activity. Figure 5–8 provides more recent figures for U.S. acquirers.

Much of the European insurance acquisition activity has been directed toward the U.S. market. Figure 5–9 shows the dollar value of cross-border M&A insurance transactions into and out of the

173

FIGURE 5–8

AMERICAN CROSS-BORDER ACQUISITIONS OF FINANCIAL INSTITUTIONS,
1985–1993

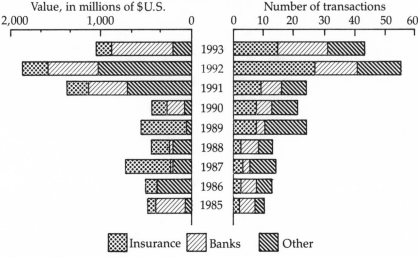

SOURCE: Wasserstein Perella & Co.

United States for 1987 through 1993. Clearly, foreign acquirers have been more active than U.S. acquirers. The most notable U.S. acquisitions since 1988 have been:

- the $970 million acquisition of the Home Insurance Company by a group of investors led by Trygg-Hansa (Sweden) in 1991
- the $5.2 billion purchase of the Farmers Group (tenth largest U.S. nonlife insurance group) by B.A.T. Industries (U.K. and Bermuda) in 1988
- the $740 million purchase of the Maryland Casualty Company by Zurich Insurance (Switzerland) in 1989
- the $3.1 billion sale of Fireman's Fund in 1991 to Allianz (Germany)
- the $1.0 billion investment in The Equitable by Group AXA (France) in 1991

U.S.-owned insurers in foreign markets realized revenues of $36.2 billion in 1991. As figure 5–10 shows, Europe is the largest market for U.S. insurers. Most revenue is from nonlife operations, although some U.S. life insurers recently have become more active internationally. Figure 5–10 also shows revenues of $72.9 billion for the U.S. insurance operations of foreign-owned insurers. The extensive European interest in the U.S. market is evident.

FIGURE 5–9

CROSS-BORDER INSURANCE MERGER AND ACQUISITION TRANSACTIONS INTO
AND OUT OF THE UNITED STATES, 1987–1993

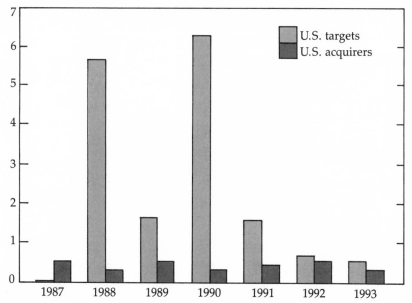

SOURCE: Wasserstein Perella & Co.

The 1993 market share by foreign interests in the U.S. market probably exceeds 12 percent. U.S. insurers' share of the EU market is less than 2 percent, and the total foreign share of the Japanese domestic insurance market is less than 3 percent, a figure little changed over many years.[23]

Establishment within the Japanese insurance market is particularly difficult. Besides government-created impediments to entry, certain market structure impediments exist. These include private procurement practices associated with *keiretsu*, a highly concentrated industry structure, and barriers in the distribution system.[24]

The Japanese *keiretsu* system of extensive cross-corporate linkages, either through equity participation or through shared traditions, interlocking boards, or other factors, is claimed to limit market access. Each *keiretsu* includes or is centered on one or more large Japanese industrial companies and usually includes a variety of other

---

23. Bedore (1991) and OECD (1994).
24. USTR (1994).

FIGURE 5–10: REVENUES OF FOREIGN-OWNED INSURANCE COMPANIES,
FROM U.S. PERSPECTIVE, 1993
($U.S. millions)

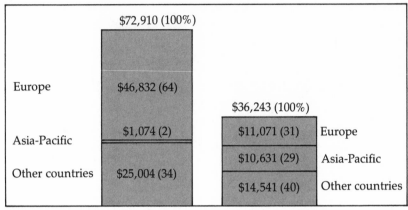

Foreign-owned
insurers in the United States

U.S.-owned
insurers abroad

NOTE: Revenue equals premium plus investment plus other income for insurance affiliates 10 percent or more owned by any one foreign person.
SOURCE: U.S. Department of Commerce, 1994.

industrial and service firms, including banks and insurers. Financial transactions generally and insurance purchases in particular take place largely among *keiretsu* family companies. As a consequence, little opportunity exists for nonfamily insurers to penetrate a *keiretsu*.

A 1993 study commissioned by the American Chamber of Commerce in Japan found that 11 *keiretsu* member insurers accounted for more than 80 percent of the total Japanese nonlife insurance market. Moreover, at least 92 percent of the insurance business of the eight major horizontally connected *keiretsu* and of six randomly selected vertically integrated *keiretsu* was handled by financially related insurers. The study further noted that several large groups, including Mitsubishi, Mitsui, Sumitomo, Sony, and NEC transacted business almost exclusively with related insurers.[25] These procurement-practice limitations plus the market power allowed by a highly concentrated Japanese market and the inability to acquire an ownership interest in many major insurers—because they are mutuals or members of *keiretsu*—operate as significant structural entry barriers. Similar circumstances are said to exist in Korea with the *chaebol*.

25. *Japanese Insurance Procurement Practices within* Keiretsu *Groups* (1993).

Regulatory transparency also has been a problem for firms seeking entry into the Japanese and some other insurance markets. Japanese and some other countries' insurance laws are written very generally, with interpretation and details of implementation left to administrative guidance. As a result, a foreign insurer is often unable to know specific entry requirements in advance and is unable to determine readily whether it is treated according to the same standards as domestic firms. Also, the absence of detailed written standards greatly hinders foreign insurers' ability to question or challenge arbitrary or unreasonable actions of the regulator.[26]

Given the great size of their financial institutions, it is surprising to some that the Japanese have not been very active internationally in insurance acquisitions. They have taken important minority interests in a few European and U.S. insurers, but these stakes are relatively small. To some extent this reluctance is attributable to culture and to a failure to develop fully competitive techniques in insurance, fostered by overly restrictive regulation. The long-term expectation is that, with upcoming governmental reforms within the Japanese financial service sector and with an improving Japanese economy, Japanese insurers will increasingly flex their considerable financial muscle worldwide.

The insurance production process. An understanding of the insurance production process will distinguish those aspects that are largely domestic from those that are not. The production of insurance services—as with other financial services—relies on financial and human capital. Financial capital underpins all operations. The most important functional operations in the production process include insurance pricing, underwriting, and claims handling; investment management; and distribution.

The role of capital and surplus. Financial capital provides a cushion against the possibility that actual expenses, claims, and investment results may deviate negatively from those implicit in the insurer's pricing. As insurance policies are contingent claim contracts that rely on pricing inversion (that is, the product is priced before actual production costs are known), a margin for pricing error must be provided if the market is to perceive that the insurer can meet its obligations. Insurers, in effect, can borrow additional capital (capacity) through the purchase of reinsurance. In general, the greater an insurer's capital, as against its premium writings and liabilities (that is, the less its

---

26. USTR (1994).

leverage), the greater the perceived security and the more favorable its reception among informed buyers and their representatives.

Herein lies the most significant consumer problem in insurance. Consumers pay now for the promise of future payment under contractually defined conditions. Yet what assurance does the buyer have that the insurer will be able to pay? A strong capital position is desirable, but how is the consumer to know what is "strong"? A firm's capital (net worth) is the simple difference between assets and liabilities. Even if the consumer determines what is a strong capital position, can the consumer be assured that the firm's apparent capital position is not inflated through asset overvaluation or liability undervaluation? This particular information asymmetry problem is magnified if a foreign insurer is involved. The balance sheets of foreign insurers, prepared using their domiciliary countries' asset and liability valuation and accounting standards, are not comparable with those of domestic insurers. The buyer, therefore, has even less basis for confidence. This issue is addressed more fully later.

Pricing, underwriting, and claims handling. The principal technical elements of the insurance production process relate to pricing, underwriting, and claims handling. Insurance prices (premiums) are determined by trained mathematicians (actuaries) using their best estimates as to future losses and expenses, with an eye toward competitiveness. Because of time lags between the receipt of premiums and loss payments, the competitive premium will be the present value of expected losses, expenses, and profits. The greater the average period between premium payment and loss payout, the greater the influence of investment returns in setting rates. Thus, investment results are exceedingly important in life insurance and in the so-called long-tail nonlife lines, such as medical malpractice and general liability insurance, and less so in other lines.

To the extent that a liberal discount factor (a high investment return) is factored into its rates, an insurer's exposure to pricing errors and possible insolvency is heightened. Accurate insurance pricing requires a knowledge of local loss characteristics but usually does not require a local presence.

Product innovation and price competitiveness often are understandably crucial determinants of success, especially for new entrants. In countries such as Japan, Korea, and many developing countries where product innovation and price competition are thwarted by government, new firms are discouraged from entering the market, or if they enter, they find themselves at a competitive disadvantage compared with entrenched firms. Thus, national treatment in the context of a restrictive regulatory regime does not necessarily provide effective market access.

Underwriters are skilled practitioners who determine whether and on what terms to issue a requested insurance policy. On complex cases, an underwriter may work with an actuary. The underwriter must assemble information about the person or object of the insurance in order to assess its loss potential. For large or unusual risks, the underwriting process can be quite complex. It requires a knowledge of local conditions and the local environment. If continuous monitoring and local knowledge acquisition are necessary—as is usually desirable in the personal lines of insurance—a local presence would be competitively useful but not essential. For complex risks, underwriters ordinarily can secure needed selection and classification information from local sources—for example, engineers or surveyors—and through brokers (see below).

The expertise required of claims personnel varies directly with the nature of the loss. With large, complex losses—such as loss of a freighter or an airplane crash—claims settlement may take months of careful technical and legal investigation and negotiation. A local presence will be required, but usually for the period of settlement only.

At the other extreme, claims under life insurance policies typically can be settled easily by the beneficiary completing a simple claim form and providing the insurer with a copy of the insured's death certificate. A local presence is not required.

Even with fairly complex claims, such as with health insurance, no local presence is necessary. Indeed, several U.S. insurers' health-claim settlement operations are conducted from Ireland, where workers analyze and settle U.S. health claims. Such decentralization of the insurance production cycle is becoming increasingly common.

In lines of insurance where losses are more frequent and require on-site examination, such as in personal automobile and homeowner's insurance, some type of national presence is typically desirable, especially if the insurer wishes to develop a reputation for efficient, quick service. Even here, however, independent claim adjustment firms can be hired.

Claims personnel, sometimes with the assistance of an actuary, estimate amounts to be established as balance sheet liabilities (reserves) for unpaid nonlife claims. In life insurance, liabilities for future claims are typically established by the actuarial department based on mathematical formulas, mortality tables, and assumptions as to future investment earnings. The investment manager may provide input into this process. A local presence is not required with either nonlife or life insurance reserve setting.

The principal consumer protection issue within the insurance pricing, underwriting, and claim settlement process relates to contract situs in connection with claims. For foreign-owned, locally established subsidiaries, the insurer and insured reside in the same jurisdiction, so conflicts do not arise. The national treatment standard suffices. The same logic generally applies to agencies and branches. For cross-border business, the question of whose law applies—home or host country—is potentially of great importance. For commercial insurance and reinsurance, the parties typically agree as to contract situs. Such an approach is reasonable with informed parties.

Less informed customers who have taken the initiative in seeking cross-border insurance have placed themselves within the insurer's jurisdiction and, in effect, must be considered to have forfeited any home-country protection. When the foreign insurer solicits such customers, a different situation arises. Home-country rules arguably should apply.

Investment management. Insurers in general and especially life insurers manage significant investment portfolios. Insurers have strong incentives to maximize investment returns, as this can be a major factor in determining product competitiveness and profitability. A poorly diversified or low-quality portfolio can lead to financial difficulties and even failure, as several recent, large U.S. insurer failures demonstrate.

Nothing inherent in the investment management function requires a local presence. Indeed, one large U.S. insurer monitors much of its American pension clients' funds through operations in Ireland.

Investment management requires decisions on investment quality and quantity, including asset liability matching and diversification. Foreign investments can exacerbate the buyer's (and regulator's) information asymmetry problem, as judging the quality of such investments can be difficult. For this reason, national insurance regulation typically places severe limits on foreign investments by domestic insurers.[27]

A related but different concern arises with cross-border insurance trade. Unlike the situation with locally established, foreign-owned firms whose assets typically must be maintained locally, the

---

27. Such limitations find less justification with the increasing internationalization of securities markets.

assets backing cross-border insurance liabilities are not ordinarily maintained in the host country. If the foreign firm fails to meet its obligations, the host-country insured could be at a legal, not to mention practical, disadvantage relative to home-country insureds and creditors in attaching the insurer's assets. The resolution of this issue is essential if cross-border insurance is to grow.

Distribution. Insurance is distributed (sold) in one or more of four ways. Some insurers sell directly to customers, without the use of intermediaries, via the internet, mail, telephone solicitation, newspaper advertisements, or other means. Relatively little insurance is sold worldwide through such direct solicitation, although the proportion is growing in some markets.

The great majority of both life and nonlife insurance worldwide is sold through intermediaries—agents and brokers. The technical distinction between them is that agents usually are the legal representatives of the insurer, whereas brokers usually represent the consumer. For obvious competitive reasons, a local distribution network is essential for many insurance lines.

Two broad classes of agents are found internationally. Some agents sell exclusively for one company. These agents are referred to as exclusive or tied agents. Independent agents represent several insurers.

Brokers, expected to be knowledgeable about the insurance market generally, work with larger clients. Insurance brokers, as well as independent agents, reinforce product and price competition by rectifying to some extent the information imbalance between the buyer and the seller.

Table 5–6 lists the world's twenty largest brokerage firms in 1993, along with their worldwide income. In contrast to the situation where relatively few U.S. insurers operate outside U.S. borders, the large U.S. brokerage houses have a major international presence.

Banks are important insurance outlets in some markets. In the overwhelming majority of instances, the bank serves as an agent for either an affiliated insurer or an insurer with whom the bank has a special arrangement. The latter situation is less common. In no OECD country are banks broadly permitted directly to underwrite insurance.[28] Restrictions in the United States limit banks' ability to participate in *bancassurance,* much to the chagrin of U.S. bankers.

Countries wherein banks are responsible for important shares of domestic insurance markets are shown in table 5–7, along with their

---

28. OECD (1992).

TABLE 5–6

TWENTY LARGEST INSURANCE BROKERAGE FIRMS WORLDWIDE,
RANKED IN ORDER, 1993
(thousands of $U.S.)

Company (Ranked in Order)	Gross Revenues
Marsh & McLennan Cos. Inc. (U.S.)	3,175,300
Alexander & Alexander Services Inc. (U.S.)	1,341,600
Sedgwick Group P.L.C. (U.K.)	1,216,169
Rollins Hudig Hall Group Inc. (U.S.)	1,215,000
Willis Corroon Group P.L.C. (U.K.)	1,057,000
Johnson & Higgins (U.S.)	962,000
Bain Hogg Group (U.K.)	397,097
Acordia Inc. (U.S.)	364,779
JIB Group P.L.C. (U.K.)	346,962
Minet Group P.L.C. (U.K.)	325,080
Arthur J. Gallagher & Co. (U.S.)	317,663
C. E. Heath P.L.C. (U.K.)	289,357
Jauch & Huebener KGaA (Germany)	183,315
Gras Savoye S.A. (France)	144,740
Hilb, Rogal & Hamilton Co. (U.S.)	134,954
Lowndes Lambert Group Holdings P.L.C. (U.K.)	125,311
ABN-AMRO Verzekeringen B.V. (Netherlands)	123,686
CECAR (France)	98,880
Poe & Brown Inc. (U.S.)	95,570
Groupe le Blanc de Nicolay (France)	90,761

SOURCE: Business Insurance (1994).

national market shares. Banks have been most successful in selling simple, commodity-type life insurance products.

The success of an insurer is directly tied to the success of its distribution system. Insurance distribution channels are of vital importance to new entrants—both foreign and domestic. For this reason, an overview of prominent insurance distribution channels in the United States, Europe, and Japan is given below.

Each of the four distribution channels is found in the United States. Generally, the exclusive agency system has been most successful in the nonlife personal lines and, to a lesser extent, with some life insurers. Most life and nonlife insurance is sold in the United States through thousands of independent agents and brokers. With the exception of annuities, banks remain relatively unimportant distribution channels in the United States.

Within the EU, distribution concerns are said to be driving the

TABLE 5–7

BANKS' PERCENTAGE OF TOTAL INSURANCE PREMIUMS
FOR SELECTED COUNTRIES, 1992

	Life	Nonlife
France	40	2
Sweden	25	3
Germany	20	3
Denmark	17	3
Britain	15	5
Holland	15	13
Spain	15	3
Italy	5	0

SOURCE: Boston Consulting Group.

restructuring of insurance markets, especially regarding bank and insurer linkages.[29] The three traditional means of linkage include:

- insurer owns bank
- bank owns insurer
- special arrangement without equity interest

All are found in Europe. A new form of *bancassurance* has recently been tried in the Netherlands.[30] Perhaps the best known such new conglomerate is the Internationale Nederlanden Groep (ING). Resulting from the merger of Nationale Nederlanden (NN) and NMB-Postbank in 1991, ING seeks to become an integrated financial services firm rather than a conglomerate of separate, affiliated firms. The Dutch group *Fortis* seems also to be moving in this direction. In each instance, the firms distinguish themselves from their *allfinanz (bancassurance)* competitors through their internal integration of banking and insurance and by using multichannel distribution, through which a full range of bank and insurance products is offered.[31]

Aside from bank-insurer linkages as distribution channels, distribution methods differ from country to country throughout Europe. In general, brokers and independent agents predominate in northern European countries, especially in the Netherlands and the United Kingdom. Tied agents predominate in Germany, France, Switzerland, Austria, Spain, and Italy. The lack of major independent agent

29. Bedore (1991).
30. See Pluym (1993).
31. See Holsboer (1993).

and broker networks in some European countries serves as a structural barrier to entry for *de novo* insurance operations.

Few brokers and no independent agents exist in Japan, although under the 1994 United States-Japan Framework Agreement, the government of Japan agreed to permit the introduction of the brokerage system. Nor are banks permitted to sell insurance or to be affiliated with insurers via equity participation. The great majority of insurance—both life and nonlife—is sold by thousands of part-time, tied agents. Most are housewives, but many are service-station attendants, automobile dealers, real estate agents, and the like who sell policies to their relatives, friends, and customers. As a result, aspiring new insurer entrants to the Japanese insurance market meet with substantial distribution impediments.

Consumer protection concerns attach to insurer marketing efforts. Where distribution is via local establishment, such as an agency, branch, or subsidiary, local regulation and a national treatment standard are sufficient. Cross-border distribution, however, may not ensure local consumers adequate protection against marketing abuses.

As with questions of contract situs in connection with claim settlement, the issue of adequate consumer protection from marketing abuses may not warrant government concern relative to reinsurance or commercial insurance lines. Individuals are arguably more vulnerable to such abuses, and a mechanism to ensure host-country protection may be warranted in a liberalized insurance world.

Government Intervention into Insurance Markets

Insurance is regulated in every country. The degree of regulation varies with the incumbent government's philosophy and capability, the nature of the domestic insurance industry, the country's level of economic development, and the sociocultural elements of the nation. With all countries, the stated goal of regulation is consumer protection. With many, especially developing countries, an additional goal may be the promotion of the domestic insurance industry and ensuring that the national insurance industry contributes to general economic development.

Insurance laws and regulations determine who may sell and underwrite insurance within a market and the circumstances under which they may do so. Minimum reserve, asset quality and quantity, and capital requirements are usually laid down. Special accounting standards are often mandated. In many countries, prices and policy conditions are regulated.

The extent of regulation varies from light to heavy worldwide. Thus, for example, the United Kingdom, Ireland, Hong Kong, and the Netherlands generally rely more on market forces to ensure a viable insurance market, with regulation principally relating to prudential matters. At the other extreme, Germany, Japan, Korea, and Switzerland have historically practiced intensive regulation, focusing not only on insurer prudential matters but on product pricing and content and on market stability. The Canadian and U.S. regulatory styles fall between the two extremes, being closer to the light end of the spectrum.

This section begins with a discussion of the rationale for insurance regulation and then presents an overview of the common areas of regulation. Barriers to trade in international insurance are discussed throughout.

Rationales for Government Intervention into Insurance. Within a competitive economy, government intervention is deemed desirable only where (1) actual or potential market failures exist; (2) failures do or could lead to meaningful consumer harm or abuse; and (3) government action can ameliorate the harm or abuse. Conversely, if at least one of the three conditions is not met, no government intervention is warranted.

The need for government regulation of insurance, therefore, will be explored by an analysis of insurance market failures. This examination will be structured around the eight market failure categories presented in chapter 2 of this volume. It should then be possible to examine the extent to which a liberalized international insurance trading system could exacerbate market failures, and whether some further governmental action, such as harmonization, might permit liberalization to move forward. The underlying premise, of course, is that a liberalized international insurance market is desirable.

Market power. As White notes in chapter 2, market power can arise when a market has entry barriers and few sellers. Varying degrees of market power are found within insurance markets worldwide. Several countries have monopolistic markets (including China and India), and many others are oligopolistic (such as Japan and Korea). Explicit or implicit collusion has historically been common in many insurance markets internationally, especially as relates to pricing. So-called tariff markets—wherein all sellers charge the same price—remain common in many developing countries and for certain insurance lines in Austria, Germany, Switzerland, Japan, and other

185

FIGURE 5–11

MARKET CONCENTRATION INDICATORS FOR LIFE AND NONLIFE INSURERS, FOR SELECTED OECD COUNTRIES, 1989

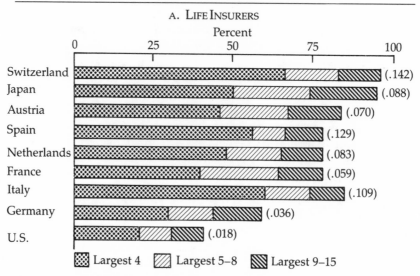

A. LIFE INSURERS

Percent

🔲 Largest 4   ⬜ Largest 5–8   ⬛ Largest 9–15

developed countries, although the EU single market program is minimizing the practice.

National tax regimes can lead to the creation of market power. Some countries assess higher premium taxes on the local business of foreign insurers than they do on the local business of domestic insurers. Such practices are analogous to trade tariffs and can be expected to have similarly adverse economic consequences.

Even when a national treatment standard is applied in insurer taxation, differences in national tax regimes can result in market power. Thus, if the United Kingdom taxes its insurers at a lower effective rate than France taxes its insurers, U.K. insurers doing business in France can enjoy a tax-related competitive advantage over French insurers. The issue of how best to deal with such situations is of critical importance but remains unresolved.

Concentration within markets varies from low (as in the United States) to high (as in Japan). Figure 5–11 compares fifteen-firm concentration ratios and Herfindahl indexes within selected OECD insurance markets for both life and nonlife insurance. Some insurance markets worldwide are witnessing a trend toward less concentration, thanks to increasing national and international competition. Other markets seem to be moving toward greater concentration, primarily through mergers and acquisitions.

FIGURE 5–11 (continued)

B. NONLIFE INSURERS

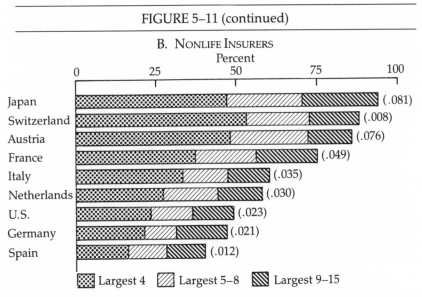

SOURCE: Swiss Reinsurance Co. (1992).

Market power in insurance arises also from structural impediments to entry. Examples include the Japanese *keiretsu* system, extensive cross-shareholdings within Germany, and the lack of independent distribution systems within several markets.

National licensing requirements are entry barriers. Licensing requirements include minimum capitalization and fitness qualifications and, in some jurisdictions, detailed operating plans. Some countries will not grant a new license unless a market need to do so is established. Other governments will not grant new licenses under any circumstances.[32] Transparency in the licensing process is less than desired in many markets, with numerous unwritten rules. Indeed, one of the U.S. insurance industry's most vociferous complaints in the 1994 United States-Japan Framework Agreement negotiations dealt with the Japanese market's alleged lack of transparency.

Within the United States, insurance is regulated primarily by the individual states, and an insurer wishing to be licensed throughout the United States must obtain a separate license from each state. This licensing process itself is believed by some observers, including the European Commission, to constitute a barrier to entry.[33] Studies of

---

32. See OECD (1983), Skipper (1987), and Carter and Dickinson (1992).
33. European Commission (1992).

the U.S. insurance market nonetheless find few meaningful economic[34] or regulatory[35] entry barriers.

Economies of scale. Increasing returns to scale over an industry's relevant output range can be expected, of course, to give rise to a natural monopoly. This market failure is considered to require detailed government intervention.

Studies on insurance scale economies generally find increasing returns to scale for smaller firms and either constant or modestly increasing returns for larger firms.[36] No compelling empirical evidence exists of a tendency toward a natural monopoly. Market observation supports this view, as competitive markets seem to be able to support a range of insurer sizes. Even relatively small insurers compete successfully with larger firms, either as careful niche players or through exploitation of technology. With market widening and deepening, there should arguably be even less concern about market failures because of scale economies.[37]

Externality effects. Examples of both negative and positive externalities can be identified in insurance. Perhaps the most significant negative insurance-related externality is the deliberate destruction of property and the occasional murder that occur in order to collect insurance proceeds. From 5 to 15 percent of all nonlife insurance claims in many markets are believed to involve fraud. Such destruction represents a dead-weight loss to society that is a "cost" associated with insurance.[38]

Governments have had a long-standing, understandable preoccupation with systemic risks—created by negative externalities—in the banking and securities sectors. Systemic risks exist if the difficulties of financial intermediaries could cause meaningful disruptions elsewhere within an economy. Earlier in this volume, Dermine (chapter 3) and White (chapter 2) note two types of systemic risk. The first—dubbed *cascading failures*, or a *domino effect*—exists if the failure of one financial institution is the proximate cause of the failure of

34. See Grace and Barth (1993) and Cummins and Weiss (1991).

35. Skipper and Gardner (1992).

36. For recent studies of life insurance, see Keller and Mathewson (1988), Grace and Timme (1992), and Gardner (1992). For recent studies on nonlife insurance, see Suret (1991) and Weiss (1991).

37. Economies of scope across financial services also could give rise to market failures. Little is known about the economies of joint production of insurance and banking services.

38. See D'Arcy (1994) for a more complete discussion of these and other insurance-related costs to society.

others. This can occur when one bank defaults on its short-term credit obligations to other banks, thus precipitating other firm failures—ultimately causing harm to the "real" economy.

The second type of systemic risk is that of depositor runs—caused by the real or imagined fear of bank insolvency. The failure of one or more banks can then precipitate depositor runs on otherwise solvent banks, causing their failure. Similar runs in securities markets can lead to crashes, as happened in 1929.

The potential for cascading failures exists in insurance, at least in theory, through reinsurance. Some reinsurer failures have led to direct-insurer failures, but these instances are rare and economic effects limited and isolated. The failures have been related to diversifiable risks only; in other words, they were not caused by catastrophic (nondiversifiable) events. They have been within the nonlife branch only. The prevention of such cascading failures is within management control through careful selection of reinsurers.

A potential also exists for cascading failures through reinsurance of nondiversifiable risks. Massive insured losses caused by particularly severe earthquakes or hurricanes, significant global warming, terrorist or accidental detonation of nuclear devices, or a host of other catastrophic events could rip through direct insurers' and reinsurers' surpluses to such an extent as to cause widespread failures. The resulting loss of capacity could imperil the viability of the real economy. This theoretical possibility is believed by most observers to be remote, but it cannot be dismissed outright.

Runs have occurred in the insurance industry, but only within the life branch. Policyholders of the two largest U.S. life insurer failures—Executive Life and Mutual Benefit Life—initiated runs, as have policyholders of smaller failed insurers. To date, runs on life insurers have not been the cause of the failure of sound insurers. The possibility of such contagion effects exists, however, and with the continued move by life insurers to offer bank-like products, the risk should not be ignored.

Runs have not occurred with nonlife insurance. These products have no savings component and are easily replaced. Therefore, it appears that the insurance industry has only minimal exposure to systemic risks—unlike the situation with banks and securities firms.[39]

39. Harrington and Niehaus (1992) found no evidence through life insurer share prices of contagion effects in connection with three major 1991 life company failures. Fields et al. (1994), however, found a statistically significant, although modest (2.1 percent), decline in market value associated with Executive Life's $466 million loss announcement, which occurred eight days prior to its seizure by the California insurance department.

Positive externalities possibly exist to some degree in insurance. Historically, for example, insurers have only rarely sought protection under intellectual property law for their product, processing, or service innovations.[40] As a consequence, a tendency may exist for firms to engage in less such development than they would otherwise.

Public goods. It is not clear that extensive public goods exist in insurance, that is, insurance services whose positive externalities are substantial and pervasive. Certain insurer loss prevention and reduction activities might constitute a public good to the extent that spillovers inure to the public. For example, an insurer-induced disaster recovery plan for an important firm (such as a city's water purification plant, or an electrical generating facility) may be a public good.

Some governments apparently believe that important positive externalities attach to insurance by its very nature. Thus, substantial and pervasive positive externalities may result from a domestic insurance industry's contributions to national security. For example, two large Arab insurance groups were said to have been created, in part, for national security reasons.[41]

Uncertainty and the absence of complete knowledge. Neither insurance buyers nor insurance sellers possess complete knowledge; hence, they face some uncertainty. Environmental factors—such as the economy, inflation, new laws and regulations, and changing consumer attitudes and preferences—present great uncertainty to both buyers and sellers, thus rendering decision-making suboptimal. These and like situations are addressed through actions such as diversification, creation of insolvency guaranty funds, and reliance on independent rating agencies.

Private insurers will not supply every type of insurance demanded by consumers. Such market failures occur when insurers cannot diversify the loss exposure. Thus, the private insurance mechanism generally offers limited or no unemployment, flood, or earthquake insurance or liability insurance in connection with nuclear-powered electrical generating facilities. In each instance, insurers

---

40. Foudree and Trzyna (1992) argue that substantial change is occurring in the extent to which insurers can and do use copyright, patent, misappropriation, trade secret, and trademark law to protect innovations.

41. UNCTAD (1982). Also, the London insurance and reinsurance market's suspension of transportation insurance on Argentine ships, aircraft, and cargo during the U.K.-Argentine Falkland Islands conflict was said to have "again demonstrated . . . the intimate links relating to insurance and reinsurance with the complete exercise of national sovereignty." Quoted in Skipper (1987).

perceive too much uncertainty occasioned by a change in the state of nature or state of the world.[42] If such exposures are to be insured, government itself or some government-subsidized private arrangement typically provides the insurance.

Asymmetric information. The problem of the seller possessing more knowledge than the buyer is perhaps the most critical market failure in insurance. Individuals and small businesses are not well equipped to evaluate and monitor the financial condition of insurance enterprises. Because insurance is a financial future-delivery product tied closely to the public interest, this particular information imbalance is judged by governments to warrant substantial insurer solvency oversight. The public, especially the ill informed, must be protected from abuse by the unscrupulous.

As discussed earlier, insurer solidity is a function of its net worth—assets less liabilities. The use of common accounting conventions is required to render financial statements comparable. Two consumer problems arise from these efforts. First, in many countries, including the United States, the required accounting conventions can mask the true financial condition of insurers through the use of historical cost, book value, amortized value, and other arbitrary valuations of assets and liabilities, rather than market value. Second, since each nation has its own accounting conventions, interpretation of financial statements by foreigners proves even more problematical. Both problems exacerbate consumer information difficulties, thus weakening market discipline.

The market has evolved some solutions to these consumer problems. Rating agencies monitor the insurer's financial condition, rendering opinions as to its solidity. Their services are widely used in the United States but less so in other countries. Also, insurance intermediaries, especially independent agents and brokers, provide their own evaluations of insurance solidity. The large brokerage firms are noted for the assistance provided to their customers in selecting sound insurers and monitoring their financial condition.

Information asymmetry problems arise with insurance products themselves. Insurance policies are complex legal documents whose language may not be understood by laypersons. Similarly, it can be

---

42. That is, a high positive correlation exists between individual loss exposures, giving rise to background risk. See Schlesinger and Doherty (1985) and Doherty and Dionnne (1987). In addition, consumers are not always willing to pay the premium even if such insurance were available: for example, the private cost to insurers may exceed the perceived private benefit to consumers. See Anderson (1974) and Kunreuther et al. (1978).

difficult for the buyer to distinguish a "good" from a "poor" policy, especially in life insurance, because of the complexities of policy illustrations. These problems are much less prominent for sophisticated insurance purchasers.

Government responses to these problems have ranged from prohibiting the use of misleading policy terms, to requiring that policies be written in simplified language, to mandating certain policy wording. Additionally, certain cost and policy disclosures may be required during the sales process, especially in life insurance.

Of course, the insurance buyer is often better informed than the seller with respect to other issues. Adverse selection and moral hazard problems exist for insurers. Thus, insurance applicants—being more knowledgeable than the insurer about their own health—can use this information to secure deals that are in their best interests and against the interests of the insurer (adverse selection). Also, because insureds may have a reduced incentive to engage in loss prevention, claims will be higher than otherwise (moral hazard).

A central purpose of insurance companies' underwriting and claims-settling processes is to minimize instances of adverse selection and moral hazard. Additionally, the extreme versions of these problems are addressed through laws that limit an insured's recovery under policies that were procured through misrepresentation or where the insured purposefully caused the loss. Mere carelessness is ordinarily covered.

Individuals who are unable to know their own best interests. The "widows and orphans" problem is believed to exist in insurance. The premise of social insurance programs is that individuals will not or cannot make adequate arrangements for their own financial security, so government must force them to do so. Laws requiring the purchase of automobile liability and no-fault insurance are grounded in similar logic.

Other examples exist in insurance. Some insurance products (pure endowments) and provisions of insurance products (warranties) are deemed to be subject to such marketplace abuse that their use is banned. The premise is that consumers are incapable of looking after their own interests.

Problems of second best. Problems of second best do not seem prevalent in most insurance markets. Some developing countries may contend that an exception flows from the "infant industry" protection argument. Developing countries often erect entry barriers to foreign insurance in order to promote their domestic insurance industries. The domestic industry is sheltered to minimize foreign exchange outflow, to promote domestic employment, to encourage local saving, to achieve balanced economic development, or to enhance national sovereignty.[43] Irrespective of the goal and its validity, in perhaps every instance more efficient means of accomplishing the goal exist than erecting trade barriers in insurance. In this sense, therefore, infant industry protection may represent a second-best solution.

The Nature of Government Intervention into Insurance Markets. In chapter 2, White lists three categories of regulation: economic, health-safety-environmental, and information. Each type is found in varying degrees within all insurance markets, as the following discussion highlights.

Economic regulation. Nearly all governments intervene economically in their insurance markets. Economic regulation of insurance addresses market power concerns generally and economies of scale concerns specifically. Insurers or certain lines of insurance are treated similarly to public utilities in some markets, where profit and product standards may be strictly regulated. Such strict regulation, often associated with capture, is intended to avoid "destructive competition" or to create an "orderly market." It does not flow from concerns about monopoly power.

Expense and commission limitations exist in some markets. Many governments exercise control over insurance prices. In some markets, the government itself or a government-sanctioned cartel sets prices that all insurers charge. In this way regulation creates market power. At the other extreme, insurers in other markets or in some lines are completely free to set prices as they deem appropriate. Variations exist between these two extremes. In many markets, collusive price-setting is illegal, although the practice of sharing loss statistics is permitted.

The government may determine that it should be a supplier of insurance where the market has failed to provide it. Thus, as noted earlier, the government may provide insurance coverage for damage caused by floods, earthquakes, crime, or nuclear liability. Governments also usually apply competition (antitrust) law to insurance to limit undue concentrations of power through merger, acquisition, and other activities that restrain competition unduly. Competition law also establishes rules against abuse of dominant position and against collusive practices. Such laws are examples of economic regu-

---

43. See Skipper (1987) and Carter and Dickinson (1992) for a discussion of these and other rationales.

lation, and they generally apply equally to domestic and foreign insurers.

Finally, some governments assert macroeconomic justifications for their actions. Thus, some countries purposely erect barriers to foreign-firm market entry to promote their local insurance industry (infant industry argument).

Health-Safety-Environment regulation. H-S-E regulation is prominent in insurance, primarily because of potentially severe information problems. Elaborate market access rules exist in every major national market and are justified because of consumer ignorance about insurer solvency. Thus, an insurer wishing to conduct business within a country must first obtain a license.

In many countries, citizens may not purchase insurance from unlicensed insurers, and intermediaries may not sell insurance for unlicensed insurers. Advertising restrictions often apply to unlicensed insurers. If a citizen nonetheless purchases insurance from such a nonadmitted insurer, tax concessions may be denied the insured or the contract may be unenforceable in local courts. Governments thus attempt to minimize the chances that their citizens deal with financially unsound insurers.

To become licensed, a foreign insurer must usually establish a local presence as an agency, branch office, or subsidiary. In some countries, the only means of market access for a foreign insurer is to create a locally incorporated subsidiary, often with majority local ownership.

In other markets, various degrees of cross-border insurance trade are permitted. For example, in the United States, nonlife insurance may be placed by a broker with an unlicensed (domestic or foreign) insurer if licensed insurers refuse to provide requested coverage. In the United Kingdom, no such rule exists for the insurance to be placed with an unlicensed insurer.

To obtain and retain a license, an insurer must meet the country's minimum capital and surplus requirements and possibly meet certain fitness stipulations. National treatment is the rule in some markets, although direct and indirect discrimination against foreign interests is not uncommon.[44] Continuing prudential oversight involves mandatory periodic financial reporting to the regulator by licensed insurers, usually in a prescribed format using mandated (or generally accepted) accounting standards.

Investments are usually subject to qualitative and quantitative

---

44. See Carter and Dickinson (1992).

restrictions, and guidelines for valuing liabilities are laid down. Most countries require that the overwhelming majority of assets backing the policy reserves of a domestic subsidiary or branch of a foreign concern be invested locally. Some countries also require a localization of reserves on cross-border reinsurance. Periodic, on-site financial examinations of licensed insurers are common. These examinations are intended to verify the accuracy of reported information and to investigate insurer financial solidity and performance.[45]

Both market access and national treatment difficulties encountered by foreign insurance concerns are often justified on grounds of H-S-E-type consumer protection. Strict national treatment, however, may lead to market access difficulties. The Japanese system of strict regulation of product prices and structure applies equally to domestic and to foreign undertakings. U.S. firms believe that they are penalized through such regulation, as their many product innovations cannot be easily introduced into the Japanese market.

Consumer protection (H-S-E) considerations extend to minimizing loss to insureds from insolvent insurers. Regulators often exert heroic efforts to avoid consumer harm by trying to arrange mergers, acquisitions, industrywide salvage activities, or other actions with respect to insolvent insurers.

Several countries have insolvency guaranty funds. Such funds may involve relatively modest (as in the EU) or generous (as in the United States) indemnity limits. The insured may be fully indemnified up to maximum amount (United States), or some loss-sharing by the insured may be included (United Kingdom). The fund may be government-run (some EU countries) or operated and financed by the insurance industry (Canada).

Guaranty funds diminish market discipline. If buyers know that they will be made whole in the event of an insolvency, they have less incentive to investigate and monitor solvency. Also, if no distinction for insurer riskiness is made in the guaranty-fund assessment mechanism, the opportunity for moral hazard by firms is enhanced, thus further weakening market discipline.

Guaranty funds in insurance are rationalized on the basis of consumer information asymmetry problems. They are rationalized in banking more because of systemic risk concerns.

Information regulation. The mandatory disclosure of product and other information is common in insurance markets worldwide. The

---

45. See OECD (1993a) for a more complete discussion of solvency regulation within OECD countries and OECD (1988) for a survey of member country supervision.

primary purpose of information regulation in insurance is to rectify consumer information asymmetry problems. Disclosure of financial statements to national insurance supervisors is universal. In many countries (including Germany and Switzerland), however, much of this information may be considered privileged and therefore not available to the insurance buying public. In other countries (including the United States and the United Kingdom), such financial information is largely available for public scrutiny.

Limited mandatory disclosure to consumers may be required in personal lines of nonlife insurance. More extensive disclosure is typically required with individual life insurance and annuity products. This disclosure usually includes price and product information.

Information regulation also includes limitations on information disclosure. Thus, it is illegal for insurers or their agents to make inaccurate or incomplete statements if the effect is to mislead consumers. In many markets, competitors may not denigrate each other in any way.

A Synopsis and Comparison. It can be seen from the preceding discussion that the intensity of regulatory oversight varies from market to market. In all markets, oversight is greatest for insurance purchased by individuals and, within this category, still more intense with insurance closely linked to public policy. The more informed the purchaser, the lighter the oversight. The following schematic illustrates this relationship:

Insurance Type	Degree of Regulatory Oversight
Personal auto	*Great*
Personal life and health	
Homeowners'	↑
Group life and health	
Small business	
Commercial and industrial	
Aviation and marine	
Reinsurance	*Slight/None*

Also, as can be gleaned from the preceding discussion, insurance regulators and banking regulators share similar concerns, especially regarding institutional solvency. Key differences also exist. Bank regulators are more concerned with macroeconomic issues and with financial system integrity than are insurance regulators.[46] Insurance

---

46. See OECD (1993b).

regulators, however, are far more concerned with product and marketing issues than are banking regulators. The chart below illustrates this difference in emphasis.

Degree of Regulatory Concern

	Insurance	Banking
Prudential considerations	+ + +	+ + +
Product and marketing issues	+ + +	+
Macroeconomic issues/system stability	+	+ + +

These differences may continue to diminish with financial services integration. At present, however, they are important and should be considered in the harmonization versus competition debate.

Is Regulatory Harmonization Necessary for Insurance Liberalization?

The market-economy model continues to be embraced worldwide. The linchpin of this model, of course, is that competitive markets are most efficient at allocating resources and at optimizing consumer choice and value. As such, moves to render markets more competitive—such as liberalization—are to be encouraged, subject to reasonable safeguards for market failures.

As the market-economy model was winning the political battle of economic systems, gains in transportation, information, and communication technology have driven the internationalization of financial services. With increasing international penetration of domestic insurance and other financial services markets, national regulators have experienced difficulties in ensuring that consumers are appropriately protected. The overriding policy issue concerns how governments should respond to this evolution.

Regulatory harmonization is initially a most appealing response. This chapter's central issue, therefore, may be stated as follows: Is regulatory harmonization a necessary condition precedent for a liberalized international market in insurance?

Drawing on information presented in the earlier sections, this section presents the arguments for and against harmonization. It also details recent harmonization experiences. Before embarking on this discussion, however, the meanings of certain key terms must be clear.

The meaning of liberalization. In general, liberalization denotes a reduction of government or other barriers to economic activity. As used in this study, liberalization connotes a diminution in government or other barriers to market access by foreigners. Questions then center on whether access should be on a most-favored-nation basis and on the definition of access.

As noted earlier, access can be via cross-border trade or establishment. The most liberal approach is to permit foreign undertakings to determine their own mode of access.

If access is via establishment, then the national treatment principle would ordinarily be considered the most liberal. If access is cross-border, the most liberal approach is mutual regulatory recognition, with complete freedom for foreign suppliers to solicit domestic customers and for domestic customers to seek cover from foreign firms.

Most-favored-nation treatment requires that trade concessions extended to one country be extended to all trading partners: that is, that there be no favoritism among trading partners. National treatment requires that foreign firms receive no less favorable treatment than domestic firms in like circumstances.

Historically, reciprocity has played an important role in financial services establishment trade. Reciprocity means, in effect, that one country extends to another country's firms treatment that is equivalent to what the second country extends to the first country's firms. Conceptually, reciprocity can result in treatment more favorable than that of national treatment. Its application, however, more often results in less favorable treatment. So-called mirror-image reciprocity can be particularly trade restricting.

Outcomes from reciprocity-based liberalization are uncertain, largely because reciprocity is a negotiation, not an economic, concept. Reciprocity-based liberalization potentially requires industry-specific and country-specific analyses. Such analyses call for a substantial bureaucratic structure and a great potential for conflict with an accompanying need for dispute resolution mechanisms.

Figure 5–12 is a simplified schematic illustration of the above degrees of liberalization. Variations are possible within each level. For example, a greater degree of liberalization could be extended to well-informed buyers (such as industrial organizations) than to individuals.

Also, the conditions for cross-border market access can vary. Cross-border solicitation could be based on host-country licensing (and control) and national treatment, a less liberal approach, or on home-country control. Mutual recognition could form the basis for home-country control, with or without regulatory harmonization.

The meaning of harmonization. Regulatory harmonization can be forced by governments making their laws and regulations virtually

FIGURE 5–12

RELATIVE LEVELS OF INSURANCE MARKET LIBERALIZATION

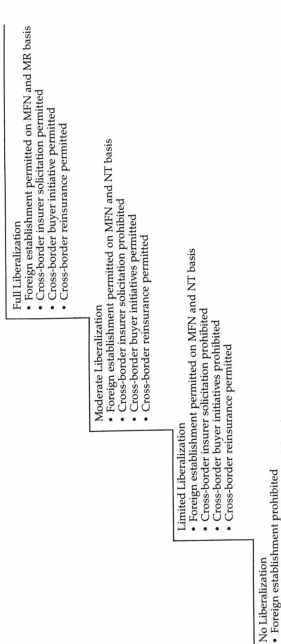

Full Liberalization
• Foreign establishment permitted on MFN and MR basis
• Cross-border insurer solicitation permitted
• Cross-border buyer initiative permitted
• Cross-border reinsurance permitted

Moderate Liberalization
• Foreign establishment permitted on MFN and NT basis
• Cross-border insurer solicitation prohibited
• Cross-border buyer initiatives permitted
• Cross-border reinsurance permitted

Limited Liberalization
• Foreign establishment permitted on MFN and NT basis
• Cross-border insurer solicitation prohibited
• Cross-border buyer initiatives prohibited
• Cross-border reinsurance permitted

No Liberalization
• Foreign establishment prohibited
• Cross-border insurer solicitation prohibited
• Cross-border buyer initiatives prohibited
• Cross-border reinsurance restricted

SOURCE: Author.

identical, or harmonization can evolve by disparate market participants cajoling their governments to seek common regulatory approaches. Harmonization could be de jure, with relevant countries'
laws and regulations being mirror images of each other, or it could be
de facto, with laws and regulations being, in substance, equivalent to
each other, but without being identical. In either instance, the quality
and nature of enforcement are as critical as the laws and regulations
themselves.

Harmonization could take place across all elements of regulation
(complete harmonization) or across selected elements only (minimum
harmonization). With minimum harmonization, the question arises
as to which regulatory elements should be included.

Deregulation and liberalization. Deregulation connotes a lessening
of national regulation. Liberalization connotes market opening. Deregulation and liberalization efforts may move in parallel as a government places greater reliance on market forces, but there is no inherent
reason for them to do so. In fact, liberalization efforts may dictate the
need for additional, not reduced, regulation.

Arguments in Favor of Harmonization. The arguments in favor of
insurance regulatory harmonization are no different conceptually
from those for regulatory harmonization in other financial services.
As noted in chapter 2, harmonization may be justified where regulatory diversity magnifies market failures or impedes liberalization, or
where it can reduce transaction costs. Divergent regulatory approaches cause few difficulties when financial services markets are
insulated from each other and largely national in character. The continued internationalization of financial services, however, could be
impeded by regulatory diversity. Moreover, it is possible that internationalization could magnify the negative effects of market failures,
thus undermining national regulatory effectiveness. Is it reasonable
to expect individual countries to exercise complete regulatory control
today over the financial service activities within their borders?

Magnification of market failures. In addition to the liberalization and
internationalization trends, we are also witnessing a trend toward
financial services deregulation. These three trends are expected to
stimulate competition and thereby create incentives for innovation
and enhanced efficiency. At the same time, pressure increases on
market suppliers to merge or to enter into various forms of cooperative arrangements. Such actions can lead to anticompetitive behavior,
thus nullifying hoped-for efficiency gains. Figure 5–13 illustrates this
chain.

FIGURE 5–13

The Case for Strengthened Competition Regulation

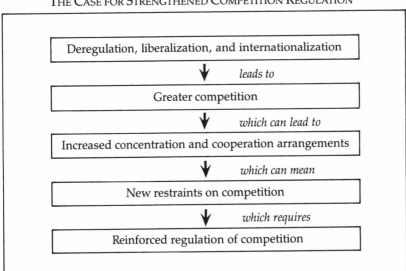

Source: Author.

Competition law is intended to prevent these types of market-power abuses. All countries and the EU have such laws, although their scope and enforcement vary.[47] Variability has led to jurisdictional conflict and, with increasing globalization, can be expected to lead to more frequent conflict and possibly to gaps in enforcement. Harmonization of insurance antitrust laws and regulations could minimize conflicts and fill gaps, thus leading to more competitive markets.

With increasing internationalization, foreign insurers arguably could more easily avoid regulation designed to protect consumers against unfair marketing practices and products and to ensure adequate information disclosure to consumers. Harmonization of essential marketing and disclosure regulation could nullify such attempts.

Also, it has been argued that without harmonization, regulatory arbitrage will lead to a regulatory "race to the bottom," as insurers locate in or move to less intrusive (costly) regulatory jurisdictions. This argument seems as applicable to insurance as to any other financial service.

---

47. See Swiss Reinsurance Company (1992) for a discussion of the different approaches to such oversight.

Impediments to liberalization. The failure to harmonize at least essential regulation could lead to greater protectionism. Governments may legitimately perceive a need for more stringent domestic trade-related regulation as they respond to the potential for more severe market failures brought on by internationalization. Regulatory harmonization, therefore, could not only check the need for such protectionistic actions, but could lead to an absolute decrease in trade-restricting insurance regulation.

Another increasingly prevalent problem for which harmonization may be a solution relates to so-called cross-border insurer insolvencies, which involve insureds in a jurisdiction different from that of the insurer. This situation might arise through cross-border trade in insurance or where an agency or a branch of the insurer operates in a foreign jurisdiction.

No internationally accepted rules exist for dealing with cross-border insolvencies of financial services firms, and with the exception of the EU, no multilateral and few bilateral agreements exist.[48] The insolvency of an international insurer can lead to enormously complex legal issues and will almost certainly involve a conflict of laws. The harmonization of insurer liquidation and rehabilitation laws could lead to greater reliance on national laws, which could permit a greater degree of liberalization.

Finally, besides purely economic arguments for liberalization via harmonization, there may be even more persuasive political arguments for harmonization. Cross-border trade in financial services can give rise to concerns by domestic firms that they are at a competitive disadvantage with foreign firms. Capitalization requirements or taxation may be lower for foreign insurers than for domestic insurers. Foreign insurers may use excessive profits derived from their cartel-controlled domestic market or from a lower cost of capital to afford their foreign operations a competitive advantage vis-à-vis domestic firms' operations.

That is, the fair-trade evils of subsidies and dumping could be invoked in support of pleas for a level playing field. Never mind that few economists would agree as to the need or even desirability to level the playing field in this way. Local politicians routinely agree. The result may be protectionism in the name of fair trade. Harmonization arguably could minimize the chances of such protectionism by creating the appearance of a level playing field. It has been argued that the Basel Accord establishing minimum capital requirements for certain banks was and remains more of a political than an economic

---

48. See Fletcher (1993), Player (1993), and Schwab et al. (1991).

necessity.[49] Regulatory harmonization may be a desirable defensive palliative.

Increased transactional costs. Insurers incur additional costs in monitoring and complying with diverse national regulations. Differing policy language and readability requirements sometimes necessitate separate policy forms and applications for each jurisdiction. Local marketing and claim settlement standards vary by jurisdiction. Different financial statements may have to be maintained for each jurisdiction in which the insurer wishes to be licensed. All these and a host of other differing requirements add to insurer operational costs and thereby lead to higher prices.[50] Harmonization could reduce these costs.

Arguments against Harmonization. The issue here is less whether harmonization should be avoided and more whether alternative means of fostering competition would be more effective. Perhaps the central argument for avoiding regulatory harmonization is that it could stifle competition by hindering regulatory innovation that competition among different regulatory philosophies and approaches would bring.

Financial services are regulation intensive. As a result, a nation's regulations are an important element in determining whether the country has a comparative advantage in a particular financial service. States that develop the best rules offer their firms a competitive advantage in international competition. If one country's approach to addressing a particular market failure proves superior to other countries' approaches, other countries have but to adopt the superior approach. If multiple approaches to addressing the particular market failure prove equally effective, then countries may comfortably continue their efforts, without the need for time-consuming regulatory changes and the risks of "getting it wrong." In this way, necessary regulatory harmonization could evolve from market forces, not from governmental edicts.[51] If there appears to be no gain from harmonization, unproductive effort and risk are thereby avoided.

---

49. See chapter 3.

50. Insurers operating throughout the United States routinely complain about the additional costs they incur to comply with each state's peculiar laws and regulations. It has been argued that such diversity handicaps U.S. insurers in international competition. See Skipper (1993).

51. Of course, adoption of such an approach does not answer the critically important question of how one would proceed from market forces to government action where action is justified by market forces. More research is needed on this point.

As for the regulatory arbitrage concern, it may be more apparent than real. It is true that insurers and especially reinsurers have been established in offshore regulatory havens. Many of these are captive insurers that do not pose significant consumer-protection problems. The failure of some offshore reinsurers, however, has led to difficulties for some domestic insurers. In each instance, the domestic insurer failed to utilize reasonable management judgment or was a victim of fraud, sometimes by its owners or managers.[52] As for poor judgment, no amount of regulation can prevent management stupidity, and no reason exists to believe that management actions would have been less egregious or have had fewer adverse consequences had the stupidity involved domestic reinsurance only. As for fraud by owners or managers, there is no evidence that regulators or auditors would have detected it any sooner had it been perpetrated exclusively by locals.

In neither of the above situations is it obvious that regulatory harmonization would have played any constructive deterrent or enforcement role. The problem lies in failures by management and by the domestic regulator, not with diverse regulation.

Moreover, insurers have natural motivations to locate in strong regulatory jurisdictions. Insurers sell security. An insurer can offer its insureds no greater security than that which it possesses itself. The financially sound insurer wishes to tout its soundness as a competitive advantage. Such insurers (and reinsurers) are interested in regulation that validates their soundness, not that calls it into question. The sanction of a regulator known to be lax is of no or even of negative market value. Thus, it is far from obvious that a regulatory race to the bottom would materialize.

A possible exception exists in lines of insurance where the insured cares little about the insurer's financial solidity. A lack of caring may stem from a belief—rightly or wrongly—that insolvency guaranty funds would make good any consumer loss or from failure to know how to assess an insurer's solidity. One or both of these conditions would more likely arise with certain personal lines of insurance, such as automobile or homeowners insurance. In instances such as these, a race to the bottom is conceivable, although techniques other than harmonization arguably could prevent such.

A further problem with government-driven as opposed to market-driven harmonization is that governments may harmonize the wrong elements or harmonize at the wrong levels.[53] Harmonizing the

---

52. See *Failed Promises* (1990).

53. The qwerty typewriter keyboard is often cited as an example of standardization (harmonization) at the wrong level. See David (1985).

wrong regulatory elements would needlessly increase transactional costs and decrease market efficiency. Trade in some insurance lines—such as reinsurance, transportation insurance, and industrial insurance—already functions smoothly within a relatively liberalized international setting, without regulatory harmonization. Market-driven harmonization has worked well. There is no evidence that government-driven harmonization is desirable for such lines.

Harmonizing at the wrong level could create entry barriers (for example, by setting capital requirements too high) or expose buyers to unacceptable risks (by setting capital requirements too low). In other words, the chances and resultant negative consequences of government failure may present too great a risk.

In addition, great diversity exists internationally in legal traditions, culture, social philosophy, language, level of economic development, and regulatory sophistication. Even if negotiations were limited to countries of similar levels of development and philosophy, the odds of achieving agreement on even minimum standards for harmonization appear small.

The most critical element of consumer protection and most logical target for harmonization relates to prudential regulation in insurance, the most important component of which relates to insurer capital. The harmonization of minimum capital requirements would require that participating governments agree to a minimum capital standard that relied either on some broad procedure for defining capital, with each nation using its own definition, or on a specific procedure set forth in the harmonization accord. In the first instance, a risk exists that governments would cheat or at least interpret national laws to the maximum benefit of domestic insurers.

An insurer's capital (and surplus) is the simple difference between its assets and its liabilities. Each country's insurance accounting conventions (and, hence, definitions of assets and liabilities) are different, often substantially so. Thus, a U.S. insurer, a U.K. insurer, and a German insurer may be identical in terms of actual assets, liabilities, and policies in force, yet because of national accounting differences may appear to have vastly different capital levels. Such a situation arguably is unsatisfactory. In fact, one might legitimately question whether such an unstructured approach even rises to the level of harmonization.

The second approach—that of agreeing on relevant definitions and procedures—would seem to require, first, some reasonable degree of standardization in insurance accounting principles. No serious effort is underway to accomplish this ambitious goal. In any event, the effort is highly unlikely to evolve separately from the broad issue of international accounting harmonization.

This second approach presumably would also require some entity to determine whether signatory nations were in compliance and remain so. A dispute resolution mechanism would also seem desirable. Whether governments would cede sovereignty to any such supranational entity seems doubtful.

One of the most compelling arguments for harmonization of banking capital requirements relates to the need to "strengthen the stability of the international banking system"—in other words, because of systematic risk concerns.[54] There is not a parallel need to "strengthen the stability of the international insurance system." Systemic risks, at present, are minimal in insurance.[55]

Even if governments reached an agreement and "got it right," with harmonization including the appropriate elements at the right levels, there is no assurance—and for some areas, there is considerable doubt—that harmonization could lead to greater efficiency. For one thing, harmonization of laws and regulation does not necessarily lead to equivalent enforcement or interpretation. The harmonization police no doubt would be busy. For another, government reaction routinely lags behind market developments. With the ever-increasing pace of change, the question must be asked whether it is reasonable to expect a set of regulatory harmonization parameters negotiated by governments ever to be timely.[56]

Finally, regulatory harmonization does not necessarily deal with the problem of conflict of laws and of differing tax regimes. French insureds and creditors of an insolvent French insurer will probably continue to enjoy priority over Canadian insureds and creditors of that insurer. And foreign insurers selling insurance in Illinois will continue to have to pay higher taxes on their Illinois income than will Illinois domestic insurers. In each instance, the issue revolves around the inferior treatment of foreign citizens and firms vis-à-vis that of domestic firms and citizens. Cross-border insurance trade accompanied by (harmonized) home-country control does not ensure equality.

---

54. Cooke (1990).

55. Of course, with increasing convergence, this situation could change.

56. A further problem can occur when certain aspects of (harmonized) regulation become obsolete and need to be updated. Portions of a regulated industry may derive market power under the obsolete standard or oppose it because of high switching costs, which new entrants could avoid. The social costs of such "excess inertia" could be magnified through harmonization. See Farrell and Soloner (1985).

Recent Insurance Harmonization Experiences. As alluded to earlier, the international insurance community has no equivalent to the banking community's Basel Accord. This result should not be surprising, given the less prominent role of insurance in international finance and national monetary control. The world economy has not faced insurance crises of the types that have pushed central bankers to work more closely with their international counterparts. The tradition of regulatory consultation and cooperation found among national banking regulators of the G10 finds no counterpart in insurance. Moreover, bankers are generally far more international than insurers—probably two decades ahead of their insurance counterparts.

This situation is changing, although not with the intensity found in banking or securities. The most recent effort at cooperation is a 1993 agreement among representatives of more than fifty governments to create an International Association of Insurance Supervisors (IAIS). The IAIS is to be a purely deliberative body. Concrete efforts at insurance regulatory harmonization, however, can be found from the experiences of the EU, the OECD, and the United States. Each is discussed below.

The EU harmonization experience. The completion of the Single European Market in insurance relies on liberalization to promote competition. The first step was the adoption in 1964 of the Reinsurance Directive that provided for freedom of establishment and of cross-border trade in reinsurance. The First Nonlife Insurance Directive, adopted in 1973, and the First Life Directive, adopted in 1979, laid the foundation for rights of establishment in direct insurance within the EU. These directives had little impact on integration and competition, as national insurance regulation by most EU member states remained highly restrictive.[57]

Until 1985 the European Commission believed that complete harmonization was a necessary precondition for liberalization. Years of debate and frustration as to how to achieve this ambitious goal gave way in 1985, with the adoption of the EC White Paper's concept of minimum harmonization of only essential legal provisions.

Through minimum harmonization, the EU is establishing common regulatory standards considered essential to protect the public interest and to create a level playing field. Minimum harmonization of the tax regimes has not been achieved, nor is the prospect bright for such to be realized in the near term. The most important area

---

57. Kollias (1991).

FIGURE 5–14
THE EU CHAIN APPROACH TO LIBERALIZATION

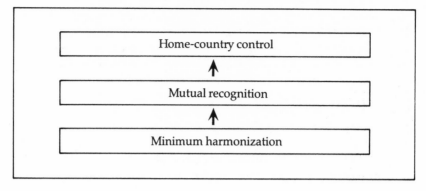

SOURCE: Author.

of insurance harmonization relates to prudential standards, wherein minimum requirements are laid down for technical reserves, solvency margins, and guarantee funds.

Technical reserve standards relate to the calculation of life and nonlife insurer technical reserves (liabilities), the permissible classes of assets to back technical reserves, asset valuation principles, and quantitative asset limitations. Solvency margin standards relate to the calculation of the minimum amount of free surplus that insurers must maintain as a function of premiums written, claims incurred, or reserves. The requirements also involve types of assets qualified to back the solvency margin. Finally, insurers are to maintain guarantee funds of at least certain minimum levels. Guarantee funds, in EU terminology, correspond to minimum capital and surplus requirements in the United States and have no relationship to the U.S. concept of insolvency guaranty funds.

The EU relies on competition among national regulatory systems to coordinate nonharmonized aspects of the integration process. The idea is that over the longer term, regulatory convergence will take place as market forces compel member states to adjust their regulations and tax systems to those of the most efficient system.

The EU concept of minimum harmonization permits mutual recognition of regulatory regimes and thereby home-country control, as illustrated in figure 5–14. A two-stage liberalization approach has been followed, involving the second and third generation insurance directives. The Second Nonlife and Life Directives, promulgated in 1988 and 1990 respectively, were to liberalize cross-border trade in certain insurance services. For nonlife insurance, more sophisticated, large industrial, and commercial risks (large risks) could be insured on a services (cross-border) basis, with home-country control applying. Insurance purchased by less sophisticated, small customers (mass risks) remained under host-country control. For life insurance, home-country control applied only for cross-border insurance sought at the buyer's own initiative. Otherwise, host-country control applied.

The Third Nonlife and Life Framework Directives, both promulgated in 1992, are intended to complete the single market in insurance. They provide for complete freedom of virtually all cross-border trade in insurance and for home-country control.

The EU experience, while insightful and interesting, is unique. The objective was to create a single integrated market in financial services. Liberalization is the understandable vehicle for doing so. Minimum harmonization is arguably necessary to create such a market. The objective was not liberalization, per se, yet the effects of liberalization are evident, as isolated national markets give way to EU-wide integrated markets. New products and lower prices are emerging. Mergers, acquisitions, and bank-insurer links are now common.

The EU experience illustrates the enormous complexity of achieving even minimal harmonization under what must be considered quite favorable conditions—a small group of countries with geographical affinity, roughly equivalent levels of economic development, and a commitment to create a single market.

The OECD harmonization experience. The OECD policy framework for international trade in financial services, including insurance, relies on two instruments: the Code of Liberalization of Capital Movements and the Code of Liberalization of Current Invisible Operations. These codes, adopted by the OECD Council in 1961, legally bind the twenty-five OECD-member countries to permit foreign establishment and cross-border trade in services. A separate, nonbinding document, the National Treatment Instrument, prohibits discrimination against foreign-established suppliers.

Insurance regulatory harmonization had been the goal of the OECD Insurance Committee since its inception. The concept had been that harmonization would render the invisibles code more effective. During the 1960s and early 1970s, the committee developed and submitted to the Council of Ministers proposals for OECD members to adopt certain minimum solvency levels for life and nonlife insurers. The council never adopted these or other harmonization proposals submitted to it by the committee, apparently because of EU member concern.[58]

In 1970, the Committee on Capital Movements and Invisible Transactions (CMIT) noted that harmonization efforts were both difficult and time consuming. It recommended several changes in the insurance provisions of the invisibles code, the purposes of which were to render trade barriers more obvious. It also concluded that harmonization was not an indispensable prerequisite of liberalization; that some member countries already had liberalized, efficient insurance markets without benefit of harmonization; and that there was no evidence that harmonization would inevitably lead to liberalization.

The insurance committee disagreed with the CMIT's recommendations. The conflict apparently resulted in a mid-1970's decision that the insurance committee be relegated to the role of an information sharing group.[59]

The insurance committee has since been revived. Although some discussion about regulatory harmonization continues, the committee no longer focuses on the issue; instead it seeks to promote liberalization irrespective of harmonization.

The OECD's insurance harmonization efforts have largely been abandoned as unnecessary for liberalization. Had the early harmonization initiative of the insurance committee been successful, a degree of regulatory harmonization among some OECD-member countries might have been achieved. Given that countries can freely register derogations and reservations to OECD code responsibilities and that no enforcement mechanism exists under the codes, it is questionable whether the practical effects would have been meaningful.

The U.S. harmonization experience. The U.S. system of insurance regulation is decentralized. As such, its harmonization experience may provide insights. In addition, U.S. free trade agreements, which include insurance, are of interest.

1. Insurance regulation. The United States has always relied on a state system of insurance oversight. Efforts at regulatory coordination and cooperation began formally in 1871 with the establishment of what was to become the National Association of Insurance Commissioners (NAIC). One of the NAIC's historical objectives has been to harmonize certain aspects of insurance regulation.

The NAIC, through a system of committees, develops so-called model laws and regulations intended to address perceived problems.

---

58. Shelp (1981).
59. Ibid.

The hope is that states will pattern their insurance laws and regulations after the models, thus minimizing regulatory differences.

The NAIC has been successful in some areas, such as in establishing common accounting and financial reporting standards, as well as asset-and-liability valuation requirements, among the states. In general, a type of modified home-state solvency oversight applies, but only after the insurer becomes licensed by the host state.[60]

Perhaps the most significant recent NAIC harmonization effort is the State Accreditation Program. Its intent is to ensure that states have at least certain basic prudential regulatory components in place. Nonaccredited states' financial examinations are not to be recognized by accredited states. Second examinations by an examiner from an accredited state are required for an insurer to maintain its license in accredited states. The U.S. General Accounting Office contends that several weaknesses exist with the NAIC accreditation program.[61]

The NAIC accreditation program is in the nature of minimum harmonization, somewhat akin to that of the EU. Unlike the EU program, however, the NAIC is not now moving toward a single market with home-state control. An insurer wishing to sell insurance in all fifty states still must demonstrate that it meets each state's particular licensing requirements. There remains an implicit mistrust between state insurance regulators. If the accreditation program proves successful, it could form the basis for a system of mutual (license) recognition and genuine home-state control.

In one sense, the EU and the NAIC might be perceived as moving toward the same goal, using different approaches. The NAIC approach could be perceived as attempting to create a single (U.S.) market in insurance via confidence-building—first ensure that each state is up to the task (accreditation), then remove interstate barriers (licensing) to cross-border insurance services, with the confidence that the host state can rely on the home state for prudential oversight (mutual recognition).[62] The EU, with no accreditation program, is moving toward creation of a single (European) market in insurance via minimum harmonization that supports mutual recognition and therefore home-country control, so that cross-border trade barriers can be eliminated.

---

60. See Skipper (1993) for a discussion of the system details.

61. GAO (1993).

62. As of 1996, the NAIC had no official position and had taken no action on streamlining U.S. insurance licensing practices or laws, such as mutual recognition. Some observers, however, believe that some such action is inevitable.

Many aspects of U.S. state insurance regulation are harmonized. Foreign insurance observers, nonetheless, are often surprised at the regulatory differences among the states, and at each state's requirement of a separate license and adherence to its own reporting requirements. These conditions persist, even though states have similar legal systems, cultures, language, and levels of economic development and sophistication.

2. Free trade agreements. The United States has free trade agreements with Israel and with Canada and Mexico (the North American Free Trade Agreement [NAFTA]). The United States-Israel Free Trade Agreement binds both countries to abide by the agreement's principles to the maximum extent possible, but it does not legally bind each government to do so. Insurance regulatory harmonization has not been an issue in these agreements. Reciprocal market access with national treatment (with a phase-in period with Mexico) is covered in each agreement. No exceptional insurance cross-border trade liberalization is contained in the agreements. Thus, these agreements achieve a moderate level of market liberalization. No new harmonization, mutual recognition, or home-country control issues arose in the agreements.

Conclusion

In the final analysis, this chapter's central question—whether regulatory harmonization is a necessary precondition for insurance market liberalization—cannot be answered unequivocally. The current state of economic knowledge argues against harmonization, whereas political considerations argue for it.

De Facto Harmonization. No compelling economic evidence exists that broad-based, government-driven regulatory harmonization would result in greater liberalization of or more efficient insurance markets worldwide. Unlike the situation with banks, market failures in insurance are unlikely to pose important systemic risks to a nation's financial system and especially to the international financial system—risks that prudential harmonization might minimize. Further, prosperous, liberalized national insurance markets function efficiently in many insurance lines without forced harmonization. The existing level of *economic* knowledge argues for a market-driven approach to harmonization.

Nevertheless, some degree of regulatory harmonization may prove desirable for *political* reasons. The Basel Accord establishing minimum capital standards for certain G10 banks was both politically and economically driven. The same level-playing-field logic underpinning that accord applies in insurance, although to a lesser degree.

The U.S. government and many others want to retain fair-trade retaliatory options, such as the ability to assess dumping duties. Of course, such trade-restricting devices have little or no economic justification, but they carry substantial political appeal in an era of fair-trade rhetoric. This being true, some circumscribed harmonization could minimize the likelihood of allegations of unfair trade, such as dumping or unfair subsidization, thus aiding liberalization.

If some regulatory harmonization is judged to be desirable, it is suggested that a de facto as opposed to a de jure approach be taken. The approach should probably involve only countries of comparable economic and regulatory development and philosophy that are committed to insurance liberalization. Such like-minded countries should establish a set of agreed-upon regulatory objectives. The objectives should address only those regulatory elements that touched meaningfully on international insurance trade, and should studiously avoid purely national issues.

In agreeing on trade-related regulatory objectives, governments would focus on what should be regulated, not on how it should be done, thereby permitting a high level of generality in harmonization. For example, the objective of minimizing insurer insolvencies would be widely agreed upon. Harmonization would not extend beyond agreement on a set of broad regulatory objectives. This approach could minimize conflict while permitting competition among regulatory systems. If important systemic risks emerged in insurance in the future, and if more rapid regulatory convergence seemed needed, the objectives could form the basis for deeper harmonization.[63]

Mutual Recognition as the Key to Liberalization. Irrespective of whether any type or level of harmonization proved feasible, it seems that the key to liberalization of international insurance lies in mutual regulatory recognition. If one nation believes another affords the first nation's insurance consumers adequate protection—irrespective of how it is done—the first nation arguably should be content with the

---

63. This approach is similar to that followed with the Basel Committee. The Basel Concordat, issued in 1975, established a set of supervisory principles that were revised in 1983 and led ultimately to the 1988 accord. See Cooke (1990) and Dermine, chapter 3, herein.

second's regulation, and vice versa.[64] Although unilateral recognition of regulatory adequacy would suffice to liberalize a country's market, the most politically appealing and efficient approach would seem to be mutual recognition.

For mutual recognition to form the basis for liberalization, three areas must be addressed: transparency, nondiscrimination, and national treatment. Each is discussed below.

The importance of transparency and trust. Transparency is necessary for mutual recognition. Among other things, transparency is meant to ensure that host-country regulators are informed about the effectiveness of home-country regulation. Such transparency is justified on prudential and consumer protection grounds.

Transparency also runs in the other direction: it is meant to ensure that home-country regulators and insurers are informed about the rules and regulations of the host country. This transparency is necessary for effective market access and operation by foreigners.

With both types, substantial cross-national regulatory communication, coordination, and cooperation are required. Notice, comment, and publication requirements reinforce transparency.[65]

Implicit within the transparency goal is a high level of interjurisdictional trust. National regulators must feel confident that their international counterparts are dealing openly and honestly with them before they would agree to mutual recognition. Confidence-building measures akin to those of the NAIC's accreditation program could be appealing, but implementation would likely be daunting.

The need for modified MFN treatment. The nondiscrimination principle (most-favored-nation treatment) should apply across "recognized" jurisdictions and separately across "nonrecognized" jurisdictions. Thus, the same market-access standards should apply to all entrant applicants domiciled in recognized jurisdictions. Another set of market-access standards would apply nondiscriminatorily

---

64. The U.K.-insurance regulator operates in this manner. Foreign insurers may operate in the United Kingdom if the U.K. regulator determines that the foreign insurer's home country regulates as well as the United Kingdom. The state of Pennsylvania requested and was named a "designated territory" under this U.K. law. As such, any insurer authorized to conduct business in Pennsylvania can market insurance on a cross-border basis in the United Kingdom, provided it joins the appropriate U.K. self-regulatory body.

65. In the late 1970s, the OECD proposed a model convention for establishing cooperation procedures among supervisory authorities. This document may warrant reexamination.

to applicants domiciled in nonrecognized jurisdictions. This modified MFN treatment is consistent with the concept of mutual recognition.

The national treatment dilemma. Once an insurer attains market access, national rules that discriminate against it are clear barriers to trade and are inconsistent with the goal of liberalization. The national treatment principle, which argues for applying host-country rules nondiscriminatorily to foreign and domestic suppliers, is intended to ensure equality of competitive opportunity.

The principle is appealing, but it can limit effective market access. The most blatant example is with a monopolistic insurance market, as in India, or in markets where particular lines of insurance are monopolistic, such as automobile liability insurance in some Canadian provinces. Differences between countries in rules regarding permissible activities of financial services firms, even when both apply national treatment, can create trade barriers. Thus, EU financial service firms engaged in both banking and insurance activities in their home country are barred from doing so in the United States. They may elect to engage in banking or insurance activities in the United States, but not in both.

National-treatment market-access barriers also exist when government restricts the number of competitors within its market, when it strictly regulates insurance products such that foreign innovators are hindered in exploiting their competitive advantage, and, in general, whenever restrictive government regulation accords existing (usually primarily national) firms a substantial competitive advantage over potential entrants. Thus, for example, the EU asserts that its *bancassurance* firms are barred from fully exploiting their competitive advantage in the U.S. market because U.S. law prohibits such firms from the production and marketing of both insurance and banking services. This argument is analogous to U.S. complaints that rigid Japanese insurance regulation prohibits U.S. insurers from fully exploiting their competitive advantage within the Japanese market.

In general, firms from different countries may not enjoy comparable levels of market access under a national treatment standard. This is especially likely to be true the greater the asymmetry of regulation—particularly in regulation-intensive industries such as insurance. One obvious solution to this problem is regulatory harmonization. Another is to utilize the mutual recognition concept to each country's competitive advantage. Mutual recognition can mean better treatment for foreign firms than does national treatment if the home country's rules are superior to those of the host country. Permitting such regulatory competition sets in motion a continuous process of regulatory Darwinism, leading to market-driven harmonization. As a practical matter, the national treatment principle, even with its problems, should probably be retained.

A Possible Liberalization Scheme. Whatever the degree of liberalization within a market, regulation will emanate from the host country, the home country, or both. In general, home-country control connotes greater liberalization. Mutual recognition—relying upon transparency, nondiscrimination, and national treatment—should permit greater reliance on home-country control and thus greater liberalization.

Table 5–8 sets out one possible scheme for permitting greater liberalization with or without harmonization. Three broad categories of market access are shown: (1) cross-border and agency, (2) local branch, and (3) local subsidiary. Within each category, allowance is made for different treatment between personal lines and life insurance on the one hand and commercial lines and reinsurance on the other.

The three most critical areas of government intervention are shown on the left side of table 5–8: prudential considerations (H-S-E regulation), consumer protection (economic and information regulation), and competition law (economic regulation). These areas are not exhaustive, but they will serve our purposes.

Each area of government intervention is then paired with each market access mode and insurance type. An indication appears as to whether control should rest with the home or host country or either. Thus, for locally incorporated subsidiaries of foreign insurers, complete host-country control logically applies (on a national treatment basis) across all regulatory areas. Issues of harmonization and mutual recognition do not arise. This situation is the clearest.

Branches are neither fish nor fowl—or perhaps they are both fish and fowl. They operate within the host country on an establishment basis as the foreign parent. Yet they remain a part of the parent and are not separately incorporated in the host country. As a (distant) part of a larger corporate whole, the branch's operations are of direct interest to the home-country regulator. As an operating, if indivisible, established entity selling insurance to locals, the branch's operations are also of direct interest to the host-country regulator. Herein lies the problem. Who should control?

Governments have sought to answer this question in various ways, none completely satisfactory. Thus, some host countries treat the branch as if it were, in effect, a subsidiary by requiring deposits equivalent to the minimum capital and surplus required of a subsid-

TABLE 5-8
POTENTIAL SCHEME FOR PERMITTING GREATER LIBERALIZATION

Type of Regulation	Mode of Insurance Trade					
	Cross-border/Agency		Branch		Subsidiary	
	Personal	Commercial	Personal	Commercial	Personal	Commercial
Prudential	Home	Home	Home	Home	Host	Host
Consumer protection						
Marketing	Host	Either	Host	Host	Host	Host
Situs	Host	Either	Host	Host	Host	Host
Guaranty fund	Home	Either	Host	Host	Host	Host
Liquidation	Home	Either	Host	Host	Host	Host
Competition	Host	Home	Host	Host	Host	Host

SOURCE: Author.

iary and requiring localization of assets backing policy reserves. Other countries impose lesser requirements.

As shown in table 5–8, it is suggested that home-country prudential control apply to branches. Neither host-country deposits nor asset localization would apply to branches whose parent companies were domiciled in "recognized" jurisdictions. Host-country consumer protection and competition law would, however, apply to both personal and commercial customers.

Cross-border insurance trade and trade via agency establishment would be treated in the same way. The essential difference between the two modes of entry relates to contract situs, and this difference seems minimal given the recommendation for host-country law to apply to personal lines in any event.

Foreign insurers selling cross-border insurance would be subject to home-country control of prudential matters. For commercial insurance and reinsurance customers, home-country competition law would apply. The parties may agree as to whose consumer protection law, including contract law, applies. For personal lines and life insurance customers, host-country marketing and contract law would apply, given such consumers' low knowledge level. Host-country protection can be effective only where the foreign insurer solicits the consumer. The same is true for competition law. When consumers initiate contact on their own, in effect they would be removing themselves from host-country control. No barriers should be erected to such consumer-initiated purchases.

Home-country guaranty fund protection and liquidation procedures would apply. Ideally, as part of the mutual recognition process, it would have been determined that such protection and procedures applied nondiscriminatorily between nationals and foreigners. An incentive for sound home-country regulation is created by internalizing guaranty fund costs within the home country.

A de facto approach to harmonization, structured around harmonization of regulatory objectives, would seem to hold the most promise for success. Mutual recognition—structured around de facto harmonization, transparency, nondiscrimination, and national treatment—seems to be the key to liberalization. Initially, efforts at increased liberalization should be limited to a small group of like-minded governments.

References

American Council of Life Insurance. *1995 Life Insurance Fact Book Update*, 1995.

Anderson, Dan R. "The National Flood Insurance Program— Problems and Potentials." *The Journal of Risk and Insurance*, 41 (1974), pp. 579–99.

Bedore, James M. *Industry & Trade Summary: Insurance*. Washington, D.C.: U.S. International Trade Commission, 1991.

Beenstock, M., Gerald M. Dickinson, and S. Khajuria. "The Determination of Life Premiums. An International Cross-Section Analysis." *Insurance Mathematics and Economics*, 5 (1986), pp. 261–70.

Black, Kenneth, Jr., and Harold D. Skipper, Jr. *Life Insurance*. 12th ed. Englewood Cliffs, N.J.: Prentice-Hall, Inc., 1994, chap. 34.

Carter, Robert L. "Insurance." In Patrick A. Messerlin and Karl P. Sauvant, eds., *The Uruguay Round: Services in the World Economy*. Washington, D.C.: The World Bank, 1990, pp. 60–68.

Carter, Robert L., and Gerald M. Dickinson. *Obstacles to the Liberalization of Trade in Insurance*. London: Harvester Wheatsheaf, 1992.

Cooke, Peter. "International Convergence of Capital Adequacy Measurement and Standards." In Edward P. M. Gardener, ed., *The Future of Financial Systems and Services*. New York: St. Martin's Press, 1990, pp. 310–35.

Cummins, J. David, and J. Francois Outreville. "An International Analysis of Underwriting Cycles in Property Liability Insurance." *The Journal of Risk and Insurance*, 54 (1987), pp. 246–62.

Cummins, J. David, and Jack L. VanDerhei. "A Note on the Relative Efficiency of Property Liability Insurance Distribution Systems." *The Bell Journal of Economics*, 10 (1979), pp. 709–20.

Cummins, J. David, and Mary A. Weiss. "The Structure, Conduct, and Regulation of the Property Liability Insurance Industry." In Richard W. Kopche and Richard E. Randall, eds., *The Financial Condition and Regulation of Insurance Companies*. Boston: Federal Reserve Bank of Boston, 1991, pp. 117–54.

D'Arcy, Stephen P. "The Dark Side of Insurance." In Sandra G. Gustavson and Scott E. Harrington, eds., *Insurance, Risk Management, and Public Policy*. Boston: Kluwer Academic Publishers, 1994, pp. 163–81.

David, Paul A. "Clio and the Economics of Qwerty." *AER Papers and Proceedings*, 75 (1985), pp. 143–49.

Diacon, S.R. "The Demand for U.K. Ordinary Life Insurance." *The Geneva Papers on Risk and Insurance*, 17 (1980), pp. 3–22.

Doherty, Neil A. "The Measurement of Output and Economies of Scale in Property-Liability Insurance." *The Journal of Risk and Insurance*, 48 (1981), pp. 390–402.

Doherty, Neil A., and Georges Dionne. "Insurance and Undiversifiable Risk." Université de Montreal Working Paper 8710 (1987).

European Commission. *Report on United States Trade Barriers and Unfair Trade Practices—1992*. EC: 1992.

219

Farrell, Joseph, and Garth Soloner. "Standardization, Compatibility, and Innovation." *Rand Journal of Economics*, 16 (1985), pp. 70–83.

Failed Promises: Insurance Company Insolvencies. Washington, D.C.: U.S. Government Printing Office, 1990.

Fields, Joseph, James B. Ross, Chinmoy Ghosh, and Keith B. Johnson. "Junk Bonds, Life Insurer Solvency, and Stock Market Reactions: The Case of First Executive Corporation." *Journal of Financial Services Research* (1994), pp. 95–111.

Fletcher, Ian F. "International Insolvency: A Case for Study and Treatment." *The International Lawyer*, 27 (1993), pp. 429–44.

Foreign Trade Barriers: 1994 National Trade Estimate Report. United States Trade Representative (1994).

Fondree, Bruce W., and Peter K. Trzyna. "Toward the Exclusive Right to Market Innovative Insurance Products: The Use of Intellectual Property Law in the Business of Insurance." *Drake Law Review*, 41 (1992), pp. 587–633.

Gardner, Lisa M. *An Analysis of Cost Inefficiencies in Life Insurance Companies: Sources and Measurements.* Unpublished Ph.D. dissertation, Georgia State University, 1992.

Geehan, Randall. "Economies of Scale in Insurance: Implications for Regulation." In Bernard Wasow and Raymond D. Hill, eds., *The Insurance Industry in Economic Development.* New York: New York University Press, 1986, pp. 135–59.

Grace, Martin F., and Michael M. Barth. *The Regulation and Structure of Nonlife Insurance in the United States.* Washington, D.C.: The World Bank, 1993.

Grace, Martin F., and Julie Hotchkiss. "External Impacts on the Property-Liability Insurance Cycle." *Journal of Risk and Insurance*, 62 (December 1995).

Grace, Martin F., and Michael J. Rebello. "Financing and the Demand for Corporate Insurance." *The Geneva Papers on Risk and Insurance Theory*, 18 (1993), pp. 147–72.

Grace, Martin F., and Harold D. Skipper, Jr. *An Analysis of the Demand and Supply Determinants for Nonlife Insurance Internationally.* Center for Risk Management and Insurance Research Working Paper 91-5, Georgia State University, 1991.

Grace, Martin F., and Stephen G. Timme. "An Examination of Cost Economics in the United States Life Insurance Industry." *The Journal of Risk and Insurance*, 59 (1992) pp. 72–103.

Harrington, Scott, and Greg Niehaus. "Policyholder Runs, Contagion, and Life Insurer Insolvency Risk: Hypotheses and Preliminary Evidence." *Proceedings of the International Insurance Society*, 1992, pp. 257–69.

Hirshhorn, R., and R. Geehan. "Measuring the Real Output of the

Life Insurance Industry." *Review of Economics and Statistics*, 49 (1977), pp. 211–19.

Holsboer, J.H. "Specialization and Diversification in Financial Services—Some Recent, Practical Experiences in the Netherlands." *The Geneva Papers on Risk and Insurance: Issues and Practice*, 69 (1993), pp. 388–98.

Japanese Insurance Procurement Practices within Keiretsu Groups. American Chamber of Commerce in Japan (1993).

Joskow, Paul L. "Cartels, Competition and Regulation in the Property-Liability Insurance Industry." *The Bell Journal of Economics and Management Science*, 4 (1973), pp. 327–427.

Kellner, Stephen, and G. Mathewson. "Entry Size Distribution, Scale, and Scope Economics in the Life Insurance Industry." *Journal of Business*, 56 (1988), pp. 23–44.

Key, Sydney J., and Hal S. Scott. *International Trade in Banking Services: A Conceptual Framework*. Washington, D.C.: Group of Thirty, 1991.

Kim, Doocheol. *The Determinants of Life Insurance Growth in Developing Countries, with Particular Reference to the Republic of Korea*. Unpublished Ph.D. dissertation, Georgia State University, 1988.

Kollias, Sotirios. "The Structure and Regulation of Insurance Markets in Europe." In Richard W. Kopche and Richard E. Randall, eds., *The Financial Condition and Regulation of Insurance Companies*. Boston: Federal Reserve Bank of Boston, 1991, pp. 165–79.

Kunreuther, H. C., R. Ginsberg, L. Miller, P. Sagi, P. Slovic, B. Bostein, and N. Katz. *Disaster Insurance Protection: Public Policy Lessons*. New York: Wiley, 1978.

Lewis, Mervyn. "Banking as Insurance." In Edward P.M. Gardner, ed., *The Future of Financial Systems and Services*. New York: St. Martin's Press, 1990, pp. 225–42.

Mayers, David, and Clifford W. Smith. "On the Corporate Demand for Insurance." *Journal of Business*, 55 (1982), pp. 281–96.

———. "On the Corporate Demand for Insurance: Evidence from the Reinsurance Market." *Journal of Business*, 63 (1990), pp. 19–40.

National Association of Insurance Commissioners (NAIC). *Cycles and Crises in Property-Casualty Insurance: Implications for Public Policy*. Kansas City, Mo.: NAIC, 1991.

Organization for Economic Cooperation and Development (OECD). *Insurance and Other Financial Services*. Paris: OECD, 1992.

———. *Insurance Statistics Yearbook*. Paris: OECD, 1994.

———. *International Trade in Services: Insurance*. Paris: OECD, 1983.

———. *Liberalization of Capital Movements and Financial Services in the OECD Area*. Paris: OECD, 1990.

———. *Policy Issues in Insurance*. Paris: OECD, 1993a.

———. "Report of the Working Group Set Up by the Conference of

Insurance Supervisors of the European Economic Community with Regard to Financial Conglomerates." Distributed as *Addendum 2 to Summary Record of the 50th Session of the Insurance Committee.* Paris: OECD, 1993b.

———. *Supervision of Private Insurance in Member Countries: Summary Tables of Insurance Supervision.* Paris: OECD, 1988.

Player, Thomas A. *Insurer Insolvency Laws: Comparisons and Recommendations.* Unpublished monograph prepared for the OECD, 1994.

Pluym, Gilbert T. "The Rise of 'Bancassaurs'." *Emphasis,* 4 (1993), pp. 2–5.

Schlesinger, Harris, and Neil A. Doherty. "Incomplete Markets in Insurance: An Overview." *The Journal of Risk and Insurance,* 52 (1985), pp. 402–23.

Schwab, S.W., et al. "Cross-Border Insurance Insolvencies: The Search for a Forum Concursus." *University of Pennsylvania Journal of International Business Law,* 12 (1991), pp. 303–57.

Shelp, Ronald K. *Beyond Industrialization: Ascendancy of the Global Service Economy.* New York: Praeger, 1981.

Skalicky, Steven A. "Discussion." In Richard W. Kopche and Richard E. Randall, eds., *The Financial Condition and Regulation of Insurance Companies.* Boston: Federal Reserve Bank of Boston, 1991, pp. 190–98.

Skipper, Harold D., Jr. "Insurer Solvency Regulation in the United States." In *Policy Issues in Insurance.* Paris: OECD, 1993, pp. 73–146.

———. "Protectionism in the Provision of International Insurance Services." *The Journal of Risk and Insurance,* 54 (1987), pp. 55–85.

Skipper, Harold D., Jr., and Lisa A. Gardner. "An Examination of U.S. Insurance Regulation and Taxation vis-à-vis Selected GATT Principles." *The Geneva Papers on Risk and Insurance: Issues and Practice,* 17 (1992), pp. 215–31.

Suret, Jean Marc. "Scale and Scope Economies in the Canadian Property and Casualty Insurance Market." *Geneva Papers on Risk and Insurance,* 16 (1991), pp. 236–56.

Swiss Reinsurance Company. "Competition Law: Increasing Significance for the Insurance Sector." *Sigma.* Zurich: 1992.

———. "Life Insurance in Eight Countries: Structure and Developments from 1980 to 1990." *Sigma.* Zurich: 1993a.

———. "World Insurance in 1993: Accelerating Premium Growth." *Sigma.* Zurich: 1995.

———. "World Insurance in 1991: Recovery in Europe—Stagnation and Decline in Asia and North America." *Sigma.* Zurich: 1993b.

Tenneyson, Sharon. "The Effect of Rate Regulation on Underwriting Cycles." *CPCU Journal,* 44 (1991).

United Nations Conference on Trade and Development (UNCTAD). *Insurance in Developing Countries: Developments in 1980–1981*, 1982.

U.S. General Accounting Office. *Insurance Regulation: The National Association of Insurance Commissioners' Accreditation Program Continues to Exhibit Fundamental Problems.* Washington, D.C.: 1993.

U.S. Department of Commerce. "Insurance." *U.S. Industrial Outlook 1993* (1993), pp. 52-1–52-10.

———. "Insurance." *U.S. Industrial Outlook 1994* (1994), pp. 48-1–48-9.

Wasow, Bernard. "Determinants of Insurance Penetration: A Cross-Country Analysis." In Bernard Wasow and Raymond D. Hills, eds., *The Insurance Industry in Economic Development.* New York: New York University Press, 1986.

Weiss, Mary. "Efficiency in the Property Liability Insurance Industry." *The Journal of Risk and Insurance*, 58 (1991), pp. 452–79.

6

Foreign Banks, Financial Development, and Economic Growth

Ross Levine

Can foreign banks play an important role in the economic growth of developing countries? This question asks two things: Does a country's level of financial development play an important role in determining the rate of economic growth, and does liberalizing restrictions on the ability of foreign banks to enter and function in a country importantly bolster financial development? I examine each of these questions below.

The first part of this chapter presents conceptual arguments and empirical evidence showing that financial development significantly influences economic growth. The financial system provides "real" services to the economy that are crucial for economic activity and long-run growth. Specifically, the financial system facilitates transactions, eases risk management, mobilizes saving, allocates savings, and monitors the behavior of managers after funding projects. These five financial services provide a rough definition of financial development. Financial systems that are better at providing these services are better developed financially. The conceptual section of this chapter

Opinions expressed are those of the author and do not necessarily reflect the views of the World Bank, its staff, or its member countries.

predicts that the level of financial development will affect growth by altering the economy's saving rate and by influencing the efficiency with which economies allocate resources; countries with better developed financial systems should grow faster than countries with less well developed systems, holding everything else equal. The empirical evidence confirms this prediction: in a broad cross-section of developing countries over the past thirty years, various measures of financial development predict future rates of economic growth even after controlling for many other economic and political factors. Thus, policies that support financial development, *ceteris paribus*, will accelerate economic growth.

The chapter next examines the role of foreign banks in promoting financial development in developing countries.[1] It discusses potential benefits and costs to financial development from liberalizing foreign bank entry. Because of data limitations, I cannot use rigorous statistical analyses to assess the importance of foreign banks in promoting financial development. Instead, I use evidence from individual country experiences and the conceptual framework developed by Lawrence White, in chapter 1 of this volume.

I argue that foreign banks will promote financial development directly by providing high-quality banking services and indirectly as well, by three means. First, they can spur domestic banks to improve quality and cut costs; second, they can encourage the upgrading of accounting, auditing, and rating institutions; and third, they can intensify pressures on governments to enhance the legal, regulatory, and supervisory systems underlying financial activities.[2] Importantly, easing entry restrictions on foreign banks is likely to create domestic pressures in developing countries to harmonize bank regulatory and supervisory procedures and standards with those of developed countries.

In contrast to these tangible benefits, most of the concerns voiced about easing restrictions on the entry of foreign banks into develop-

1. On the role of foreign banks, this chapter has benefited from many previous studies. In addition to citations in the text, the chapter incorporates the insights of Aliber (1984), Dermine (1993), Goldberg and Saunders (1981), Gray and Gray (1981), Grosse and Goldberg (1991), Hultman and McGee (1989), Sabi (1988), Treasury (1990), Ursacki and Vertinsky (1992), Walter (1981, 1985, 1988), and Walter and Gray (1983).

2. Some analysts contend that foreign banks promote capital inflows and these increased capital inflows stimulate economic growth in developing countries. I remain unconvinced by this argument because (a) capital accumulation does not account for the majority of economic growth and (b) historically, capital has not flowed rapidly from rich to poor countries.

ing countries are typically unsubstantiated or not directly linked to foreign bank entry. Various analysts express fears about foreign banks, ranging from concerns that they will service only select segments of the market to concerns that foreign banks will dominate the entire market. In the vast majority of developing countries, foreign banks account for less than 10 percent of total domestic assets. Thus, entry restrictions could be marginally liberalized without fear of market domination by foreign banks. At the other end of the spectrum, individual foreign banks enter countries by targeting specific market niches. These strategies, however, differ across banks, and these business tactics represent the natural market mechanism through which competitive forces operate to improve financial services. Furthermore, I disagree with the assertion that foreign banks significantly foster capital flight. Capital flight is caused by an unattractive investment climate typically produced by poor policies. Restrictions on capital outflows typically do not impede it. Foreign banks play, at most, a peripheral role in capital flight. Thus, I interpret existing evidence as suggesting that most of the major concerns about foreign banks rest on shaky foundations.

Foreign banks are unlikely to be the engines of growth in any developing country. Even in the same country, regional banks often have important advantages in terms of knowing local customers.[3] Thus, foreign banks are unlikely to play a dominant role in most countries because of cost advantages enjoyed by domestic banks in terms of acquiring information about firms, business conditions, and policy changes. Nevertheless, foreign banks can play an influential role in stimulating financial development and thereby spurring economic growth. Given the very low levels of foreign bank participation in developing country markets, our analysis suggests that most developing countries could benefit from liberalizing foreign bank entry restrictions. As long as an adequate supervisory and regulatory system is in place to ensure the safety, soundness, and transparency of the financial system, most of the potential costs of foreign banks can be circumvented while still enjoying the benefits. Indeed, liberalizing

---

3. For example, while some northern-based Italian banks operate in southern Italy and southern-based Italian banks compete for business in the north, there is an important regional concentration of business: northern-based Italian banks focus on providing banking services to firms and individuals that reside in the north (see Faini, Galli, and Giannini 1993). This is also true for Spain and many other countries (see Cuadrado, Dehesa, and Precedo 1993).

foreign bank entry restrictions may create powerful pressures to improve bank supervision and regulation.[4]

Does Finance Matter?

This section addresses the question of whether the functions performed by the financial system are important for economic development. I tackle this question conceptually and empirically. Conceptually, I review ways in which the services provided by the financial system may affect economic growth. Specifically, I outline five functions performed by the financial system and explain how these functions affect economic activity. Those countries with financial systems that are better at performing these five financial services will be more economically developed and grow at a faster pace than those with less developed financial systems. The second part of this section presents empirical evidence that confirms these predictions. Countries with larger financial sectors relative to GDP and countries where banks play a larger role relative to the central bank in allocating credit have higher levels of real per capita income and grow faster.

Theory. The financial system provides five services that are important for economic growth. These services may affect growth through two channels: either by increasing the rate of physical capital accumulation or by improving the efficiency with which economies combine capital and labor in production. If the financial system stimulates capital formation and enhances economic efficiency, foreign banks may then have an important role in economic development; foreign banks that improve the provision of growth-enhancing financial services will promote economic development.

Before describing the details, four preliminary points help clarify our conceptual approach to evaluating whether finance is significant for economic development. First, our analysis focuses on specific financial services rather than on particular financial institutions. I find this helpful conceptually because these services are the same across countries and through time, while the institutions that perform these functions differ across countries and change over time within the same country. Of course the quantity, quality, and availability of

---

4. For specifics on regulatory and supervisory issues with foreign banks, see Campbell Report (1983), Dale (1984), Key (1992), Musalem et al. (1993), and Treasury (1990).

these services differ markedly across countries.[5] Second, financial services can affect growth both by increasing the national saving rate and by improving the efficiency with which society allocates capital. Although the field of development economics has focused on the role of physical capital in economic development, our conceptual framework suggests that financial development will importantly affect economic growth by improving the efficiency with which society allocates capital. Third, I focus exclusively on how the financial system influences economic growth even though we recognize that economic development may affect the financial system. I examine only one direction of causality because this chapter is primarily concerned with the role of foreign banks in spurring financial and thereby economic development. Fourth, in reviewing and studying financial services, our conceptual approach gives a rough definition of financial development. Financial systems that provide higher quality financial services are more highly developed financially than financial systems that provide these services less well.

Channels. In 1954, Arthur Lewis, one of the pioneers of development economics, argued that "the central problem in the theory of economic development is to understand the process by which a community which was previously saving and investing 4 or 5 percent of its national income or less, converts itself into an economy where voluntary saving is running at about 12 to 15 percent of national income or more" (Lewis 1954, 155). Similarly, W. W. Rostow (1960, 8) asserted that a large jump in the saving rate is necessary, though not sufficient, for rapid economic advancement. This "capital fundamentalist" view—that rapid physical capital accumulation is the central factor underlying rapid economic development—has been a dominant and continuing feature of development economics. An important corollary of this view is that international capital inflows can importantly contribute to economic growth by increasing domestic capital accumulation. Thus, capital fundamentalism suggests that foreign banks can increase economic growth by raising the domestic saving rate or by increasing capital inflows.

As Arthur Lewis was enumerating the central role of capital in economic growth, Robert Solow (1957) found that a surprisingly small fraction of the differences in both the level of economic development and the rate of economic growth across industrialized countries is explained by physical capital. Denison (1967) similarly argued that

5. In the empirical section, we must use measures of financial institutions because it is very difficult to measure the provision and quality of financial services directly.

less than a third of the differences in income per capita or the rate of economic growth is explained by physical capital. These findings suggested that some countries were better at combining capital and labor than other countries.[6] As Paul Krugman (1993, 13) noted, "poorer countries simply have worse production functions, and hence the marginal product of capital is not in fact as high as their low capital-labor ratios would suggest." Thus, many analysts reject capital fundamentalism and argue that improvements in productivity and economic efficiency are at least as important as physical capital accumulation in explaining economic development. Thus, financial development, and therefore foreign banks, will have to improve economic efficiency to promote growth according to this productivity view of development.

In sum, there are two major channels through which financial systems may affect growth. They may alter the rate of physical capital accumulation, or they may alter the productivity and efficiency with which capital and labor are combined to produce goods and services.

Financial services. Though differing widely in quality, all financial systems provide five basic financial services that affect long-term economic development through the capital accumulation channel or the productivity channel.[7] The basic theme of this section is that these financial services constitute real value added; financial institutions are not simple balance sheets, and financial markets are not simple veils for the functioning of the real sector. The financial system provides real services that are crucial for economic activity and long-run growth. These financial services influence growth both by influencing capital accumulation and by affecting economic efficiency. Our analysis predicts, therefore, that those financial systems that are better at providing these services will provide a correspondingly greater boost to economic growth.

Financial systems facilitate trade. At the most rudimentary level, money minimizes the need for barter and thereby encourages commerce and specialization. As argued by Adam Smith over two hundred years ago, specialization in production forms the foundation of modern economies and stimulates productivity improvements. At a more sophisticated level, checks, credit cards, and the entire payment-and-clearance system simplify a wide array of economic interactions. In most industrialized economies, individuals and businesses

---

6. For recent growth accounting work on developing countries see King and Levine (1994).

7. This section draws on Merton (1992) and Levine (1996).

take the ability to write and settle financial transactions easily for granted. The absence of a reliable means for conducting trade, however, importantly impedes economic activity and economic growth. This is exemplified most notably in transitional socialist economies where insufficiently developed payment-and-clearance systems have stymied economic interactions. Thus, financial systems that make trade and commerce easy foster economic activity and promote economic growth by encouraging and supporting a more efficient allocation of resources.

Financial systems facilitate risk management. Financial systems price risk and provide mechanisms for pooling, ameliorating, and trading risk. Recent uses of options and futures contracts to hedge and trade interest-rate and exchange-rate risk have been well publicized. At a more basic level, financial institutions transform asset and liability maturities to satisfy savers and investors. The securities most useful to businesses—equities, bonds, bills of exchange—may not have the liquidity, security, and risk characteristics that savers desire. By offering attractive financial instruments to savers—liquid demand deposits, well-diversified mutual fund portfolios—financial intermediaries can tailor financial instruments for different clients and thereby manage risk for individuals. By facilitating the management, trading, and pooling of risk, financial systems can ease the interactions between savers and investors. Financial systems that are better at providing risk-management services will encourage efficient resource allocation and may also stimulate saving and investment (Levine 1991).

One particularly important type of risk is liquidity risk. Liquidity risk arises because savers frequently need quick access to their savings, yet their assets may be difficult to sell. Liquidity risk is important for long-run growth because big investments often enjoy economies of scale, promote specialization, and stimulate technological innovation, but big investments require a long-run commitment of capital. Since investors are reluctant to relinquish control of their savings for long periods, banks—and other financial arrangements—may arise to reduce liquidity risk on the part of savers while providing firms with long-term capital. As shown by Bencivenga and Smith (1991), well-functioning banks facilitate long-run investments. Making long-run, illiquid investments easier may in turn spur investment, improve resource allocation, and stimulate economic growth.

Financial systems mobilize resources. Financial intermediaries mobilize resources from disparate savers to investment in worthwhile investment projects. Some worthwhile investment projects may require large capital inputs, and some projects enjoy economies of scale. By

230

agglomerating savings, financial intermediaries enlarge the set of feasible investment projects and thereby encourage economic efficiency. Thus, efficiency and savings may be importantly linked; by facilitating resource mobilization, financial intermediaries increase the feasibility of large, high-return investment projects. As noted by Greenwood and Smith (1994), Bagehot (1873, 3–4) argued that the role of the financial system in mobilizing resources is crucial for economic development.

> We have entirely lost the idea that any undertaking likely to pay, and seen to be likely, can perish for want of money; yet no idea was more familiar to our ancestors, or is more common in most countries. A citizen of Long in Queen Elizabeth's time . . . would have thought that it was no use inventing railways (if he could have understood what a railway meant), for you would have not been able to collect the capital with which to make them. At this moment, in colonies and all rude countries, there is no large sum of transferable money; there is not fund from which you can borrow, and out of which you can make immense works.

Thus, by effectively mobilizing resources for sound investment projects, the financial system may play a crucial role in permitting the adoption of better technologies and thereby encouraging economic development.

Financial systems obtain information, evaluate firms, and allocate capital. Firms, projects, and managers are difficult to evaluate. Individual savers may not have the time, resources, or means to collect and process information on a wide array of enterprises, markets, managers, and economic conditions. Financial intermediaries may have a cost advantage in obtaining and evaluating information and then allocating capital based on these assessments. Since many firms and entrepreneurs will solicit capital, financial intermediaries that are better at selecting the most promising firms and managers will spur economic growth by fostering a more efficient allocation of capital. The higher returns to capital investment produced by financial intermediaries that better evaluate firms and allocate capital may also increase savings and capital formation, further boosting economic growth.

Financial systems provide corporate governance. Small individual investors often find it arduous, time-consuming, and costly to evaluate and monitor the performance of firm managers. Consequently, financial intermediaries are often charged with compelling managers to act in the best interests of firm claim holders (stock, debt, and loan

231

holders). That is, financial intermediaries help resolve the principal-agent problem by facilitating the ability of claim holders to oversee the actions of managers (agents). Financial systems that are more effective at mitigating the principal-agent problem will prompt managers to allocate resources more efficiently.

Summary. Theory predicts that the services provided by financial systems are crucial for economic development. The links between financial and economic development may be complex. For example, financial services may affect growth by increasing the rate of capital accumulation or by influencing the efficiency with which economies combine labor and capital in production. Further, across countries, different combinations of financial institutions, markets, and instruments provide services. Moreover, international financial systems provide very different quality financial services.

Nonetheless, the analysis suggests that the five financial services—facilitating transactions, easing risk management, mobilizing saving, allocating funds, and monitoring firm managers—are crucial determinants of economic growth. This argument conforms with Hicks's (1969) view that the industrial revolution in England required, as a precondition, the financial revolution that dramatically increased the availability of financial services. According to Hicks, the ability both to mobilize resources for permanent investment in capital goods and to provide liquid assets to savers was necessary for the massive investment and technological change that characterized the industrial revolution.[8] Thus, the basic prediction that emerges is that countries with better developed financial systems—countries that provide higher-quality financial services—should enjoy faster rates of economic growth, *ceteris paribus*, than countries with less well developed financial systems. Developing countries that encourage financial development enhance their chances of achieving long-run sustained growth. In the following section I will evaluate this prediction empirically.

Evidence. In a series of articles, King and Levine (1993a,b,c) study the link between financial development and economic growth. Using data on eighty countries over the 1960–1989 period, they show that various measures of the level of financial development are strongly associated with real per capita GDP growth, the rate of physical capital accumulation, and improvements in the efficiency with which economies employ physical capital. Moreover, King and Levine show

---

8. I learned about the views of Hicks (1969) through Bencivenga, Smith, and Starr (1995).

that the level of financial development predicts future economic growth even after controlling for other economic and political factors. These results contrast sharply with the weak links between growth and a wide array of other economic indicators, as shown by Levine and Renelt (1992) and Levine and Zervos (1993). In contrast to King and Levine (1993a,b,c), this chapter focuses on non-OECD countries.

We use two measures of financial development. The first is called DEPTH and equals the ratio of liquid liabilities of the financial system divided by GDP. Liquid liabilities consist of currency held outside the banking system plus demand and interest-bearing liabilities of banks and other financial institutions. DEPTH is the traditional measure of financial development and is designed to measure the size of the formal financial intermediary sector relative to economic activity (see McKinnon 1973 and Goldsmith 1969).

The second indicator seeks to measure the relative importance of specific financial intermediaries. For the 1960–1989 period, the only decomposition is between the central bank and deposit banks. Thus, I compute the ratio of deposit-bank domestic credit divided by deposit-bank domestic credit plus central-bank domestic credit and call this measure of financial development BANK. Banks are more likely to provide the financial services detailed above than is the central bank. Thus, higher levels of BANK should be associated with a greater provision of financial services and greater financial development.

These measures may not accurately capture the provision of growth-promoting financial services as defined above. DEPTH may not be closely related to risk management and information processing, for example. BANK does not measure the provision of financial services by nonbanks, and governments may control banks as tightly as they control central banks. Nonetheless, these different measures tell similar stories about the relationship between financial development and economic activity.

Figure 6–1 shows that the level of financial development in 1970 is closely associated with the level of real per capita GDP in 1970 for a sample of fifty-six developing countries. I rank countries by real per capita income in 1970 and break the countries into four groups with the same number of countries in each group. The poorest group of countries had a real per capita GDP of $543 (in $1987) in 1970, and the richest group of developing countries had a real per capita income of $3,710.[9] As illustrated, richer countries had higher DEPTH and BANK. Countries with larger formal financial systems and countries

---

9. These figures are from Summers and Heston (1988).

FIGURE 6–1: Real per Capita Income and Financial Development for Selected Developing Countries, 1970

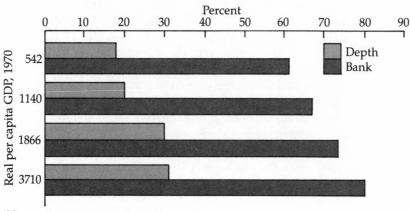

Observations per quartile = 14
Depth: liquid liabilities divided by GDP
Bank: deposit bank domestic credit divided by deposit bank domestic credit plus central bank domestic credit

Source: Author.

with larger deposit banks relative to the central bank in terms of allocating credit tended to be richer.

Figure 6–2 relates the average level of financial development over the 1960–1989 period to the average real per capita growth rate over this same period. Again, we see a close link between financial development and economic growth. Countries with better developed financial systems grew faster. These results hold even when controlling for many other economic and political factors.

Finally, figure 6–3 examines the relationship between the level of financial development in 1960 and economic growth over the next thirty years. Since I could not compute the value of BANK for many countries in 1960, I conduct this analysis only with DEPTH. Here, I am trying to abstract from the possibility that the strong association between financial development and economic activity occurs because economic activity spurs financial development. As depicted in figure 6–3, however, DEPTH in 1960 strongly predicts future economic growth. Importantly, these results hold when controlling for other factors, and these results do not hold in reverse; the level of real per capita income in 1960 does not predict improvements in DEPTH over the next thirty years. Thus, the data are consistent with the view

234

FIGURE 6–2: GROWTH AND FINANCIAL DEVELOPMENT FOR SELECTED
DEVELOPING COUNTRIES, 1960–1989

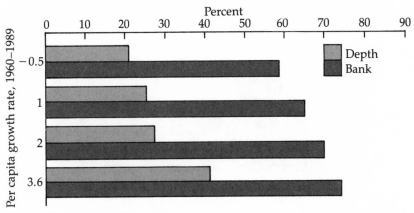

Observations per quartile = 15
Growth: per capita GDP growth
Depth: liquid liabilities divided by GDP
Bank: deposit bank domestic credit divided by bank credit plus central bank
credit

SOURCE: Author.

that financial development stimulates economic growth. Policies that
promote financial development, *ceteris paribus*, will stimulate economic development. Easing restrictions on foreign bank entry is one
policy that can help spur financial development in many developing
countries.

What Role for Foreign Banks?

Given that financial development plays an important role in promoting economic growth, this section examines the role that foreign
banks can play in stimulating financial development and thereby
spurring growth in developing countries. I could not construct a
cross-country data set with measures of foreign banks across a sufficient number of countries to quantify the importance of foreign banks
in promoting financial and economic development in a rigorous, statistical manner. Instead, this section sheds some light on the role that
foreign banks play in financial and economic development based on
individual country experiences. First, I discuss potential benefits from
permitting foreign bank entry. Second, I consider potential costs from

235

FIGURE 6–3: Initial Depth of Financial Devleopment, 1960, versus Future Growth, 1960–1989, for Selected Countries

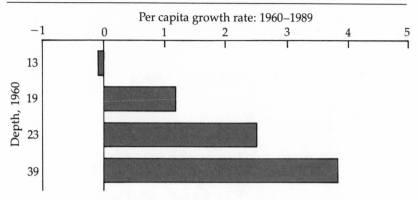

Number of observations in each quartile = 11
Growth: per capita GDP growth, 1960–1989
Depth: liquid liabilities divided by GDP, 1960

Source: Author.

liberalizing foreign bank entry. I review the case of Australia in some detail using Catherine McFadden's (1994) study. The experience of Australia highlights, first, strategies that particular foreign banks employed when entering the Australian market and a preliminary assessment of the results of those strategies, and second, the effect on the Australian financial system.

I find that while openness to foreign banks will probably not ignite rapid economic development, the benefits of liberalizing entry restrictions on foreign banks seem in most cases to be much larger than the costs. The major concerns about foreign bank entry are often only peripherally related to foreign banks, and in most cases these concerns can be allayed while still obtaining the benefits of foreign banks.

Benefits. Liberalizing entry of foreign banks may have important benefits for at least three related reasons. First, reducing impediments to foreign bank entry may improve access to international capital markets. Second, easing restrictions on foreign bank entry should improve the quality and availability of the five financial services noted above by stimulating competition in and contestability of domestic financial markets and by facilitating the application of more modern banking skills, management, and technology in the domestic market. Third, openness to foreign banks may stimulate improvements in both domestic financial policy and the financial infrastructure, which in turn will promote domestic financial development (Glaessner and Oks 1994). The financial infrastructure includes the legal system underlying financial transactions and the supervisory and regulatory system. Improvements in the financial infrastructure will facilitate the provision of financial services and make the financial system more stable. This section reviews each of these arguments and presents some evidence regarding their validity and significance.

International capital flows. In line with the capital fundamentalist approach to economic development, countries may ease restrictions on foreign bank entry as a means of encouraging capital inflows in the belief that these capital inflows will promote capital formation and economic growth. For example, Korea (Euh and Baker 1990) and Australia (Campbell Report 1983) specifically emphasized that one of the policy objectives sought in opening to foreign banks was to enhance contacts with the international financial community and thereby to increase capital inflows.[10] The efficacy of this strategy relies on two premises: first, foreign banks will facilitate capital inflows; second, capital inflows will spur economic development. I examine each of these premises.

Bhattacharaya (1993) reports individual cases in Pakistan, Turkey, and Korea, where domestically based and capitalized foreign banks helped to make foreign capital accessible to fund domestic projects. Pigott (1986) finds in a review of Pacific-Basin countries that while foreign banks rely more than domestic banks on foreign borrowing, foreign-owned banks still fund three-fourths of their domestic loans from domestic sources. Unfortunately, most of the evidence on the role of foreign banks in providing greater access to international capital markets is scant, scattered, and unsystematic. Thus, it is difficult to assess the role of foreign banks in promoting access to international capital markets.

We now turn to the second premise of the belief that foreign banks promote economic development by encouraging capital inflows. This development strategy presupposes that capital inflows are important to economic growth. There are good reasons to believe, however, that international capital flows will not play an important

---

10. As McFadden (1993, 10–11) notes, "The Australian Industries Development Association, a powerful lobby representing manufacturing, mining, and mineral processing interests, advocated foreign bank entry to develop Australian capital markets and the real economy. . . . Foreign banks were expected to bring new capital from establishing (subsidiary) operations, through access to parent capital and from international markets."

role in fostering growth in developing countries. As noted above, considerable empirical evidence suggests that the impact of capital accumulation on economic growth is surprisingly weak. Furthermore, history suggests that not much capital flows from rich to poor countries. For example, the pre–World War I period witnessed much larger capital flows relative to income than did the post–World War I period. Yet very little of this capital flowed from rich to poor countries. As documented by Nurske (1954) and Feis (1964), capital flowed from Europe to already high-income countries like Canada, New Zealand, Australia, Argentina, and the United States, where per capita incomes were as high or higher than in Britain. Little capital flowed to poor colonies such as India. More recently, the period from 1972 to 1981 is often viewed as a period of large capital flows. Yet less than 15 percent of domestic investment was financed by foreign borrowing, even in highly indebted countries, during this period. More important, these capital flows did not produce a sustained boom in economic development. Finally, it is worth considering the case of southern Italy. Faini et al. (1993) show that despite openness to banks from northern Italy and despite large capital inflows, southern Italy has not matched the performance of northern Italy over the past half century.

International capital flows are not likely to be a major engine of economic growth in developing countries. As Paul Krugman (1993, 22) argues,

> There is nothing in past historical experience to suggest that developing countries will be the recipients of large capital flows; there is no convincing evidence that rather low neoclassical estimates of the impact of capital on growth are wrong.

Thus, easing entry restrictions on foreign banks may have its greatest growth-promoting effects through channels other than stimulating international capital inflows.

Better domestic financial services. Easing restrictions on foreign bank entry should improve the quality, pricing, and availability of the five financial services to domestic firms and individuals. Foreign banks will directly bring new and better skills, management techniques, training procedures, technology, and products to the domestic market. In addition, foreign banks will indirectly force improvements in the domestic financial system by pressuring existing institutions to improve. Specifically, foreign banks will stimulate competition in and contestability of domestic financial markets, which will put downward pressure on the price of financial services and

TABLE 6–1
BANK OPERATING RATIOS, INDUSTRIAL COUNTRIES, 1977

	Open[a]	Closed[b]
Gross earnings margin to volume of business	3.21	4.48
Pretax profits to volume of business	0.58	0.78
Operating costs to volume of business	2.27	3.25

NOTE: Data are for 1977. Countries include Austria, Belgium, France, Italy, Netherlands, Switzerland, and United States under "*Open*." Countries include Australia, Canada, Finland, Norway, Spain, and Sweden under "*Closed*." Gross earnings = gross interest minus gross interest paid plus other (net) income. Volume of business refers to total assets.
a. Open: Banks in countries excluding foreign bank entry.
b. Closed: Banks in countries permitting foreign bank entry.
SOURCE: Terrell (1986).

spur existing financial institutions to improve the quality of their services to stay in business.

In terms of specifically linking foreign banks to the five financial services discussed above, foreign banks may

- stimulate improvements in transaction services by introducing credit cards or improving the payments system
- introduce, expand the availability of, and lower the cost of risk management mechanisms
- intensify credit assessment procedures and enhance information gathering techniques
- introduce improved mechanisms for monitoring firm and manager performance
- intensify the competition of mobilizing domestic resources that would expand the mobilization of domestic saving and promote better resource allocation

Thus, by intensifying competition and by directly bringing new services to bear on the domestic market, foreign banks may provoke rapid improvements in the provision of growth-promoting financial services.

There is some evidence that openness to foreign banks goes hand-in-hand with greater banking efficiency. Table 6–1 is taken from Terrell (1986) and shows that countries that permitted foreign bank entry had lower profits and were more efficient than countries that had more restrictive policies. Similarly, as Indonesia reduced restrictions on foreign bank activities in its domestic market and thereby intensified competition with domestic banks, the percentage difference between interest rates charged by domestic and foreign banks fell dramatically, as shown in table 6–2. Similarly, as noted by Bhattacharaya (1993), enhanced foreign bank competition has forced lower commission fees in Turkey; fees on letters of credit fell from 1.5 percent to 0.5 percent, and fees on letters of guarantee fell from 4 percent to 1 percent. In Australia, foreign bank competition helped pull down interest rate spreads. Whereas major corporations borrowed at 75 to 100 basis points above the Australian Treasury Bill rate before foreign bank entry liberalization, major corporations borrow at between 25 and 50 basis points above the bill rate now, as reported in McFadden (1993, 46–47).

In addition to lowering the cost of banking services, foreign banks have also introduced new and better services. For example, in Spain, Midland Bank pioneered the commercial paper market, while First Chicago introduced swaps (see Bhattacharaya 1993, 23). Furthermore, foreign banks have led the boom in credit cards and automated teller machines (ATMs) in Spain. In Turkey, foreign banks computerized most of their banking operations, used modern budgeting and planning techniques, and quickly tied themselves to the SWIFT payments system network. To remain competitive, domestic banks soon followed to remain competitive. Interestingly, although 10 percent of the employees in Turkey's banking sector had university degrees in 1980, after permitting greater foreign bank access, the figure rose to 20 percent by 1990.[11] Thus, evidence suggests that foreign banks directly improve the range and quality of financial services in countries that open to foreign banks and indirectly promote financial development by inducing domestic banks to improve their operations.

Finally, while difficult to establish unambiguously, as foreign banks enter a country, they may improve ancillary institutions and procedures that promote the flow of information about firms. As foreign intermediaries undertake brokerage and underwriting activities, they will encourage information acquisition. In addition, foreign banks may encourage the emergence of better rating agencies, accounting and auditing firms, and credit bureaus that acquire and process high-quality information on individuals, firms, and financial institutions. Similarly, these banks may improve information disclosure about banks themselves in order to attract customers by demonstrating their sound financial condition. Thus, as part of increasing competition, foreign banks may create pressures that improve the quality and availability of information about individuals, firms, and financial intermediaries.

---

11. See Bhattacharaya (1993).

TABLE 6–2

SELECTED DEPOSIT RATES OF FOREIGN AND DOMESTIC BANKS IN INDONESIA, 1978–1985

	1978	1979	1980	1981	1982	1983	1984	1985
Six-month deposit rate								
Private national banks	15.7	16.8	18.2	18.1	18.4	18.8	20.7	17.8
Foreign banks	8.4	9.8	8.7	10.2	14.3	17.0	21.4	17.0
Twelve-month deposit rate								
Private national banks	17.9	18.1	20.0	19.4	19.4	19.7	20.5	19.8
Foreign banks	10.0	9.7	12.1	11.9	15.5	17.0	19.1	16.6
Inflation % (consumer prices)	8.1	22.0	18.4	12.2	9.5	11.8	10.4	4.7

SOURCE: Cho and Khatkhate (1989), 186–87.

Financial regulation. The ease and effectiveness of financial arrangements depend importantly on the legal code governing property rights, the legal system's ability to enforce those property rights, the legal and regulatory requirements regarding information disclosure, the transparency and availability of financial statements on firms and financial intermediaries, and the supervisory and regulatory systems overseeing the financial system. When property rights are well defined and enforced, when information on firms and financial institutions is accurate, easy to obtain, and easy to understand, and when the supervisory and regulatory systems foster stability, innovation, and fairness, the financial system will provide better financial services than when these conditions are not met. As argued by Glaessner and Oks (1994), opening to foreign banks may spur improvements in the financial infrastructure and thereby promote the development of the domestic financial system. White (1995) provides a detailed assessment of when harmonization of particular regulations between countries will be optimal and when competition between regulators in different countries will lead to the best set of regulations for promoting financial development.

A developing-country perspective on regulatory harmonization. Consider the case of a small developing country that eases restrictions on foreign bank entry by developed-country banks. The developing country may also seek access to developed-country markets for its banks. In this situation, the burden of regulatory change will likely fall on the developing country. Before granting access to developing-country banks, the developed country will require evidence that the developing-country authorities "appropriately" supervise and regulate their banks. And the developed country will use its own supervisory and regulatory system to define *appropriate*. Thus, unlike the case where two or more developed economies may face regulatory competition, the burden of changing regulations and supervisory procedures will probably fall on the developing country. Developing countries will have to harmonize.

Interestingly, the pressure for harmonization may come from developing-country banks. Faced with entry and competition by developed-country banks, developing-country banks may seek rapid access to developed markets so that they can provide a competitively complete array of financial services to existing clients. Provision of competitive services may require having a subsidiary in a developed country. But entry into a developed country will require satisfying developed-country requirements about the supervisory and regulatory capacity of the developing country. Under these conditions, domestic banks may pressure domestic regulatory authorities to harmonize their supervisory and regulatory procedures and standards with those of developed countries so that the domestic bank can enter developed markets.

This harmonization will cover different types of regulation. While there may be some harmonization of economic regulations—regulations regarding limits on prices, profits, and entry and exit requirements—there will be two major forms of regulatory harmonization. The first is prudential regulation—regulations on capital, restrictions on the assets and liabilities of banks, deposit insurance, limitations on lending to insiders, and standards of approval of bank management. The second is information regulation—regulations regarding the disclosure of information about bank assets, liabilities, interest rates, fees, losses, owners, capital, related-party transactions, and so forth. To the extent that a developed country has a regulatory regime that fosters greater financial development than the developing-country regulatory regime, this harmonization will be socially beneficial to the developing country. The availability of human capital skills, however, is one important risk faced by many developing countries. Specifically, developed countries may rely on a great deal of technical expertise on the part of regulators and supervisors, which may not be available in developing countries. Thus, supervisory and regulatory regimes may not be immediately "harmonizable" in developing countries.

Consider, for example, the case of Mexico. The recently signed North American Free Trade Agreement (NAFTA) has a financial services component. Under condition-specific conditions specified in NAFTA and discussed in Glaessner and Oks (1994), Mexico will open to United States and Canadian banks, and the United States and Canada will allow Mexican banks to enter their domestic markets. To have access to the United States, Mexican banks must demonstrate to the Federal Reserve that Mexican supervisors can adequately supervise its banks and related financial institutions. Thus, as Mexico has opened its doors to U.S. banks and sought entry for its banks in the United States, there have been pressures to harmonize prudential regulations in areas such as capital adequacy, valuation and accounting principles, related-party transactions, and conflict-of-interest provisions. Furthermore, because of pressures for regulatory harmonization, Glaessner and Oks predict important improvements in Mexico's laws and regulations regarding corporate and bankruptcy law, laws regarding negotiable instruments, the functioning of registries of land, buildings, and goods in warehouses, and laws relating to

243

secured transactions. NAFTA will prompt improvements in these registries, which should lower the cost of financial intermediation.

Thus, easing foreign-entry restrictions may create incentives that improve domestic bank regulation with at least two beneficial effects on economic development. First, better bank regulation will reduce the chances for systemic bank failures. Second, better bank regulation will improve the sustained provision of growth-enhancing financial services—risk diversification, transaction facilitation, resource mobilization, resource allocation, and corporate governance. Developing-country bank regulation will move toward the developed-country norm, further emphasizing the importance of developed countries' choosing an optimal mix of competition and harmonization in fostering the development of an international regulatory regime for financial services.

Additional regulatory benefits. In addition to the regulatory benefits mentioned above, opening to foreign banks may spur regulatory improvements by removing domestic political impediments to regulatory improvements. For example, in many developing (and developed) countries, regulators may have weak incentives, inadequate staffs, and insufficient resources to acquire comprehensive information about financial groups and to supervise and regulate banks energetically. Gaining the support of bankers may be more important politically than supervising and regulating banks well. This may change with the relaxation of restrictions on foreign bank entry. To expand abroad, domestic banks must convince foreign central banks of the soundness of the domestic supervisory and regulatory system. Thus, relaxation of entry restrictions on foreign banks realigns incentives: now domestic banks and domestic regulators both seek to improve supervision and regulation to internationally accepted standards. This realignment of incentives should work to reduce capture of regulators by banks, to improve the flow and quality of information about banks, to boost the level of public resources devoted to supervision and regulation, and to clarify the goals of the regulatory agency. Thus, opening to foreign bank competition may enhance supervision and regulation by realigning incentives and reducing political impediments to improvements.

Conclusions on benefits from openness to foreign banks. Two broad conclusions emerge from this analysis. First, while openness to foreign banks may promote capital flows, international capital flows in general are unlikely to promote growth significantly in developing countries, so that opening to foreign banks will not significantly enhance economic development by improving access to foreign capital.

Second, foreign banks are likely to promote growth by stimulating improvements in the domestic banking system. Country-specific evidence suggests that openness to foreign banks is positively associated with financial development, and theory plus statistical and historical evidence imply that greater financial development boosts economic growth. These two findings suggest that opening to foreign banks will spur economic growth by encouraging development of the domestic financial system. Nevertheless, countries around the globe impose severe restrictions on foreign bank entry. A thorough understanding of the reasons underlying these restrictions is necessary for evaluating the potential role that foreign banks can play in supporting both financial and economic development.

Concerns about Foreign Bank Entry. Countries have numerous concerns about liberalizing foreign bank entry into their domestic markets. Countries are concerned that foreign bank entry may actually stymie financial development instead of enhancing the provision of financial services and capital. This section analyzes four broad categories of concerns.

International capital outflows. Foreign banks are often accused of stimulating capital flight. Through closer ties to the international financial community than domestic banks, foreign banks may facilitate capital outflows.

Closer scrutiny, however, suggests that this concern rests on shaky foundations. In the case of a country with an open capital account, Musalem et al. (1993, 4) argue that "the role of foreign institutions is little different from that of domestic institutions in countries. Both have the means to facilitate flight if there are strong incentives to do so." If a country has a closed capital account, foreign banks "may facilitate capital flight by providing contacts to their parent institutions in foreign financial centers and by facilitating arrangements for the maintenance of bank accounts and other investments in overseas markets" (Musalem et al., 1993, 4). But capital controls are almost universally ineffective when there are strong incentives for capital to flee whether foreign banks exist or not. Moreover, foreign banks do not cause capital flight; the causes underlying capital flight are poor and inconsistent policies, political uncertainty, and high and variable taxes that make the domestic market an unattractive and risky place to invest (Gordon and Levine 1989). Countries concerned about capital flight should tackle these fundamental determinants of capital flight. Thus fears of capital flight do not seem to justify restrictions on foreign bank entry.

From cream skimming to market dominance. Policy makers often express concern that foreign banks will (a) service only the most profitable market segments; (b) not service the retail market; (c) service only foreign corporations; or (d) dominate the entire domestic market. Market-based business strategy suggests that foreign banks will attempt to carve out areas of competitive advantage. Foreign banks will enter and attempt to develop products and services that they have successfully offered in other countries, and foreign banks will both follow and lead corporations from their base countries that are expanding or contemplating expansion in other countries. Similarly, foreign banks, particularly when entering developing countries, will provide more sophisticated financial services than domestic financial institutions. Thus foreign banks, like any business, may initially attempt to service only particular parts of the market. In addition to concerns that foreign banks will service only small sectors of the financial market, many countries also fear that foreign banks will dominate the entire financial sector; restrictions on foreign banks are sometimes justified on "infant industry" arguments. Thus foreign banks are criticized both for having too narrow a focus and too expansive objectives.

There are extremely few cases in which foreign banks dominate domestic financial markets. Gelb and Sagari (1990) report that foreign banks' median share of total domestic assets in a sample of twenty countries is about 6 percent. Thus in the vast majority of cases, foreign banks constitute a very small share of the domestic credit market. Countries could significantly liberalize foreign bank entry even while placing a cap, of say 40 percent, on the maximum share that foreign banks can have in the domestic market. This might ameliorate fear of domination while still permitting the benefits of foreign banks to flow into the domestic financial system.

The evidence regarding foreign banks' picking market niches is more anecdotal and difficult to interpret. The evidence supports the perspective that foreign banks initially focus on market niches where they expect to have competitive advantages. This is not a surprising or negative implication of foreign bank entry. Businesses attempt to find profitable markets, and this manifestation of market-based competition will promote improvements in the provision of financial services to domestic clients.

McFadden (1994) documents the different strategies employed by particular foreign banks as they entered the Australian market in the 1980s. Appendix 6–A reviews some of McFadden's work. Here it is worth noting that different foreign banks pursued different strategies. Some focused on attracting large Australian corporations, some focused on servicing corporations from their base countries, some focused on sophisticated financial products, and some focused on the retail market. Furthermore, some foreign banks were successful and some have experienced losses. Moreover, many Australian banks adjusted, upgraded service, and fought off foreign competition. Thus, individual banks pursued strategies based on their strengths, domestic banks often responded successfully, and domestic firms and consumers benefited from the more competitive climate.

Importantly, domestic financial policies can often create profit opportunities for foreign banks. For example, Nag and Shivaswamy (1990) note that 75 percent of foreign bank credit advanced in India went to the growing private industrial sector, while only 30 percent of domestic bank credit went to private industry. The reason underlying this difference is that the government forces domestic banks to lend to public enterprises and agriculture, which are less profitable and have high loan default rates. It is thus not surprising that foreign banks are more profitable in India and avoid lending to risky sectors. Instead of restricting foreign bank entry and stymieing financial development, countries may wish to modify directed credit programs so that domestic banks are not disadvantaged.

Local commitment. A third concern is that foreign banks will quickly retreat when faced with problems in the local market or when faced with problems in their domestic market. Thus foreign banks may enhance the fragility of the domestic financial system if they are a large component of it. Empirical evidence is scant.[12]

Supervision and the payment system. Country officials are often charged with maintaining the safety of the financial system, including the payment system. If foreign banks are permitted direct access to the payment system, then particular care must be taken to maintain a secure and reliable payment system. In the case of Australia, opening to foreign banks accelerated the development of an improved interbank payment system. Similarly, deregulation often accompanies reduced entry restrictions on foreign banks. Countries may need to enhance prudential supervision as they open to foreign banks. As noted above, NAFTA has spurred improvements in Mexico's bank supervision system. Thus, while foreign bank entry should not be allowed to overwhelm the government's ability to regulate, supervise, and support banks, opening to foreign banks may be coordinated

---

12. Bhattacharaya (1993) shows that foreign banks in the United States have not retreated during recessions. However, Vittas (1995) provides some examples of industrialized-country banks retreating from overseas markets.

with improvements in the financial infrastructure so that domestic companies and individuals can enjoy better financial services.

Final points on concerns with foreign banks. While it is natural and appropriate to be concerned about the entry of foreign banks, these concerns should, in most cases, not prohibit liberalizing entry restrictions on foreign banks. Foreign banks are unlikely to enlarge capital outflows significantly, and countries should avoid capital flight by creating an attractive investment climate, not by restricting foreign bank entry. In most countries, foreign banks play a small role, so that fear of foreign banks dominating the market should not impede easing foreign bank entry restrictions. Although individual foreign banks will attempt to identify profitable niches, these strategies will probably differ across foreign banks, and these strategies represent the natural market process through which competitive forces operate to improve financial services. While foreign banks may have a harder time entering retail markets, this probably results from high information costs, and these natural barriers may fall over time as foreign banks gain familiarity with the local market. Thus, most countries can probably obtain the benefits from foreign banks without incurring the costs, though entry should not run ahead of the ability of domestic regulators and supervisors to ensure a safe and sound financial system.

Conclusion

Using a two-part approach, this chapter has examined the role that foreign banks can play in economic development. In the first part, I presented conceptual arguments and empirical evidence that suggest that a developing country's level of financial development is important for its future rate of economic growth. The financial system provides services to the nonfinancial sector that help determine the fraction of resources devoted to productive endeavors and the efficiency with which the economy uses those resources. The data show that various measures of financial development predict how fast economies will grow in the future. Thus, policies that bolster financial development will accelerate economic development.

The second part of the chapter evaluated whether openness to foreign banks promotes financial development. Foreign banks may promote financial development directly by providing high-quality financial services to the domestic market and by exerting downward pressure on the prices of financial services. Foreign banks also enhance financial development by spurring domestic banks to improve the quality of their services and cut costs. Further, they encourage the upgrading of ancillary institutions such as accounting, auditing, and rating firms, thereby improving the quality and flow of information about firms and banks. And foreign banks will facilitate domestic financial development by intensifying pressures for governments to improve the legal, regulatory, and supervisory systems.

In comparison with these benefits, the potential negative effects of foreign banks on financial development seem remote. Foreign banks play at most a peripheral role in capital flight. In most countries, foreign banks are minor participants, so that some easing of entry restrictions should not create fears of foreign domination of the domestic financial system.

While foreign banks initially try to exploit market niches where they have exhibited competitive success in other countries, this natural business tactic will improve financial services in the domestic market. Eventually, foreign banks may attempt to compete more broadly as they gain experience about the domestic market. Thus, the belief that foreign banks will initially service some segments of the market should not deter countries from liberalizing entry restrictions. Although opening to foreign banks may place greater burdens on the supervisory system, financial liberalization efforts in general should be coordinated with improved supervisory capacity.

In sum, the benefits to be gained from easing foreign bank entry restrictions in developing countries where foreign banks currently play a very small role in the domestic financial system seem much greater than the costs and risks involved.

Appendix 6–A: McFadden's Study of Foreign Banks in Australia

Australia liberalized foreign bank entry in 1984. Prior to 1984, foreign banks had operated in Australia through finance companies and merchant banks and held 17 percent of financial assets. They had been restricted from foreign exchange transactions, deposit taking, and direct access to the payment system. The financial system was concentrated. The four largest trading banks (Westpac, National Australian Bank, ANZ, and the Commonwealth Bank of Australia) held 60 percent of financial assets and 80 percent of deposits, and had 5,500 branches nationwide.

Foreign banks had to be locally incorporated subsidiaries and were subject to the same legislative, prudential, and tax regulation as domestic trading banks. Reciprocity was required. Banks had to be at least 50 percent domestically owned to provide a broad range of banking services, although exceptions were routinely granted. Eight of the original 16 banking licenses went to wholly foreign-owned banks, including Citibank, Barclays, NatWest, Bankers Trust, and Deutsche Bank.

Citibank. Extending its global strategy and building on its preexisting finance company, Citibank pursued investment and commercial banking, foreign exchange and risk management services, and retail banking, especially for high-income individuals. Citibank targeted the 200 largest firms in Australia in attempting to expand its corporate and investment banking business. Citibank offered full electronic trade finance to corporations that greatly lowered various transaction costs. In retail banking, Citibank developed its money market, ATM credit card, mortgage instruments, and home financing products. In terms of risk management, Citibank offered full swap warehouses and other sophisticated risk-trading facilities. So far, Citibank has been generally successful, even in retail banking and home financing.

Chase Manhattan. In a joint venture with Australia Mutual Provident Society, Chase-AMP Bank is attempting to combine banking with the customer base, agents, and offices of the huge AMP insurance company to provide a wide array of services. They have taken off slowly, as Chase did not have earlier experience in Australia, and the insurance-banking mix has not yet had positive synergies.

Bank of Tokyo. Building on its existing merchant bank, Bank of Tokyo has succeeded in expanding services to primarily large Japanese corporations. This strategy has also helped Mitsubishi to expand its operations in Australia successfully.

Bankers Trust and Barclays. They have used their new banking licenses to expand operations in Australia. They are expanding their client base, providing foreign exchange and money market services, and doing more syndicated funding.

General Conclusions. Domestic banks improved their operations, invested in new technologies, cut costs, and competed intensively with foreign banks, so that foreign banks were less profitable initially than many analysts had expected. Foreign bank entry has coincided with lower interest rate margins, lower spreads over the Treasury Bill rate for corporations, and better service for individuals than were available before Australia liberalized foreign bank entry.

References

Aliber R.Z. "International Banking: A Survey." *Journal of Money, Credit and Banking*, 16, Part 2, 1984, pp. 661–78.

Bagehot, W. *Lombard Street*. Homewood Ill.: 1962 ed.

Bencivenga, Valerie R., and Bruce D. Smith. "Financial Intermediation and Endogenous Growth." *Review of Economic Studies*, 58(2), 1991, pp. 195–209.

Bencivenga, Valerie R., Bruce D. Smith, and Ross Starr. "Equity Markets, Transactions Costs, and Capital Accumulation: An Illustration." Cornell University, mimeo, 1995.

Bhattacharaya, Joydeep. "The Role of Foreign Banks in Developing Countries: A Survey of the Evidence." Cornell University, mimeo, 1993.

Boyd, J.H., and B.D. Smith. "Intermediation and the Equilibrium Allocation of Investment Capital: Implications for Economic Development." *Journal of Monetary Economics*, 30, 1992, pp. 409–32.

Cho, Y.J., and Khatkhate. *Lessons of Financial Liberalization in Asia*. World Bank: Discussion Paper no. 50, 1989.

Cuadrado, Juan Ramon, Guillermo de la Dehesa, and Andres Precedo. "Regional Imbalances and Government Compensatory Financial Flows: The Case of Spain." In A. Giovannini, ed., *Finance and Development: Issues and Experience*. Cambridge: Cambridge University Press, 1993.

Dale, R. *The Regulation of International Banking*. Cambridge: Woodhead-Faulkner, 1984.

Denison, E.F. *Why Economic Growth Rates Differ: Postwar Experience in Nine Western Countries*. Washington, D.C.: Brookings Institution, 1967.

Dermine, J. "International Trade in Banking." INSEAD, mimeo, 1993.

Euh, Y.D., and J. Baker. *The Korean Banking System and Foreign Influence*. London: Routledge, 1990.

Faini, R., G. Galli, and C. Giannini. "Finance and Development: The Case of Southern Italy." In A. Giovannini, ed., *Finance and Development: Issues and Experience*. Cambridge: Cambridge University Press, 1993.

Feis, H. *Europe, the World's Banker: 1870–1914*. New York: Kelley, 1964.

Gelb, A., and S. Sagari. "Banking." In P. Messerlin and K. Sanvant, eds., *The Uruguay Bond: Services in the World Economy*. Washington, D.C.: The World Bank and UN Centre on Transnational Corporations, 1990.

Germidis, D., and C. Michalet. *International Banks and Financial Markets in Developing Countries*. Paris: OECD Publication, 1984.

Glaessner, T., and D. Oks. "NAFTA, Capital Mobility, and Mexico's Financial System." World Bank, mimeo, 1994.

Goldberg, L.G., and A. Saunders. "The Determinants of Foreign Banking Activity in the United States." *Journal of Banking and Finance*, 5, 1 March 1981, pp. 17–32.

Goldsmith, R.W. *Financial Structure and Development*. New Haven: Yale University Press, 1969.

Gordon, D., and R. Levine. "The 'Problem' of Capital Flight: A Cautionary Note." *The World Economy*, 12(2), June 1989, pp. 237–52.

Greenwood, J., and B.D. Smith. "Financial Aid in Development, and the Development of Financial Markets." *Journal of Economic Dynamics and Control*, forthcoming.

Grosse, R., and L.G. Goldberg. "Foreign Bank Activity in the United States: An Analysis by Country of Origin." *Journal of Banking and Finance*, 15(6), December 1991, pp. 1093–112.

Gray, J.M., and P.H. Gray. "The Multinational Bank: A Financial MNC?" *Journal of Banking and Finance*, 5, 1981, pp. 33–63.

Hicks, J. "A Theory of Economic History." Oxford: Clarendon Press, 1969.

Hultman, C.W., and R. McGee. "Factors Affecting the Foreign Banking Presence in the United States." *Journal of Banking and Finance* 13 (3), July 1989, pp. 383–96.

Key, S.J. "International Trade in Banking Services." In A. Steinherr, ed., *The New European Financial Market Place*. New York: Longman, 1992.

King, R.G., and R. Levine. "Financial Intermediation and Economic Development." In C. Mayer and X. Vives, eds., *Capital Markets and Financial Intermediation*. Cambridge: Cambridge University Press, 1993 (1993a).

———. "Finance and Growth: Schumpeter Might Be Right." *Quarterly Journal of Economics*, 108(3), August 1993, pp. 717–37 (1993b).

———. "Finance Entrepreneurship and Growth: Theory and Evidence," *Journal of Monetary Economics*, 32(3), December, pp. 513–42 (1993c).

———. "Capital Fundamentalism, Economic Development, and Economic Growth." *Carnegie-Rochester Series on Public Policy*, 40, June, pp. 259–92 (1994).

Krugman, P. "International Finance and Economic Development." In A. Giovannini, ed., *Finance and Development: Issues and Experience*. Cambridge: Cambridge University Press, 1993.

Levine, R. "Unresolved Issues in the Relationship between Finance and Development." In *Financial Development and Economic Growth: Theory and Experiences from Developing Countries*, eds. N. Hermes and R. Lensink, forthcoming.

————. "Financial Development and Economic Growth: Views and Agenda." Mimeo, World Bank, Washington, D.C., 1996.

————. "Stock Markets, Growth, and Tax Policy." *Journal of Finance*, 46(4), September 1991, pp. 1,445–65.

Levine, R., and D. Renelt. "A Sensitivity Analysis of Cross-Country Growth Regressions." *American Economic Review*, 82(4), September 1992, pp. 942–63.

Levine, R., and S. Zervos. "What We Have Learned about Policy from Cross-Country Growth Regressions." *American Economic Review*, May 1993, pp. 426–30.

Lewis, W.A. "Economic Development with Unlimited Supplies of Labour." *The Manchester School of Economic and Social Studies*, 22(2), 1954, pp. 139–91.

Merton, Robert C. "Operation and Regulation in Financial Intermediation: A Functional Perspective." Harvard University, mimeo, 1992.

McFadden, Catherine. "Foreign Banks in Australia." The World Bank, mimeo, 1994.

McKinnon, R. I. "Money and Capital in Economic Development." Washington, D.C.: Brookings Institution, 1973.

Musalem, A., D. Vittas, and A. Demirguc-Kunt. "North American Free Trade Agreement: Issues on Trade in Financial Services for Mexico." *World Bank Working Paper* WPS 1153, 1993.

Nag, A.K. and K. Shivaswamy. "Foreign Banks in India—Recent Performance." Reserve Bank of India Occasional Papers, 11(4), pp. 297–328, 1990.

Nurske, R. "International Investment Today in the Light of Nineteenth-Century Experience." *Economic Journal*, 64, 1954, pp. 134–50.

Pigott, C.A. "Financial Reform and the Role of Foreign Banks in Pacific-Basin Nations." *Financial Policy and Reform in Pacific-Basin Countries*, ed. H. Cheng. Lexington: Lexington Books, 1986.

Reserve Bank of Australia. *Campbell Report*. Sydney, Australia, 1983.

Rostow, W.W. *The Stages of Economic Growth: A Non-Communist Manifesto*. Cambridge: Cambridge University Press, 1960.

Sabi, M. "An Application of the Theory of Foreign Direct Investment to Multinational Banking in LDCs." *Journal of International Banking Studies*, 19(3), 1988, pp. 433–47.

Solow, R. "Technological Change and the Aggregate Production Function." *Review of Economics and Statistics*, 39, 1957, pp. 312–20.

Summers, R., and A. Heston. "A New Set of International Comparisons of Real Product and Price Levels: Estimates for 130 Countries, 1950–1985." *Review of Income and Wealth*, 34(1), March 1988, pp. 1–25.

Terrell, H.S. "The Role of Foreign Banks in Domestic Banking Markets." In. H. Cheng, ed., *Financial Policy and Reform in Pacific-Basin Countries*. Lexington: Lexington Books, 1986.

United States Treasury, *National Treatment Study*, 1990.

Ursacki, T., and H. Vertinsky. "Choice of Entry Timing and Scale by Foreign Banks in Japan and Korea." *Journal of Banking and Finance*, 16, 1992, pp. 405–21.

Vittas, Dimitri. "Free Trade Issues in Banking and Insurance." World Bank, mimeo, 1995.

Walter, I. "Country Risk, Portfolio Decisions, and Regulation in International Bank Lending." *Journal of Banking and Finance*, 1, March 1981, pp. 77–92.

———. *Barriers to Trade in Banking and Financial Services*. Thames Lectures, Trade Policy Research Centre, London, 1985.

———. *Global Competition in Financial Services: Market Structure, Protection, and Trade Liberalization*. Cambridge: AEI Press and Ballinger, 1988.

Walter, I., and H. Peter Gray. "Protectionism and International Banking." *Journal of Banking and Finance*, 7(4), 1983, pp. 597–609.

White, Lawrence J. "Competition versus Harmonization: An Overview of International Regulation of Financial Services." Chap. 1 of this volume.

Index

Abuaf, Niso, 61
Accounting standards
    countries other than United
        States, 127
    generally accepted accounting
        principles (GAAP), 127
    related to insurance, 205
Adverse selection, 191–92
Aliber, R. Z., 224n1
Anderson, Dan, 190n41
Arbitrage
    in distant markets, 25
    regulatory, 110–14, 203
Aronson, Jonathan, 13n18, 31
Arrow, Kenneth, 16–17n26

Bagehot, W., 229–30
Baker, J., 236
Bancassurance, 74, 151, 181, 183
Bank for International Settlements
    (BIS), 55, 57t, 59t, 60t, 79t
Banking Act (1933),United States. *See*
    Glass-Steagall Act (1933)
Banking industry
    asymmetric information in,
        63–66
    categories of services, 52–53
    determinants of foreign market
        competitiveness, 61–63
    economic regulation of, 8–9, 22
    EU integration, 74–79
    foreign-based banks, 27
    guarantee in fair trade, 69

health-safety-environment regu-
    lation (H-S-E), 10
information regulation, 11
insurance market shares, 182–83
interbanking activity, 55
international competition, 27–28
Japan, 137–38
limited access to insurance mar-
    kets, 182
potential for bank runs and sys-
    temic crises, 66–69
regulation of, 53–55
scope of permissible activities of
    banks in, 71–74
supervision by Basel Committee
    and GATS, 51
U.S. dual regulation, 26–27
    See also Bancassurance
    See also Banks, foreign
Banking Law (1984), France, 133
Banking systems
    entry by foreign universal bank,
        121, 125
    Germany, 133–34
    rules for EU countries, 129
Banks, foreign
    access to U.S. markets, 128
    concerns related to entry of,
        244–48
    role in promoting economic
        growth, 234–44
    role in promotion of financial de-
        velopment, 224

255

under U.S. International Banking Act, 125–26
Baron, David, 20n33
Barriers to trade
in financial services, 50
in insurance markets, 184–95
under national treatment principle, 214–43
Barth, Michael, 157n7, 187n33
Basel Accord (1988)
harmonization through, 35–36
minimum capital standards under, 36, 40–41, 212
Basel Committee on Banking Supervision, 51, 69
Basel Concordat (1975, 1983), 129
Baumol, William, 12n16, 39n71
Bebchuk, Lucian, 28n57
Bedore, James, 169, 171, 174n22, 183n28
Beenstock, M., 161nn10,11
Behavior, individual
as factor in market failure, 17–18
health-safety-environment regulation of, 18–19
Bencivenga, Valerie, 229, 231n8
Benston, George, 6n4, 28n57, 61
Berger, Allen, 13n19, 14n22
Bhattacharaya, Joydeep, 236, 238, 240, 247n12
Black, Kenneth, Jr., 157n7, 161n12
Bloch, Ernest, 26n49
Bodner, David, 25n47
Bradley, Caroline, 25n46
Braeutigan, Ronald, 8n8
Braunstein, 39n73
Breeden, Richard, 6n2
Bronfman, Corinne, 37n68

Calomiris, Charles, 66n13
Campbell Report (1983), Australia, 236
Capital
relation to supply of insurance, 164–65, 177–78
required levels under EU, 131–33
taxation of income in EU integrated market, 78–79
Capital Adequacy Directive (CAD), European Union, 131–32, 135

Capital flows
EU directive related to, 76
influence of foreign banks in, 236–37
relation to economic growth, 236, 243
Capital markets
access to, 114–17
access to international, 235
securities firms activities in, 97–101, 105t
Capital standards
of Basel Committee, 69
EU banking industry, 76
of IOSCO, 35–36
proposals for harmonization of, 205
Carmody, Kathleen, 61
Carter, Robert, 169, 171, 186n31, 192n42, 194n43
Central banks. See European System of Central Banks (ESCB)
Chaebol practices, Korea, 176
Cho, Y. J., 239t
Choi, Frederick, 39n72
Code of Liberalization of Capital Movements, OECD, 209
Code of Liberalization of Current Invisible Operations, OECD, 209
Coffee, John, 26n49
Committee on Capital Movements and Invisible Transactions (CMIT), OECD, 209
Commodity Futures Trading Commission (CFTC), 27
Competition
firm-level, 24
Japanese securities market, 138
in the market, 24
regulatory regimes, 7, 110–11
restriction caused by international harmonization, 31
state-level regulatory regimes, 26–27
stock exchanges, 25
U.S. domestic and international financial services, 25
Conduct-of-business rules, EU, 135–36
Consumers
life and nonlife insurance, 161, 164

problems in insurance of, 177–80
protection in insurance market, 183–84
Cooke, Peter, 205n53, 213n63
Cowhey, Peter, 31n58
Cross-subsidization, 22–23
Cuadrado, Juan, 225n3
Cummins, J. David, 157n7, 161n12, 165nn16,17,18, 187n33

Dale, Richard, 50n1, 73, 225n4
D'Arcy, Stephen, 188n37
David, Paul, 204n52
Dehesa, Guillermo, 225n3
Denison, E. F., 227
Deposit insurance
    to avoid bank runs and systemic crises, 67–69
    in EU integrated market, 77–79
Deregulation
    competitive, 66
    difference from liberalization, 198
    factors in U.S. movement toward, 24
    of financial services, 200
    See also Liberalization
Dermine, Jean, 69n20, 213n63, 224n1
Developing countries
    benefits of foreign bank presence, 235–44
    concerns related to foreign bank entry, 244–48
    economic growth related to capital flows, 236, 243
    perspective on harmonization, 241–43
Diacon, S. R., 161n12
Diamond, Douglas, 52n2
Dickinson, Gerald, 161nn10,11, 186n31, 192n42, 194n43
Dionne, Georges, 190n41
Directive on Liberalization of Capital Flows (1988), European Community, 76
Dixit, Avinash, 40n75
Doherty, Neil, 164n15, 190n41
Dudley, William, 33n60

Economic growth
    relation in developing countries to capital flows, 236, 243

relation to financial development, 223, 232–34
role of financial systems in, 226–31
role of foreign banks in, 225, 234–44
Economides, Nicholas, 39n73
Economies of scale
    as cause of market failure, 13–14
    economic regulation of, 18
    as rationale for insurance regulation, 187–88
Edwards, Franklin, 5n1, 28n56
England, Catherine, 33n60
Euh, Y. D., 236
Eurobond market, 135
European Commission, 50, 55t, 78n29
European Economic Area (EEA), 77
European Free Trade Association (EFTA), 77
European System of Central Banks (ESCB), 76–77
European Union (EU)
    Capital Adequacy Directive, 131–32, 135
    conduct-of-business rules, 135–36
    First and Second Banking Directives (1977, 1988), 129
    harmonization in insurance market, 207–9
    international integration, 74–79
    Investment Services Directive, 130–31
    regulatory and market access rules, 142–43
    securities industry in, 129–37
Externalities
    effects as cause of market failure, 14–15
    effects in insurance industry, 188–89
    health-safety-environment regulation of, 18–19

Faini, R., 226n3, 238
Farrell, Joseph, 206n55
Federal Reserve Board, 125–26
Feis, H., 237
Fields, Joseph, 189n38

Financial development
    developing countries in 1960–
        1989 period, 232–34
    developing country levels in
        1970, 232–33
    measures of, 232
    role of foreign banks in, 224,
        234–44
Financial intermediation
    of insurance companies, 153
    Japan, 138
    process of, 87–97
Financial markets
    access of foreign-based securi-
        ties firms to, 144–45t
    EU conduct-of-business rules,
        135–36
Financial services
    asymmetric information in, 17
    competition in markets of, 25
    for economic growth, 226–31
    economies of scale, 14
    effect of regulation of, 107–14
    European Commission frame-
        work, 50
    externalities in, 15
    factors in developing country,
        237–40
    in GATT Uruguay Round proc-
        ess, 1–2
    internationalization of, 168
    liberalization in response to
        GATT Uruguay Round, 49
    market power in, 13
    merger and acquisition activity,
        171, 173
    national level regulation, 6
Fingleton, John, 5n1
Firms, foreign-based, 133
Fletcher, Ian, 201n47
Fondree, Bruce, 189n39
Foreign Bank Supervision Enhance-
    ment Act (1991), United States, 68
Framework Agreement (1994),
    United States-Japan, 183, 186
Free-Trade Agreement, United
    States-Israel, 211
Freund, William, 28n56

Galli, G., 225n3
Gardner, Lisa, 164n15, 187nn34,35

Geehan, R., 164n15
Gelb, A., 245
General Agreement on Tariffs and
    Trade (GATT)
    financial services omitted from
        Uruguay Round, 142
    implicit harmonization, 31
    liberalization of financial ser-
        vices in response to, 49
    Uruguay Round rules for, 1–2
General Agreement on Trade in Ser-
    vices (GATS), 66, 68
    Committee on Trade in Financial
        Services, 142
    Council for Trade in Services
        under, 142
    Dispute Settlement Body under,
        142
    industries covered by, 141
    provisions and parts, 140
Generally accepted accounting prin-
    ciples (GAAP), United States, 11,
    28, 39, 127
George, Eddy, 35n63
Giannini, C., 225n3
Gilbert, Alton, 13n17
Glaessner, T., 235, 241, 242
Glass-Steagall Act (1933)
    banks as Section 20 securities af-
        filiates, 126, 133
    distortions of, 145
    function of, 71, 73
    under International Banking Act
        (1978), 125
    proposals for repeal, 129
    restrictions on foreign banks,
        125, 133
Goals, formulation, 19
Goldberg, L. G., 60t, 224n1
Goldsmith, R. W., 232
Gordon, D., 244
Gorton, Gary, 66n13
Governance, corporate, 230–31
Government failure
    concept of, 7
    reasons for, 19–21
    role of weak incentives in, 19
Government role
    in insurance markets, 184–95
    intervention through regulation,
        8

See also Deregulation; Glass-Steagall Act (1933); Harmonization; Regulation

Grace, Martin, 153n3, 157n7, 161n13, 165n17, 187nn33,35

Gray, H. Peter, 224n1

Gray, J. M., 224n1

Greenwood, J., 229

Grosse, R., 224n1

Gruenspecht, Howard, 10n14, 23n40

Grundfest, Joseph, 6n3

Guy, Paul, 6n2

Hannan, Timothy, 13n19

Harmonization
    arguments against, 203–6
    arguments for insurance regulation harmonization, 200–2
    conditions for regulatory, 66, 69–70
    developing country perspective on, 241–43
    EU insurance market experience, 207–9
    of insurance regulation, 196–212
    potential effects of, 7
    proposed de facto, 212–13, 218
    regulatory, 198
    of U.S. dual banking regulations, 26
    of U.S. state-level regulation, 211

Harmonization, international
    examples of economic regulation, 30–32
    principles applied to financial services, 29–30
    securities prices and markets, 37–40
    systemic risk, 32–36

Harrington, Scott, 189n38

Hawawini, Gabriel, 61

Herring, Richard, 50n1

Heston, A., 232n9

Hicks, John, 231

Hiraki, Takato, 139n22

Hirshhorn, R., 164n15

Holsboer, J. H., 183n30

Hoshi, Takeo, 62n5

Host country conduct-of-business rules, 135–36

Hotchkiss, 165n17

Hultman, Charles, 50n1, 62, 224n1

Humphrey, David, 33n60

Hunter, William, 14n22

Information
    disclosure of, 135–36
    effect of inadequate, 20
    regulation of, 11–12
    role of financial systems in provision of, 230

Information, asymmetric
    in banking markets, 63–66
    as factor in market failure, 16–17
    in insurance industry, 190–92
    regulation of, 19

Insider trading, 135

Insurance
    cross-border trade in, 169–70, 179–80
    differences in social and private, 154–55
    direct insurance and reinsurance, 156–57
    establishment trade in, 169–77
    importance within national economies, 159
    keiretsu practices associated with, 174–84
    life and nonlife, 155
    market power in, 185–87
    market shares of life and nonlife, 158–59
    personal and commercial, 155–56
    production process, 177
    rationale for regulation of, 184–85
    terms of life insurance, 155
    See also Deposit insurance

Insurance Committee, OECD, 209–10

Insurance companies
    international, 166
    merger and acquisition activity, 173–75
    OECD countries, 165–66
    presence in markets of foreign, 171–72
    world's largest, 165–67

Insurance industry
    economic regulation of, 9–10

economies of scale, 14
harmonization arguments, 200–6
harmonization experiences, 206–12
health-safety-environment regulation, 11
information regulation in, 11–12
market power of, 13
permissible activities in, 71–72
regulation of banks in, 71–72
U.S. accreditation program, 210–11
See also Bancassurance
Insurance markets
banking industry limits to access, 182
determinants of demand and supply, 160–84
determinants of structure, 157
differences in national, 165
Japan, 174–76
measurement of size, 157–58
offshore, 203
regulatory oversight, 195–96
role of government in, 184–95
shares by selected country groupings, 159–60
Interbank activity, international, 55
International Association of Insurance Supervisors (IAIS), 31, 207
International Banking Act (1978), U.S., 125–26
International Organization of Securities Commissions (IOSCO), 31, 35–36
Interstate Banking Act (1994), 128
Investment Advisers Act (1940), 127
Investment services
access to, 117–43
securities firms, 102–7
Investment Services Directive (ISD), 130–31
Isaac, William, 26nn49,51
Iwahara, Shinsaku, 36n67, 41n76, 61n4, 69n19

Japan
access to insurance market in, 174–76

proposed reform of Glass-Steagall look-alike rules, 137–38
securities industry in, 137–40
Johnson, Philip McB., 27n54
Joskow, Paul, 8n8, 22n38, 24n44, 157n7

Kane, Edward, 6n4, 27n54, 109n3, 110n5, 111
Karmel, Roberta, 6n3
Kashyap, Anil, 62n5
Kasper, Daniel, 31n58
Kaufman, George, 116t
Kay, John, 63n7
Keiretsu practices, Japan, 174–76
Kellner, Stephen, 187n35
Key, Sydney, 28n57, 34n62, 50n1, 70, 71n21, 171n22, 225n3
Khajuria, S., 161nn10,11
Khatkhate, 239t
Kim, Doocheol, 161n10
King, R. G., 227n6, 231, 232
Klass, Michael, 22n38, 24n44
Klevorick, Alvin, 12n16
Klinkerman, Steve, 26n50
Kokkalenios, Vickie, 39n70
Kollias, Sotirios, 207n56
Kopke, Richard, 11n15
Kosters, Marvin, 5n1
Krozner, Randall, 94t
Krueger, Anne, 20n34
Krugman, Paul, 227, 237
Kunreuther, Howard, 190n41
Kwoka, John, 24n45

Laboul, 210n59
Lancaster, K., 18n27
Lave, Lester, 10n14, 23n40
Lender-of-last-resort, 67–68
Levich, Richard, 39n72, 109n4
Levine, R., 4, 227n6, 228n7, 229, 231–32, 244
Lewis, Mervyn, 151n1
Lewis, W. A., 227
Liberalization
defined, 197
EU approach for securities industry, 129–37
of international insurance markets, 213

national treatment principle in negotiations on, 71–74
potential scheme for, 215–18
reciprocity-based, 197–99
See also Deregulation
Lipsey, R. G., 18n27
Litan, Richard, 50n1

Maastricht Treaty on Economic and Monetary Union (1991), 76–77
McAuley, Robert, 61
McFadden, 234, 236n10, 240, 245
McGee, Suzanne, 25n47, 27n55, 62, 224n1
McKinnon, Ronald, 232
Malkiel, Burton, 39n71
Market access
commitment under GATS, 141–43
determinants of security firms', 121
Market failure
asymmetric information in banking as factor in, 63–66
banking fair trade issues, 69–70
banking regulations to guard against, 63–71
categories of, 12–13
concept of, 7
potential for bank runs and systemic crises, 66–69
potential in international banking, 50–51
Market power
as cause of market failure, 12–13
economic regulation of, 18
factors protecting, 22
as rationale for insurance regulation, 185–87
reinforced through international harmonization, 31
Markets
competition in, 24
factors impeding function of, 21–22
widening scope of, 24–28
See also Financial markets; Insurance markets; Offshore markets
Mathewson, G., 187n35
Mayers, David, 153n3

Meltzer, Allan, 5n1
Merton, Robert, 64n8, 228n7
Misback, Ann, 69
Moral hazard, 191–92
Most favored nation (MFN)
GATS rules based on obligations of, 140
requirement for modified, 214
U.S. exemption, 142
Musalem, A., 25n4, 244
Mutual funds, European Union (EU), 136–37

Nag, A. K., 247
National Association of Insurance Commissioners (NAIC), United States, 210–11
National treatment principle
defined, 60–61
under European Union, 130, 134–35
under General Agreement on Trade in Services, 141
in insurance markets, 197–98
in Japan, 60–61
in negotiations on trade liberalization, 71
problems of, 214–15
related to banking, 70–71
Net regulatory burden (NRB)
conditions for lower levels of, 121
of financial firms, 109–14
See also Arbitrage, regulatory
Niehaus, Greg, 189n38
Noll, Roger, 20n34, 21n35, 24n44
North American Free Trade Agreement (NAFTA)
financial services component, 242
insurance markets under, 211–12
regulatory and market access rules, 142–43
NRB. *See* Net regulatory burden (NRB)
Nurske, Ragnar, 237

Offshore markets
currency and bond markets, 111
financial markets, 110–11
insurance and reinsurance, 203

Oks, D., 235, 241, 242
Okun, Arthur, 21n37
Ordahl, James, 37
Organization for Economic Coopera-
    tion and Development (OECD),
    55, 56t, 187n32, 195n45, 196n46
    Code of Liberalization of Capital
        Movements, 209
    Code of Liberalization of Cur-
        rent Invisible Operations, 209
    Committee on Capital Move-
        ments and Invisible Transac-
        tions, 209
    harmonization in insurance mar-
        ket, 209–10
Outreville, J. Francois, 165nn16,17,18

Packer, Frank, 61n4
Patrick, Hugh, 5n1
Pecchioli, Rinaldo, 50n1
Peltzman, Sam, 21n35
Philips, Almarin, 22n38
Pigott, C. A., 236
Player, Thomas, 201n47
Pluym, Gilbert, 183n29
Posner, Richard, 21nn35,36
Postlewaite, Andrew, 15n23
Precedo, Andres, 225n3
Primary Dealers Act (1988), 126–27
Protectionism, 201
Public goods
    as cause of market failure, 16
    defined, 15
    health-safety-environment regu-
        lation of, 18–19
    in insurance industry, 189–90
Pugel, Thomas, 13n20

Quinn, Brian, 6n2

Randall, Richard, 11n15
Rebello, Michael, 153n3
Reciprocity
    in EU integrated market, 78
    in financial services trade,
        197–98
Regulation
    costs of, 23
    as determinant of financial struc-
        tures, 107–14
    developing country perspective
        on harmonization, 241–43

economic, 8–10
effect in international markets,
    26
in EU banking industry, 75
evasion of, 26
of financial services, 86
harmonization of U.S. state
    level, 211
health-safety-environment,
    10–11
information, 11–12
in insurance markets, 184,
    192–95
international harmonization of,
    29–31
justification for, 12–24
national-level banks, 53–55,
    63–66
national rules as barriers to
    trade, 50
regulatory regimes, 71
See also Arbitrage, regulatory;
    Deregulation; Net regulatory
    burden (NRB)
Regulatory oversight, insurance mar-
    kets, 195–96
Reinsurance
    markets, 156–57
    offshore markets for, 203
Renelt, D., 232
Rent creation, 21
Rent-seeking, 20–21
Resource mobilization, 229–30
Risk
    of capital, 165
    management of, 229
Risk, systemic
    potential in insurance industry,
        188–89
    scenarios of, 32–33
Rose, Nancy, 8n8, 22n38, 24n44
Rostow, W. W., 227

Sabi, M., 224n1
Sagari, S., 245
Santomero, Anthony, 66n11
Saunders, Anthony, 13n19, 103,
    224n1
Scharfstein, David, 62n5
Schlesinger, Harris, 190n41
Schmikat, Harold, 39n70

Schwab, S. W., 201n47
Scott, Hal, 28n57, 34n62, 36n67, 41n76, 50n1, 61n4, 69n19, 70, 171n21
Scott, Kenneth, 26n49
Second best problem
    as factor in market failure, 18
    in insurance industry, 192
    regulation of, 19
Securities Acts Amendments (1975), 126
Securities and Exchange Commission (SEC), 27
    regulation of securities activities, 126
    rule changes by, 127
    rules benefiting foreign securities firms, 128–29
Securities and Exchange Law (1948), Japan, 54, 73, 135–36
Securities industry
    access to national markets of foreign-based, 143–45
    barriers to access, 214–43
    competition in, 27–28
    corporate finance activities, 101–2
    determinants of market access, 121
    directives for and supervision of EU firms in, 130
    economic regulation of, 9
    EU liberalization of, 137
    foreign firms in Japanese market, 138–40
    health-safety-environment regulation, 10–11
    information regulation, 11
    international activities, 84–86, 97–107
    market power of, 13
    permissible activities of banks in, 73–74
    regulation of banks in, 72–73
    relevance to Japanese banks of markets in, 137–38
    United Kingdom, 134
Seidman, Lawrence, 39n70
Self-insurance programs, international, 166
Self-regulatory organizations (SROs), United Kingdom, 65

Semkow, Brian, 62, 73
Shapiro, May, 28n56
Shelp, Ronald, 209n57
Shivaswamy, K., 247
Siegel, Daniel, 5n1
Skill, Michael, 61
Skipper, Harold, 15n23, 157n7, 161nn12,13, 186n31, 187n34, 190n40, 192n42, 202n49, 210n60
Smith, Bruce, 229, 231n8
Smith, Clifford, 153n3
Smith, Roy, 98f, 117n9
Soloner, Garth, 206n55
Solow, Robert, 227
Spence, A. Michael, 40n75
Sprague, Irwin, 33n60
Stansell, Stanley, 5n1
Starr, Ross, 231n8
Steil, Benn, 6nn3,4, 28n57, 137n21, 143n23
Stigler, George, 21n35
Stiglitz, Joseph, 16n25, 20n32, 40n75
Stoll, Hans, 5n1
Summers, R., 232n9
Suret, Jean Marc, 187n35
Swary, 60t

Tenneyson, 165n17
Terrell, H. S., 238
Timme, Stephen, 14n22, 187n35
Topf, 60t
Torres, Craig, 28n56, 39n70
Trade
    in financial services, 1–2
    role of financial systems in, 228–29
    trend to liberalize financial services, 49–50
Trade, international
    in financial services, 55, 57
    free-trade agreements, 211–12
    importance of banking industry in, 55–56
    insurance market cross-border, 169–77
    OECD policy framework, 209
Trading conduct, 136
Transparency
    under GATS, 140
    in insurance market mutual recognition, 213–14
Trzyna, Peter, 189n39

Uncertainty
    as factor in market failure, 16
    in insurance industry, 190
U.S. Department of the Treasury, National Treatment Study, 58–60
Ursacki, T., 224n1

Vanderhei, Jack, 157n7
Vertinsky, H., 224n1
Vickers, John, 63n7
Viscusi, W. Kip, 23n40
Vittas, Dimitri, 247n12
Vives, Xavier, 15n23

Walker, David, 6n2
Walter, Ingo, 50n1, 73, 98f, 103, 109n4, 117n9, 139n22, 224n1
Wasow, Bernard, 161n11

Watson, Ronald, 66n11
Weiss, Leonard, 13n19, 22n38, 24n44
Weiss, Mary, 161n12, 164n15, 187nn33,35
White, Lawrence, 3, 5n1, 6n5, 7n7, 13n19, 19n30, 22n39, 23nn40,43, 24nn44,45, 28n57, 31n58, 34n61, 39n73, 64n9, 86, 241
Winston, Clifford, 24n44
Wolf, C., Jr., 7n7, 19n30
World Trade Organization (WTO), 2, 78
Worth, Nancy, 6n3
WTO. *See* World Trade Organization (WTO)

Zervos, S., 232
Zimmer, Steven, 61
Zimmerman, Gary, 60, 62

A NOTE ON THE BOOK

This book was edited by
Cheryl Weissman of the publications staff
of the American Enterprise Institute.
The figures were drawn by Hordur Karlsson.
The index was prepared by Shirley Kessel.
The text was set in Palatino, a typeface
designed by the twentieth-century Swiss designer
Hermann Zapf. Coghill Composition Company of
Richmond, Virginia, set the type,
and Edwards Brothers Incorporated
of Lillington, North Carolina,
printed and bound the book,
using permanent acid-free paper.

The AEI Press is the publisher for the American Enterprise Institute for Public Policy Research, 1150 Seventeenth Street, N.W., Washington, D.C. 20036; *Christopher DeMuth*, publisher; *Dana Lane*, director; *Ann Petty*, editor; *Leigh Tripoli*, editor; *Cheryl Weissman*, editor; *Lisa Roman*, editorial assistant (rights and permissions).

The American Enterprise Institute for Public Policy Research

Founded in 1943, AEI is a nonpartisan, nonprofit, research and educational organization based in Washington, D.C. The Institute sponsors research, conducts seminars and conferences, and publishes books and periodicals.

AEI's research is carried out under three major programs: Economic Policy Studies; Foreign Policy and Defense Studies; and Social and Political Studies. The resident scholars and fellows listed in these pages are part of a network that also includes ninety adjunct scholars at leading universities throughout the United States and in several foreign countries.

The views expressed in AEI publications are those of the authors and do not necessarily reflect the views of the staff, advisory panels, officers, or trustees.

William M. Landes
Clifton R. Musser Professor of
  Economics
University of Chicago Law School

Sam Peltzman
Sears Roebuck Professor of Economics
  and Financial Services
University of Chicago
  Graduate School of Business

Nelson W. Polsby
Professor of Political Science
University of California at Berkeley

George L. Priest
John M. Olin Professor of Law and
  Economics
Yale Law School

Murray L. Weidenbaum
Mallinckrodt Distinguished
  University Professor
Washington University

Research Staff

Leon Aron
Resident Scholar

Claude E. Barfield
Resident Scholar; Director, Science
  and Technology Policy Studies

Cynthia A. Beltz
Research Fellow

Walter Berns
Resident Scholar

Douglas J. Besharov
Resident Scholar

Robert H. Bork
John M. Olin Scholar in Legal Studies

Karlyn Bowman
Resident Fellow

John E. Calfee
Resident Scholar

Lynne V. Cheney
W. H. Brady, Jr., Distinguished Fellow

Dinesh D'Souza
John M. Olin Research Fellow

Nicholas N. Eberstadt
Visiting Scholar

Mark Falcoff
Resident Scholar

John D. Fonte
Visiting Scholar

Gerald R. Ford
Distinguished Fellow

Murray F. Foss
Visiting Scholar

Diana Furchtgott-Roth
Assistant to the President and Resident
  Fellow

Suzanne Garment
Resident Scholar

Jeffrey Gedmin
Research Fellow

Patrick Glynn
Resident Scholar

Robert A. Goldwin
Resident Scholar

Robert W. Hahn
Resident Scholar

Thomas Hazlett
Visiting Scholar

Robert B. Helms
Resident Scholar; Director, Health
  Policy Studies

Glenn Hubbard
Visiting Scholar

Douglas Irwin
Henry Wendt Scholar in Political
  Economy

James D. Johnston
Resident Fellow

Jeane J. Kirkpatrick
Senior Fellow; Director, Foreign and
  Defense Policy Studies

Marvin H. Kosters
Resident Scholar; Director,
  Economic Policy Studies

Irving Kristol
John M. Olin Distinguished Fellow

Dana Lane
Director of Publications

Michael A. Ledeen
Resident Scholar

James Lilley
Resident Fellow; Director, Asian
  Studies Program

John H. Makin
Resident Scholar; Director, Fiscal
  Policy Studies

Allan H. Meltzer
Visiting Scholar

Joshua Muravchik
Resident Scholar

Charles Murray
Bradley Fellow

Michael Novak
George F. Jewett Scholar in Religion,
  Philosophy, and Public Policy;
  Director, Social and
  Political Studies

Norman J. Ornstein
Resident Scholar

Richard N. Perle
Resident Fellow

William Schneider
Resident Scholar

William Shew
Visiting Scholar

J. Gregory Sidak
F. K. Weyerhaeuser Fellow

Herbert Stein
Senior Fellow

Irwin M. Stelzer
Resident Scholar; Director, Regulatory
  Policy Studies

W. Allen Wallis
Resident Scholar

Ben J. Wattenberg
Senior Fellow

Carolyn L. Weaver
Resident Scholar; Director, Social
  Security and Pension Studies